THE FUNDAMENTALS OF POLITICAL SCIENCE RESEARCH

Paul M. Kellstedt's and Guy D. Whitten's *The Fundamentals of Political Science Research* provides an introduction to the scientific study of politics, supplying students with the basic tools needed to be both critical consumers and producers of scholarly research in political science. The book begins with a discussion of what it means to take a scientific approach to the study of politics. At the core of such an approach is the development of causal theories. Because there is no magic formula by which theories are developed, the authors present a series of strategies and develop an integrated approach to research design and empirical analyses that allows students to determine the plausibility of their causal theories. The text's accessible presentation of mathematical concepts and regression models with two or more independent variables is a key component to this process, along with the integration of examples from political science and the real world to help students grasp the key concepts.

Paul M. Kellstedt is Associate Professor of Political Science and Director of the American Politics Program at Texas A&M University. He is the author of *The Mass Media and the Dynamics of American Racial Attitudes* (2003), which won the Goldsmith Book Prize. Professor Kellstedt is also the author or co-author of articles appearing in scholarly journals such as *American Journal of Political Science*, *British Journal of Political Science*, and *Political Analysis*, as well as several book chapters. He has been an Academic Visitor at Nuffield College, Oxford, and a Harvard University Fellow in the Joan Shorenstein Center on the Press, Politics, and Public Policy in the Kennedy School of Government.

Guy D. Whitten is Associate Professor of Political Science and Director of the European Union Center at Texas A&M University. He has published a variety of papers in scholarly journals, including *American Journal of Political Science*, *British Journal of Political Science*, and *Electoral Studies*. Professor Whitten serves on the editorial board of *Electoral Studies* and has previously served on the editorial boards of *Journal of Politics* and *Political Research Quarterly*. He has been a visiting researcher at the University of Amsterdam and is a frequent instructor at the Summer School for Social Science Data Analysis and Collection at the University of Essex in the United Kingdom.

THE FUNDAMENTALS OF

Political Science Research

Paul M. Kellstedt

Texas A&M University

Guy D. Whitten

Texas A&M University

CAMBRIDGE
UNIVERSITY PRESS

CAMBRIDGE UNIVERSITY PRESS
Cambridge, New York, Melbourne, Madrid, Cape Town, Singapore,
São Paulo, Delhi, Dubai, Tokyo

Cambridge University Press
32 Avenue of the Americas, New York, NY 10013-2473, USA

www.cambridge.org
Information on this title: www.cambridge.org/9780521697880

First published 2009
Reprinted 2009 (twice)

Printed in the United States of America

A catalog record for this publication is available from the British Library.

Library of Congress Cataloging in Publication data

Kellstedt, Paul M., 1968–
The fundamentals of political science research / Paul M. Kellstedt, Guy D. Whitten.
    p.   cm.
Includes bibliographical references and index.
ISBN 978-0-521-87517-2 (hardback) – ISBN 978-0-521-69788-0 (pbk.)
1. Political science – Research. I. Whitten, Guy D., 1965– II. Title.
JA86.K45   2009
320.072 – dc22   2008035250

ISBN 978-0-521-87517-2 Hardback
ISBN 978-0-521-69788-0 Paperback

Dedicated to

Lyman A. Kellstedt, Charmaine C. Kellstedt,

David G. Whitten, and Jo Wright-Whitten,

the best teachers we ever had

– PMK and GDW

Contents

Figures

Tables

Acknowledgments

An inevitable part of the production of a book like this is an accumulation of massive intellectual debts. We have been overwhelmed by both the quality and quantity of help that we have received from our professional (and even personal) contacts as we have gone through every stage of this project.

This book arose out of more than 20 years of combined teaching experience at Brown University, the University of California, Los Angeles, the University of Essex, the University of Minnesota, and Texas A&M University. We tried out most of the examples in this book on numerous classes of students before we refined them into their present state. We thus owe a debt to every student who raised his or her hand or showed us a furrowed brow as we worked our way through these attempts to explain the complicated processes of scientifically studying politics.

More immediately, this project came out of separate and skeptical conversations that each author had with Ed Parsons during his visit to Texas A&M in the spring of 2006. Without Ed's perfect balance of candor and encouragement, this book would not have been started. At every stage in the process he has helped us immensely. He obtained three sets of superbly helpful reviews and seemed always to know the right times to be in and out of touch as we worked our way through them. It has been a tremendous pleasure to work with Ed on the book.

Throughout the process of writing this book, we got a steady stream of support, understanding, and patience from Christine, Deb, Abigail, and Elizabeth. We thank them for putting up with our crazy hours and for helping us to keep things in perspective as we worked on this project.

For both authors, the lines separating family, friends, and professional colleagues are pretty blurry. We relied on our combined networks quite heavily at every stage in the production of this book. Early in the process of putting the manuscript together, we received sage advice from Jeff Gill about textbook writing for social scientists and how to handle early versions of our chapters. Our fathers, Lyman A. "Bud" Kellstedt and David

G. Whitten, provided their own unique and valuable perspectives on early drafts of the book. In separate but related ongoing conversations, John Transue and Alan M. Brookhart engaged us in lengthy debates about the nature of experiments, quasi-experiments, and observational studies. Other colleagues and friends provided input that also improved this book, including Harold Clarke, Geoffrey Evans, John Jackson, Marisa Kellam, Eric Lawrence, Christine Lipsmeyer, Evan Parker-Stephen, David Peterson, James Rogers, Randy Stevenson, Georg Vanberg, Rilla Whitten, and Jenifer Whitten-Woodring.

Despite all of this help, we remain solely responsible for any deficiencies that persist in the book. We look forward to hearing about them from you so that we can make future editions of this book better.

Throughout the process of writing this book, we have been mindful of how our thinking has been shaped by our teachers at a variety of levels. We are indebted to them in ways that are difficult to express. In particular, Guy Whitten thanks the following, all from his days at the University of Rochester: Larry M. Bartels, Richard Niemi, G. Bingham Powell, Lynda Powell, William H. Riker, and David Weimer. Paul Kellstedt thanks Al Reynolds and Bob Terbog of Calvin College; Michael Lewis-Beck, Vicki Hesli, and Jack Wright at the University of Iowa; and Jim Stimson and John Freeman at the University of Minnesota.

Although we have learned much from the aforementioned professors, we owe our largest debt to our parents: Lyman A. "Bud" Kellstedt, Charmaine C. Kellstedt, David G. Whitten, and Jo Wright-Whitten. We dedicate this book to the four of them – the best teachers we ever had.

THE FUNDAMENTALS OF POLITICAL SCIENCE RESEARCH

1 The Scientific Study of Politics

OVERVIEW

Most political science students are interested in the substance of politics and not in its methodology. We begin with a discussion of the goals of this book and why a scientific approach to the study of politics is more interesting and desirable than a "just-the-facts" approach. In this chapter we provide an overview of what it means to study politics scientifically. We begin with an introduction to how we move from causal theories to scientific knowledge, and a key part of this process is thinking about the world in terms of *models* in which the concepts of interest become variables that are causally linked together by theories. We then introduce the goals and standards of political science research that will be our rules of the road to keep in mind throughout this book. The chapter concludes with a brief overview of the structure of this book.

Doubt is the beginning, not the end, of wisdom.
    – Chinese proverb

1.1 POLITICAL *SCIENCE?*

"Which party do you support?" "When are you going to run for office?" These are questions that students often hear after announcing that they are taking courses in political science. Although many political scientists are avid partisans, and some political scientists have even run for elected offices or have advised elected officials, for the most part this is not the focus of modern political science. Instead, political science is about the scientific study of political phenomena. Perhaps like you, a great many of today's political scientists were attracted to this discipline as undergraduates because of intense interests in a particular issue or candidate. Although we are often drawn into political science based on political passions, the most respected political science research today is conducted in a fashion that makes it impossible to tell the personal political views of the writer.

Many people taking their first political science research course are surprised to find out how much science and, in particular, how much math are involved. We would like to encourage the students who find themselves in this position to hang in there with us – even if your answer to this encouragement is "but I'm only taking this class because they require it to graduate, and I'll never use any of this stuff again." Even if you never run a regression model after you graduate, having made your way through these materials should help you in a number of important ways. We have written this book with the following three goals in mind:

- *To help you consume academic political science research in your other courses.* One of the signs that a field of research is becoming scientific is the development of a common technical language. We aim to make the common technical language of political science accessible to you.
- *To help you become a better consumer of information.* In political science and many other areas of scientific and popular communication, claims about causal relationships are frequently made. We want you to be better able to evaluate such claims critically.
- *To start you on the road to becoming a producer of scientific research on politics.* This is obviously the most ambitious of our goals. In our teaching we often have found that once skeptical students get comfortable with the basic tools of political science, their skepticism turns into curiosity and enthusiasm.

To see the value of this approach, consider an alternative way of learning about politics, one in which political science courses would focus on "just the facts" of politics. Under this alternative way, for example, a course offered in 1995 on the politics of the European Union (EU) would have taught students that there were 15 member nations who participated in governing the EU through a particular set of institutional arrangements that had a particular set of rules. An obvious problem with this alternative way is that courses in which lists of facts are the only material would probably be pretty boring. An even bigger problem, though, is that the political world is constantly changing. In 2008 the EU is made up of 27 member nations and has some new governing institutions and rules that are different from what they were in 1995. Students who took a facts-only course on the EU back in 1995 would find themselves lost in trying to understand the EU of 2008. By contrast, a theoretical approach to politics helps us to better understand why changes have come about and their likely impact on EU politics.

In this chapter we provide an overview of what it means to study politics scientifically. We begin this discussion with an introduction to how we move from causal theories to scientific knowledge. A key part of this process is thinking about the world in terms of *models* in which the concepts of interest become **variables**[1] that are causally linked together by theories. We then introduce the goals and standards of political science research that will be our rules of the road to keep in mind throughout this book. We conclude this chapter with a brief overview of the structure of this book.

1.2   APPROACHING POLITICS SCIENTIFICALLY: THE SEARCH FOR CAUSAL EXPLANATIONS

I've said, I don't know whether it's addictive. I'm not a doctor. I'm not a scientist.
> – Bob Dole, in a conversation with Katie Couric about tobacco during the 1996 U.S. presidential campaign

The question of "how do we know what we know" is, at its heart, a philosophical question. Scientists are lumped into different disciplines that develop standards for evaluating evidence. A core part of being a scientist and taking a scientific approach to studying the phenomena that interest you is always being willing to consider new evidence and, on the basis of that new evidence, change what you thought you *knew* to be true. This willingness to always consider new evidence is counterbalanced by a stern approach to the evaluation of new evidence that permeates the scientific approach. This is certainly true of the way that political scientists approach politics.

So what do political scientists do and what makes them scientists? A basic answer to this question is that, like other scientists, political scientists develop and test theories. A **theory** is a tentative conjecture about the causes of some phenomenon of interest. Once a theory has been developed, we can restate it into one or more testable hypotheses. A **hypothesis** is a theory-based statement about a relationship that we expect to observe. For every hypothesis there is a corresponding **null hypothesis**. A null hypothesis is also a theory-based statement but it is about what we would expect to observe if our theory was incorrect. **Hypothesis testing** is a process in which scientists evaluate systematically collected evidence to make a judgement of

---

[1] When we introduce an important new term in this book, that term appears in boldface type. We discuss variables at great length later in this and other chapters. For now, a good working definition is that a variable is something that varies. An example of a variable is voter turnout; researchers usually measure it as the percentage of voting-eligible persons in a geographically defined area who cast a vote in a particular election.

Causal theory

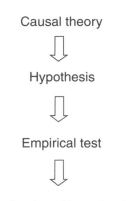

Hypothesis

Empirical test

Evaluation of hypothesis

Evaluation of causal theory

Scientific knowledge

Figure 1.1. The road to scientific knowledge.

whether the evidence favors their hypothesis or favors the corresponding null hypothesis. If a hypothesis survives a series of rigorous tests, scientists start to gain confidence in that hypothesis rather than in the null hypothesis, and thus they also gain confidence in the theory from which they generated their hypothesis.

Figure 1.1 presents a stylized schematic view of the path from theories to hypotheses to scientific knowledge.[2] At the top of the figure, we begin with a **causal** theory to explain our phenomenon of interest. We then derive one or more hypotheses about what our theory leads us to expect when we measure our concepts of interest (which we call **variables** – as subsequently discussed) in the real world. In the third step, we conduct **empirical** tests of our hypotheses.[3] From what we find, we evaluate our hypotheses relative to corresponding null hypotheses. Next, from the results of our hypothesis tests, we evaluate our causal theory. In light of our evaluation of our theory, we then think about how, if at all, we should revise what we consider to be scientific knowledge concerning our phenomenon of interest.

A core part of the scientific process is skepticism. On hearing of a new theory, other scientists will challenge this theory and devise further tests. Although this process can occasionally become quite combative, it is a necessary component in the development of scientific knowledge. Indeed, a core component of scientific knowledge is that, as confident as we are in a particular theory, we remain open to the possibility that there is still a test out there that will provide evidence that makes us lose confidence in that theory.

It is important to underscore here the nature of the testing that scientists carry out. One way of explaining this is to say that scientists are *not* like lawyers in the way that they approach evidence. Lawyers work for a particular client, advocate a particular point of view (like "guilt" or "innocence"), and then accumulate evidence with a goal of proving their case to a judge or jury. This goal of *proving* a desired result determines

---

[2] In practice, the development of scientific knowledge is frequently much messier than this step-by-step diagram. We show more of the complexity of this approach in later chapters.
[3] By "empirical" we simply mean "based on observations of the real world."

their approach to evidence. When faced with evidence that conflicts with their case, lawyers attempt to ignore or discredit such evidence. When faced with evidence that supports their case, lawyers try to emphasize the applicability of the supportive evidence. In many ways, the scientific and legal approaches to evidence couldn't be further apart. Scientific confidence in a theory is achieved only after hypotheses derived from that theory have run a gantlet of tough tests. At the beginning of a trial, lawyers develop a strategy to *prove* their case. In contrast, at the beginning of a research project, scientists will think long and hard about the most rigorous tests that they can conduct. A scientist's theory is never *proven* because scientists are always willing to consider new evidence.

The process of hypothesis testing reflects how hard scientists are on their own theories. As scientists evaluate systematically collected evidence to make a judgment of whether the evidence favors their hypothesis or favors the corresponding null hypothesis, they *always* favor the null hypothesis. Statistical techniques allow scientists to make probability-based statements about the empirical evidence that they have collected. You might think that, if the evidence was 50–50 between their hypothesis and the corresponding null hypothesis, the scientists would tend to give the nod to the hypothesis (from their theory) over the null hypothesis. In practice, though, this is not the case. Even when the hypothesis has an 80–20 edge over the null hypothesis, most scientists will still favor the null hypothesis. Why? Because scientists are very worried about the possibility of falsely rejecting the null hypothesis and therefore making claims that others ultimately will show to be wrong.

Once a theory has become established as a part of scientific knowledge in a field of study, researchers can build upon the foundation that this theory provides. Thomas Kuhn wrote about these processes in his famous book *The Structure of Scientific Revolutions*. According to Kuhn, scientific fields go through cycles of accumulating knowledge based on a set of shared assumptions and commonly accepted theories about the way that the world works. Together, these shared assumptions and accepted theories form what we call a **paradigm**. Once researchers in a scientific field have widely accepted a paradigm, they can pursue increasingly technical questions that make sense only because of the work that has come beforehand. This state of research under an accepted paradigm is referred to as **normal science**. When a major problem is found with the accepted theories and assumptions of a scientific field, that field will go through a revolutionary period during which new theories and assumptions replace the old paradigm to establish a new paradigm. One of the more famous of these scientific revolutions occurred during the 16th century when the field of astronomy was forced to abandon its assumption that the Earth was the center of the known universe. This was an assumption that had informed theories about planetary movement for thousands of years. In the book *On Revolutions of the Heavenly Bodies*, Nicolai Copernicus presented his theory that the Sun was the center of the known universe. Although this radical theory met many challenges, an increasing body of evidence convinced astronomers that Coperinicus had it right. In the aftermath of this paradigm shift, researchers developed new assumptions and theories that established a new paradigm, and the affected fields of study entered into new periods of normal scientific research.

It may seem hard to imagine that the field of political science has gone through anything that can compare with the experiences of astronomers in the 16th century. Indeed, Kuhn and other scholars who study the evolution of scientific fields of research have a lively and ongoing debate about where the social sciences, like political science, are in terms of their development. The more skeptical participants in this debate argue that political science is not sufficiently mature to have a paradigm, much less a paradigm shift. If we put aside this somewhat esoteric debate about paradigms and paradigm shifts, we can see an important example of the evolution of scientific knowledge about politics from the study of public opinion in the United States.

In the 1940s the study of public opinion through mass surveys was in its infancy. Prior to that time, political scientists and sociologists assumed that U.S. voters were heavily influenced by presidential campaigns – and, in particular, by campaign advertising – as they made up their minds about the candidates. To better understand how these processes worked, a team of researchers from Columbia University set up an in-depth study of public opinion in Erie County, Ohio, during the 1944 presidential election. Their study involved interviewing the same individuals at multiple time periods across the course of the campaign. Much to the researchers' surprise, they found that voters were remarkably consistent from interview to interview in terms of their vote intentions. Instead of being influenced by particular events of the campaign, most of the voters surveyed had made up their minds about how they would cast their ballots long before the campaigning had even begun. The resulting book by Paul Lazarsfeld, Bernard Berelson, and Hazel Gaudet, titled *The People's Choice*, changed the way that scholars thought about public opinion and political behavior in the United States. If political campaigns were not central to vote choice, scholars were forced to ask themselves what *was* critical to determining how people voted.

At first other scholars were skeptical of the findings of the 1944 Erie County study, but as the revised theories of politics of Lazarsfeld et al. were evaluated in other studies, the field of public opinion underwent a change

ex of
shift

that looks very much like what Thomas Kuhn calls a "paradigm shift." In the aftermath of this finding, new theories were developed to attempt to explain the origins of voters' long-lasting attachments to political parties in the United States. An example of an influential study that was carried out under this shifted paradigm is Richard Niemi and Kent Jenning's seminal book from 1974, *The Political Character of Adolescence: The Influence of Families and Schools*. As the title indicates, Niemi and Jennings studied the attachments of schoolchildren to political parties. Under the pre–Erie County paradigm of public opinion, this study would not have made much sense. But once researchers had found that voter's partisan attachments were quite stable over time, studying them at the early ages at which they form became a reasonable scientific enterprise. You can see evidence of this paradigm at work in current studies of party identification and debates about its stability.

1.3 THINKING ABOUT THE WORLD IN TERMS OF VARIABLES AND CAUSAL EXPLANATIONS

So how do political scientists develop theories about politics? A key element of this is that they order their thoughts about the political world in terms of concepts that scientists call *variables* and causal relationships between variables. This type of mental exercise is just a more rigorous way of expressing ideas about politics that we hear on a daily basis. You should think of each variable in terms of its *label* and its *values*. The **variable label** is a description of what the variable is, and the **variable values** are the denominations in which the variable occurs. So, if we're talking about the variable that reflects an individual's age, we could simply label this variable "Age" and some of the denominations in which this variable occurs would be years, days, or even hours.

It is easier to understand the process of turning concepts into variables by using an example of an entire theory. For instance, if we're thinking about U.S. presidential elections, a commonly expressed idea is that the incumbent president will fare better when the economy is relatively healthy. If we restate this in terms of a political science theory, the state of the economy becomes the **independent variable**, and the outcome of presidential elections becomes the **dependent variable**. One way of keeping the lingo of theories straight is to remember that the value of the "dependent" variable "depends" on the value of the "independent" variable. Recall that a theory is a tentative conjecture about the causes of some phenomenon of interest. In other words, a theory is a conjecture that the independent variable is causally related to the dependent variable; according to our theory, change in the value of the independent variable *causes* change in the value of the dependent variable.

This is a good opportunity to pause and try to come up with your own causal statement in terms of an independent and dependent variable; try filling in the following blanks with some political variables:

_____ **causes** _____

Sometimes it's easier to phrase causal propositions more specifically in terms of the values of the variables that you have in mind. For instance,

higher _____ **causes lower** _____

or

higher _____ **causes higher** _____

Once you learn to think about the world in terms of variables you will be able to produce an almost endless slew of causal theories. In Chapter 4 we will discuss at length how we design research to evaluate the causal claims in theories, but one way to initially evaluate a particular theory is to think about the causal explanation behind it. The causal explanation behind a theory is the answer to the question, "why do you think that this independent variable is causally related to this dependent variable?" If the answer is reasonable, then the theory has possibilities. In addition, if the answer is original and thought provoking, then you may really be onto something. Let's return now to our working example in which the state of the economy is the independent variable and the outcome of presidential elections is our dependent variable. The causal explanation for this theory is that we believe that the state of the economy is *causally related* to the outcome of presidential elections *because* voters hold the president responsible for management of the national economy. As a result, when the economy has been performing well, more voters will vote for the incumbent. When the economy is performing poorly, fewer voters will support the incumbent candidate. If we put this in terms of the preceding fill-in-the-blank exercise, we could write

economic performance causes presidential election outcomes,

or, more specifically, we could write

higher economic performance causes higher incumbent vote.

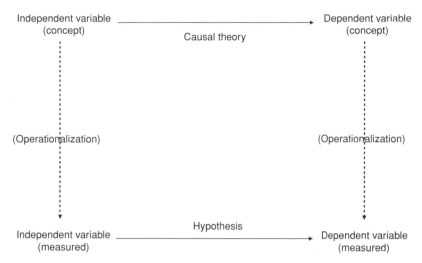

Figure 1.2. From theory to hypothesis.

For now we'll refer to this theory, which has been widely advanced and tested by political scientists, as "the theory of economic voting."

To test the theory of economic voting in U.S. presidential elections, we need to derive from it one or more testable hypotheses. Figure 1.2 provides a schematic diagram of the relationship between a theory and one of its hypotheses. At the top of this diagram are the components of the causal theory. As we move from the top part of this diagram (Causal theory) to the bottom part (Hypothesis), we are moving from a general statement about how we think the world works to a more specific statement about a relationship that we expect to find when we go out in the real world and measure (or **operationalize**) our variables.[4]

At the theory level at the top of Figure 1.2, our variables do not need to be explicitly defined. With the economic voting example, the independent variable, "Economic Performance," can be thought of as a concept that ranges from very strong to very poor. The dependent variable, "Incumbent Vote," can be thought of as a concept that ranges from very high to very low. Our causal theory is that a stronger economic performance causes the incumbent vote to be higher.

Because there are many ways in which we can measure each of our two variables, there are many different hypotheses that we can test to find out how well our theory holds up to real-world data. We can measure economic performance in a variety of ways. These measures include inflation,

---

[4] Throughout this book we will use the terms "measure" and "operationalize" interchangeably. It is fairly common practice in the current political science literature to use the term "operationalize."

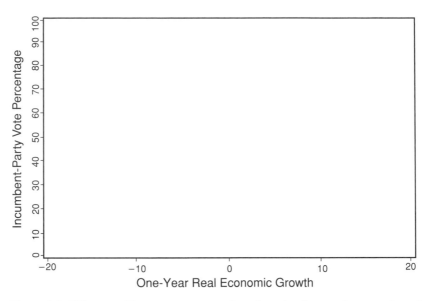

Figure 1.3. What would you expect to see based on the theory of economic voting?

unemployment, real economic growth, and many others. "Incumbent Vote" may seem pretty straightforward to measure, but here there are also a number of choices that we need to make. For instance, what do we do in the cases in which the incumbent president is not running again? Or what about elections in which a third-party candidate runs? Measurement (or operationalization) of concepts is an important part of the scientific process. We will discuss this in greater detail in Chapter 5, which is devoted entirely to variable measurement. For now, we imagine that we are operationalizing economic performance with real economic growth, as defined by official U.S. government measures of the one-year rate of inflation-adjusted economic growth at the time of the election. We operationalize our dependent variable as the percentage of the popular vote, as reported in official election results, for the party that controlled the presidency at the time of the election.

Figure 1.3 shows the axes of the graph that we could produce if we collected the measures of these two variables. We could place each U.S. presidential election on the graph in Figure 1.3 by identifying the point that corresponds to the value of both "One-Year Real Economic Growth" (the horizontal, or *x*, axis) and "Incumbent-Party Vote Percentage" (the vertical, or *y*, axis). For instance, if these values were (respectively) 0 and 50, the position for that election year would be exactly in the center of the graph. Based on our theory, what would you expect to see if we collected these measures for all elections? Remember that our theory is that a stronger *economic performance* causes the *incumbent vote* to be higher. And we can restate this theory in reverse such that a weaker *economic performance* causes the *incumbent vote* to be lower. So, what would this lead us to expect to see if we plotted real-world data onto Figure 1.3? To get this answer right, let's make sure that we know our way around this graph. If we move from left to right on the horizontal axis, which is labeled "One-Year Real Economic Growth," what is going on in real-world terms? We can see that, at the far left end of the horizontal axis, the value is −20. This would mean that the U.S. economy had shrunk by 20% over the past year, which would represent a very poor performance (to say the least). As we move to the right on this axis, each point represents a better economic performance up to the point where we see a value of +20, indicating that the real economy has grown by 20% over the past year. The vertical axis depicts values of "Incumbent-Party Vote Percentage." Moving upward on this axis represents an increasing share of the popular vote for the incumbent party, whereas moving downward represents a decreasing share of the popular vote.

Now think about these two axes together in terms of what we would expect to see based on the theory of economic voting. In thinking through these matters, we should always start with our independent variable. This is because our theory states that the value of the independent variable exerts a causal influence on the value of the dependent variable. So, if we start with a very low value of *economic performance* – let's say −15 on the horizontal axis – what does our theory lead us to expect in terms of values for the *incumbent vote*, the dependent variable? We would also expect the value of the dependent variable to be very low. This case would then be expected to be in the lower-left-hand corner of Figure 1.3. Now imagine a case in which economic performance was quite strong at +15. Under these circumstances, our theory would lead us to expect that the incumbent-vote percentage would also be quite high. Such a case would be in the upper-right-hand corner of our graph. Figure 1.4 shows two such hypothetical points plotted on the same graph as Figure 1.3. If we draw a line between these two points, this line would slope upward from the lower left to the upper right. We describe such a line as having a positive slope. We can therefore hypothesize that the relationship between the variable labeled "One-Year Real Economic Growth" and the variable labeled "Incumbent-Party Vote Percentage" will be a **positive relationship**. A positive relationship is one for which higher values of the independent variable coincide with higher values of the dependent variable.

Let's consider a different operationalization of our independent variable. Instead of economic growth, let's use "Unemployment Percentage" as our operationalization of economic performance. We haven't changed our theory, but we need to rethink our hypothesis with this new measurement or operationalization. The best way to do so is to draw a picture like

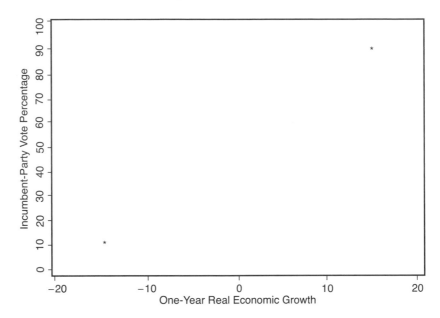

Figure 1.4. What would you expect to see based on the theory of economic voting? Two hypothetical cases.

Figure 1.3 but with the changed independent variable on the horizontal axis. This is what we have in Figure 1.5. As we move from left to right on the horizontal axis in Figure 1.5, the percentage of the members of the workforce who are unemployed goes up. What does this mean in terms

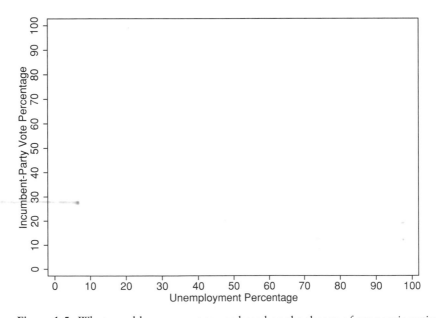

Figure 1.5. What would you expect to see based on the theory of economic voting?

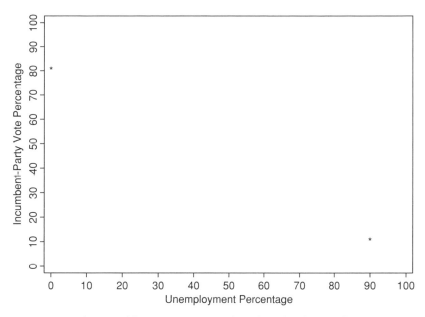

Figure 1.6. What would you expect to see based on the theory of economic voting? Two hypothetical cases.

of economic performance? Rising unemployment is generally considered a poorer economic performance whereas decreasing unemployment is considered a better economic performance. Based on our theory, what should we expect to see in terms of incumbent vote percentage when unemployment is high? What about when unemployment is low?

Figure 1.6 shows two such hypothetical points plotted on our graph of unemployment and incumbent vote from Figure 1.5. The point in the upper-left-hand corner represents our expected vote percentage when unemployment equals zero. Under these circumstances, our theory of economic voting leads us to expect that the incumbent party will do very well. The point in the lower-right-hand corner represents our expected vote percentage when unemployment is very high. Under these circumstances our theory of economic voting leads us to expect that the incumbent party will do very poorly. If we draw a line between these two points, this line would slope downward from the upper-left to the lower-right. We describe such a line as having a negative slope. We can therefore hypothesize that the relationship between the variable labeled "Unemployment Percentage" and the variable labeled "Incumbent-Party Vote Percentage" will be a **negative relationship**. A negative relationship is one for which higher values of the independent variable coincide with lower values of the dependent variable.

In this example we have seen that the same theory can lead to a hypothesis of a positive or a negative relationship. The operationalization of the independent and the dependent variables determines the direction of the hypothesized relationship. It is often very helpful to draw a picture like Figure 1.3 or 1.5 to translate our theories into hypotheses. Once we have such a figure with the axes properly labeled, we can determine what our expected value of our dependent variable should be if we observe both a high and a low value of the independent variable. And once we have placed the two resulting points on our figure, we can tell whether our hypothesized relationship is positive or negative.

Once we have figured out our hypothesized relationship, we can collect data from real-world cases and see how well these data reflect our expectations of a positive or negative relationship. This is a very important step that we can carry out fairly easily in the case of the theory of economic voting. Once we collect all of the data on economic performance and election outcomes, we will, however, still be a long way from confirming the theory that economic performance *causes* presidential election outcomes. Even if a graph like Figure 1.3 produces compelling visual evidence, we will need to see more rigorous evidence than that. Chapters 8–12 focus on the evaluation of hypotheses by use of statistics. The basic logic of statistical hypothesis testing is that we assess the probability that the relationship we find could be due to random chance. The stronger the evidence that such a relationship *could not* be due to random chance, the more confident we would be in our hypothesis. The stronger the evidence that such a relationship *could* be due to random chance, the more confident we would be in the corresponding null hypothesis. This in turn reflects on our theory.

We also, at this point, need to be cautious about claiming that we have "confirmed" our theory, because social scientific phenomena (such as elections) are usually complex and cannot be explained completely with a single independent variable. Take a minute or two to think about what other variables, aside from economic performance, you believe might be causally related to U.S. presidential election outcomes. If you can come up with at least one, you are on your way to thinking like a political scientist. Because there are usually other variables that matter, we can continue to think about our theories two variables at a time, but we need to qualify our expectations to account for other variables. We will spend Chapters 3 and 4 expanding on these important issues.

1.4   MODELS OF POLITICS

When we think about the phenomena that we want to better understand as dependent variables and develop theories about the independent variables that causally influence them, we are constructing **theoretical models**.

Political scientist James Rogers provides an excellent analogy between models and maps to explain how these abstractions from reality are useful to us as we try to understand the political world:

> . . . the very unrealism of a model, if properly constructed, is what makes it useful. The models developed below are intended to serve much the same function as a street map of a city. If one compares a map of a city to the real topography of that city, it is certain that what is represented in the map is a highly unrealistic portrayal of what the city actually looks like. The map utterly distorts what is *really* there and leaves out numerous details about what a particular area looks like. But it is precisely *because* the map distorts reality – because it abstracts away from a host of details about what is really there – that it is a useful tool. A map that attempted to portray the full details of a particular area would be too cluttered to be useful in finding a particular location or would be too large to be conveniently stored. (2006, p. 276, emphasis in original)

The essential point is that models *are* simplifications. Whether or not they are useful to us depends on what we are trying to accomplish with the particular model. One of the remarkable aspects of models is that they are often more useful to us when they are inaccurate than when they are accurate. The process of thinking about the failure of a model to explain one or more cases can generate a new causal theory. Glaring inaccuracies often point us in the direction of fruitful theoretical progress.

1.5 RULES OF THE ROAD TO SCIENTIFIC KNOWLEDGE ABOUT POLITICS

In the chapters that follow, we will focus on particular tools of political science research. As we do this, try to keep in mind our larger purpose – trying to advance the state of scientific knowledge about politics. As scientists, we have a number of basic rules that should never be far from our thinking:

- Make your theories causal.
- Don't let data alone drive your theories.
- Consider only empirical evidence.
- Avoid normative statements.
- Pursue both generality and parsimony.

1.5.1 Make Your Theories Causal

All of Chapter 3 deals with the issue of causality and, specifically, how we identify causal relationships. When political scientists construct theories, it is critical that they always think in terms of the causal processes that drive the phenomena in which they are interested. For us to develop a better understanding of the political world, we need to think in terms of causes and not mere **covariation.** The term covariation is used to describe a situation in which two variables vary together (or **covary**). If we imagine two variables, *A* and *B*, then we would say that *A* and *B* covary if it is the case that, when we observe higher values of variable *A*, we generally also observe higher values of variable *B*. We would also say that *A* and *B* covary if it is the case that, when we observe higher values of variable *A*, we generally also observe lower values of variable *B*.[5] It is easy to assume that when we observe covariation we are also observing causality, but it is important not to fall into this trap.

1.5.2   Don't Let Data Alone Drive Your Theories

This rule of the road is closely linked to the first. A longer way of stating it is "try to develop theories before examining the data on which you will perform your tests." The importance of this rule is best illustrated by a silly example. Suppose that we are looking at data on the murder rate (number of murders per 1000 people) in the city of Houston, Texas, by months of the year. This is our dependent variable, and we want to explain why it is higher in some months and lower in others. If we were to take as many different independent variables as possible and simply see whether they had a relationship with our dependent variable, one variable that we might find to strongly covary with the murder rate is the amount of money spent per capita on ice cream. If we perform some verbal gymnastics, we might develop a "theory" about how heightened blood sugar levels in people who eat too much ice cream lead to murderous patterns of behavior. Of course, if we think about it further, we might realize that both ice cream sales and the number of murders committed go up when temperatures rise. Do we have a causally plausible explanation for why temperatures and murder rates might be causally related? It is pretty well known that people's tempers tend to fray when the temperature is higher. People also spend a lot more time outside during hotter weather, and these two factors might combine to produce a plausible relationship between temperatures and murder rates.

---

[5] A closely related term is **correlation.** For now we use these two terms interchangeably. In Chapter 8, you will see that there are precise statistical measures of covariance and correlation that are closely related to each other but produce different numbers for the same data.

What this rather silly example illustrates is that we don't want our theories to be crafted based entirely on observations from real-world data. We are likely to be somewhat familiar with empirical patterns relating to the dependent variables for which we are developing causal theories. This is normal; we wouldn't be able to develop theories about phenomena about which we know nothing. But we need to be careful about how much we let what we see guide our development of our theories. One of the best ways to do this is to think about the underlying causal process as we develop our theories and to let this have much more influence on our thinking than patterns that we might have observed.

1.5.3 Consider Only Empirical Evidence

As we previously outlined, we need to always remain open to the possibility that new evidence will come along that will decrease our confidence in even a well-established theory. A closely related rule of the road is that, as scientists, we want to base what we know on what we see from *empirical* evidence, which, as we have said, is simply "evidence based on observing the real world." Strong logical arguments are a good start in favor of a theory, but before we can be convinced, we need to see results from rigorous hypothesis tests.[6]

1.5.4 Avoid Normative Statements

Normative statements are statements about how the world ought to be. Whereas politicians make and break their political careers with normative statements, political scientists need to avoid them at all costs. Most political scientists care about political issues and have opinions about how the world ought to be. On its own, this is not a problem. But when normative preferences about how the world "should" be structured creep into their scientific work, the results can become highly problematic. The best way to avoid such problems is to conduct research and report your findings in

---

[6] It is worth noting that some political scientists use data drawn from experimental settings to test their hypotheses. There is some debate about whether such data are, strictly speaking, empirical or not. We discuss political science experiments and their limitations in Chapter 4. In recent years some political scientists have also made clever use of simulated data to gain leverage on their phenomena of interest, and the empirical nature of such data can certainly be debated. In the context of this textbook we are not interested in weighing in on these debates about exactly what is and is not empirical data. Instead, we suggest that one should always consider the overall quality of data on which hypothesis tests have been performed when evaluating causal claims.

such a fashion that it is impossible for the reader to tell what your values are or your normative preferences about the world are.

This does not mean that good political science research cannot be used to change the world. To the contrary, advances in our scientific knowledge about phenomena enable policy makers to bring about changes in an effective manner. For instance, if we want to rid the world of wars (normative), we need to understand the systematic dynamics of the international system that produce wars in the first place (empirical and causal). If we want to rid America of homelessness (normative), we need to understand the pathways into and out of being homeless (empirical and causal). If we want to help our favored candidate win elections (normative), we need to understand what characteristics make people vote the way they do (empirical and causal).

1.5.5 Pursue Both Generality and Parsimony

Our final rule of the road is that we should always pursue generality and parsimony. These two goals can come into conflict. By "generality," we mean that we want our theories to be applied to as general a class of phenomena as possible. For instance, a theory that explains the causes of a phenomenon in only one country is less useful than a theory that explains the same phenomenon across multiple countries. Additionally, the more simple or **parsimonious** a theory is, the more appealing it becomes.[7]

In the real world, however, we often face trade-offs between generality and parsimony. This is the case because, to make a theory apply more generally, we need to add caveats. The more caveats that we add to a theory, the less parsimonious it becomes.

1.6 A QUICK LOOK AHEAD

You now know the rules of the road. As we go through the next 11 chapters, you will acquire an increasingly complicated set of tools for developing and testing scientific theories about politics, so it is crucial that, at every step along the way, you keep these rules in the back of your mind. The rest of this book can be divided into three different sections. The first section, which includes this chapter through Chapter 4, is focused on the development

---

[7] The term "parsimonious" is often used in a relative sense. So, if we are comparing two theories, the theory that is simpler would be the more parsimonious. Indeed, this rule of the road might be phrased "pursue both generality and simplicity." We use the words "parsimony" and "parsimonious" because they are widely used to describe theories.

of theories and research designs to study causal relationships about politics. In Chapter 2, "The Art of Theory Building," we discuss a range of strategies for developing theories about political phenomena. In Chapter 3, "Evaluating Causal Relationships," we provide a detailed explanation of the logic for evaluating causal claims about relationships between an independent variable, which we call "X," and a dependent variable, which we call "Y." In Chapter 4, "Research Design," we discuss the research strategies that political scientists use to investigate causal relationships.

In the second section of this book, we expand on the basic tools that political scientists need to test their theories. Chapter 5, "Measurement," is a detailed discussion of how we measure (or operationalize) our variables. Chapter 6, "Descriptive Statistics and Graphs," introduces a set of tools that can be used to summarize the characteristics of variables one at a time. Chapter 7, "Statistical Inference," is an introduction to the logic of statistical hypothesis testing. In Chapter 8, "Bivariate Hypothesis Testing," we begin to apply the lessons from Chapter 7 to a series of empirical tests of the relationship between pairs of variables.

The third and final section of this book introduces the critical concepts of the regression model. Chapter 9, "Bivariate Regression Models," introduces the two-variable regression model as an extension of the concepts from Chapter 8. In Chapter 10, "Multiple Regression Models I: The Basics," we introduce the multivariate-regression model, with which researchers are able to look at the effects of independent variable X on dependent variable Y while controlling for the effects of other independent variables. Chapter 11, "Multiple Regression Models II: Crucial Extensions," and Chapter 12, "Multiple Regression Models III: Applications," provide in-depth *discussions of* and *advice for* commonly encountered research scenarios involving multivariate-regression models.

CONCEPTS INTRODUCED IN THIS CHAPTER

causal	null hypothesis
correlation	operationalize
covary (or covariation)	paradigm
dependent variable	paradigm shift
empirical	parsimonious
hypothesis	theoretical models
hypothesis testing	theory
independent variable	variable
normal science	variable label
normative statements	variable values

EXERCISES

1. Think about something in the political world that you would like to to better understand. Try to think about this as a variable with high and low values. This is your dependent variable at the conceptual level. Now think about what might cause the values of your dependent variable to be higher or lower. Try to phrase this in terms of an independent variable, also at the conceptual level. Write a paragraph about these two variables and your theory about why they are causally related to each other.

2. Identify something in the world that you would like to see happen (normative). What scientific knowledge (empirical and causal) would help you to pursue this goal?

3. The 1992 U.S. presidential election, in which challenger Bill Clinton defeated incumbent George H. W. Bush, has often been remembered as the "It's the economy, stupid," election. How can we restate the causal statement that embodies this conventional wisdom – "Clinton beat Bush because the economy had performed poorly" – into a more general theoretical statement?

   For Exercises 4 and 5, consider the following statement about the world: "If you care about economic success in a country, you should also care about the peoples' political rights in that country. In a society in which people have more political rights, the victims of corrupt business practices will work through the system to get things corrected. As a result, countries in which people have more political rights will have less corruption. In countries in which there is less corruption, there will be more economic investment and more economic success."

4. Identify at least two causal claims that have been made in the preceding statement. For each causal claim, identify which variable is the independent variable and which variable is the dependent variable. These causal claims should be stated in terms of one of the following types of phrases in which the first blank should be filled by the independent variable and the second blank should be filled by the dependent variable:

   _____ **causes** _____

   higher _____ **causes lower** _____

   higher _____ **causes higher** _____

5. Draw a graph like Figure 1.3 for each of the causal claims that you identified in Exercise 4. For each of your figures, do the following: Start on the left-hand side of the horizontal axis of the figure. This should represent a low value of the independent variable. What value of the dependent variable would you expect to find for such a case? Put a dot on your figure that represents this expected location. Now do the same for a case with a high value of the independent variable. Draw a line that connects these two points and write a couple of sentences that describe this picture.

6. Find an article in a political science journal that contains a model of politics. Provide the citation to the article, and answer the following questions:

(a) What is the dependent variable?

(b) What is one of the independent variables?

(c) What is the causal theory that connects the independent variable to the dependent variable?

(d) Does this seem reasonable?

2 The Art of Theory Building

OVERVIEW

In this chapter we discuss the art of theory building. Unfortunately there is no magical formula or cookbook for developing good theories about politics. But there are strategies for developing theories that will help you to develop good theories. We discuss these strategies in this chapter.

2.1 GOOD THEORIES COME FROM GOOD THEORY-BUILDING STRATEGIES

In Chapter 1 we discussed the role of theories in developing scientific knowledge. From that discussion, it is clear that a "good" theory is one that, after going through the rigors of the evaluation process, makes a contribution to scientific knowledge. In other words, a good theory is one that changes the way that we think about some aspect of the political world. We also know from our discussion of the rules of the road that we want our theories to be causal, empirical, nonnormative, general, and parsimonious. This is a tall order, and a logical question to ask at this point is "How do I come up with such a theory?"

Unfortunately, there is neither an easy answer nor a single answer. Instead, what we can offer you is a set of strategies. "Strategies?" you may ask. Imagine that you were given the following assignment: "Go out and get struck by lightning."[1] There is no cut-and-dried formula that will show you how to get struck by lightning, but certainly there are actions that you can take that will make it more likely. The first step is to look at a weather map and find an area where there is thunderstorm activity, and if you were to go to such an area, you would increase your likelihood of getting struck.

---

[1] Our lawyers have asked us to make clear that this is an illustrative analogy and that we are in no way encouraging you to go out and try to get struck by lightning.

You would be even more likely to get struck by lightning if, once in the area of thunderstorms, you climbed to the top of a tall barren hill. But you would be still more likely to get struck if you carried with you a nine iron and, once on top of the barren hill, in the middle of a thunderstorm, you held that nine iron up to the sky. The point here is that, although there are no magical formulae that make the development of a good theory (or getting hit by lightning) a certain event, there are strategies that you can follow to increase the likelihood of it happening.

2.2 IDENTIFYING INTERESTING VARIATION

A useful first step in theory building is to think about phenomena that vary and to focus on general patterns. Because theories are designed to explain variation in the dependent variable, identifying some variation that is of interest to you is a good jumping-off point. In Chapter 4 we present a discussion of two of the most common research designs – cross-sectional and time-series observational studies – in some detail. For now it is useful to give a brief description of each in terms of the types of variation in the dependent variable. These should help clarify the types of variation to consider as you begin to think about potential research ideas.

When we think about measuring our dependent variable, the first things that we need to identify are the time and spatial dimensions over which we would like to measure this variable. The **time dimension** identifies the point or points in time at which we would like to measure our variable. Depending on what we are measuring, typical time increments for political science data are annual, quarterly, monthly, or weekly measures. The **spatial dimension** identifies the units that we want to measure. There is a lot of variability in terms of the spatial units in political science data. If we are looking at survey data, the spatial unit will be the individual people who answered the survey (known as survey respondents). If we are looking at data on U.S. state governments, the typical spatial unit will be the 50 U.S. states. Data from international relations and comparative politics often take nations as their spatial units. Throughout this book, we think about measuring our dependent variable such that one of these two dimensions will be static (or constant). This means that our measures of our dependent variable will be of one of two types. The first is a **time-series measure**, in which the spatial dimension is the same for all cases and the dependent variable is measured at multiple points in time. The second is a **cross-sectional measure**, in which the time dimension is the same for all cases and the dependent variable is measured for multiple spatial units. Although it is possible for us to measure the same variable across both time and space, we strongly recommend thinking in terms of variation across only one of these

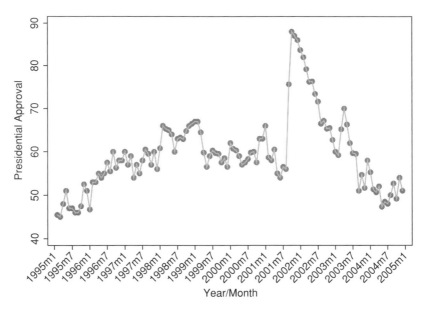

Figure 2.1. Presidential approval, 1995–2005.

two dimensions as you attempt to develop a theory about what causes this variation.[2] Let's consider an example of each type of dependent variable.

2.2.1   Time-Series Example

In Figure 2.1 we see the average monthly level of U.S. presidential approval displayed from 1995 to 2005. We can tell that this variable is measured as a time series because the spatial unit is the same (the United States), but the variable has been measured at multiple points in time (each month). This measure is comparable across the cases; for each month we are looking at the average percentage of people who reported that they approved of the job that the president was doing. Once we have a measure like this that is comparable across cases, we can start to think about what independent variable might *cause* the level of the dependent variable to be higher or lower.

If you just had a mental alarm bell go off telling you that we seemed to be violating one of our rules of the road from Chapter 1, then congratulations – you are doing a good job paying attention. Our second rule of the road is "don't let data alone drive your theories." Remember that we

---

[2] As we mentioned in Chapter 1, we will eventually theorize about multiple independent variables simultaneously causing the same dependent variable to vary. Confining variation in the dependent variable to a single dimension helps to make such multivariate considerations tractable.

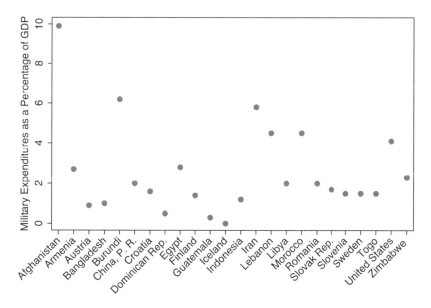

Figure 2.2. Military spending in 2005.

also can phrase this rule as "try to develop theories before examining the data on which you will perform your tests." So what this means is that we might develop a theory about U.S. presidential approval using Figure 2.1, but we would want to test that theory by using a different set of data that may or may not contain the data depicted in Figure 2.1.

2.2.2 Cross-Sectional Example

In Figure 2.2 we see military spending as a percentage of gross domestic product (GDP) in 2005 for 24 randomly selected nations. We can tell that this variable is measured cross sectionally, because it varies across spatial units (nations) but does not vary across time (it is measured for the year 2005 for each case). When we measure variables across spatial units like this, we have to be careful to choose appropriate measures that are comparable across spatial units. To better understand this, imagine that we had measured our dependent variable as the amount of money that each nation spent on its military. The problem would be that country currencies – the Afghan afghani, the Armenian dram, and Austrian euro – do not take on the same value. We would need to know the currency exchange rates in order to make these comparable across nations. Using currency exchange rates, we would be able to convert the absolute amounts of money that each nation had spent into a common measure. We could think of this particular measure as an operationalization of the concept of relative military "might." This would be a perfectly reasonable dependent variable for theories about what makes one nation more powerful than another. Why, you might ask, would we want to measure military spending as a percentage of GDP? The answer is that this comparison is our attempt to measure the percentage of the total budgetary effort available that a nation is putting into its armed forces. Some nations have larger economies than others, and this measure allows us to answer the question of how much of their total economic activity each nation is putting toward its military. We can theorize about what would *cause* a nation to put more or less of its available economic resources toward military spending.

Of course, as we discussed in the previous subsection, we would not want to develop our theory by using data from these 24 cases and then test it by using only the same set of cases.

2.3   LEARNING TO USE YOUR KNOWLEDGE

One of the common problems that people have when trying to develop a theory about a phenomenon of interest is that they can't get past a particular political event in time or a particular place about which they know a lot. It is helpful to know some specifics about politics, but it is also important to be able to distance yourself from the specifics of one case and to think more broadly about the underlying causal process. To use an analogy, it's fine to know something about trees, but we want to theorize about the forest. Remember, one of our rules of the road is to try to make our theories general.

2.3.1   Moving from a Specific Event to More General Theories

For an example of this, return to Figure 2.1. What is the first thing that you think most people notice when they look at Figure 2.1? Once they have figured out what the dimensions are in this figure (U.S. presidential approval over time), many people look at the fall of 2001 and notice the sharp increase in presidential approval that followed the terrorist attacks on the United States on September 11, 2001. This is a period of recent history about which many people have detailed memories. In particular, they might remember how the nation rallied around President Bush in the aftermath of these attacks. There are few people who would doubt that there was a causal linkage between these terrorist attacks and the subsequent spike in presidential approval.

At first glance, this particular incident might strike us as a unique event from which general theoretical insights cannot be drawn. After all, terrorist attacks on U.S. soil are rare events, and attacks of this magnitude are even more rare. The challenge to the scientific mind when we have strong confidence about a causal relationship in one specific incident is to push the core concepts around in what we might call thought experiments: How might a less-effective terrorist attack affect public opinion? How might other types of international incidents shape public opinion? Do we think that terrorist attacks lead to similar reactions in public opinion toward leaders in other nations? Each of these questions is posed in general terms, taking the specific events of this one incident as a jumping-off point. The answers to these more general questions should lead us to general theories about the causal impact of international incidents on public opinion.

In the 1970s John Mueller moved from the specifics of particular international incidents and their influence on public opinion towards a general theory of what causes rallies (or short-term increases) in public opinion.[3] Mueller developed a theory that presidential popularity would increase in the short term any time that there was international conflict. Mueller thought that this would occur because, in the face of international conflict, people would tend to put their partisan differences and other critiques that they may have of the president's handling of his job aside and support him as the commander and chief of the nation. In Mueller's statistical analysis of time-series data on presidential approval, he found that there was substantial support for his hypothesis that international conflicts would raise presidential approval rates, and this in turn gave him confidence in his theory of public opinion rallies.

2.3.2 Know Local, Think Global: Can You Drop the Proper Nouns?

Physicists don't have theories that apply only in France, and neither should we. Yet many political scientists write articles with one particular geographic context in mind. Among these, the articles that have the greatest impact are those that advance general theories from which the proper nouns have been removed.[4] An excellent example of this is Michael Lewis-Beck's article titled "Who's the Chef?" Lewis-Beck, like many observers of French politics, had observed the particularly colorful period from 1986 to 1988 during which the president was a socialist named François Mitterrand and the prime minister was Jacques Chirac, a right-wing politician from the Gaullist RPR party. The height of this political melodrama occurred when both leaders showed up to international summits of world leaders claiming to be the rightful representative of the French Republic. This led to a famous photo of the leaders of the G-7 group of nations that contained eight

---

[3] See Mueller (1973).

[4] By "proper nouns," we mean specific names of people or countries. But this logic can and should be pushed further to include specific dates, as we subsequently argue.

people.[5] Although many people saw this as just another colorful anecdote about the ever-changing nature of the power relationship between presidents and prime ministers in Fifth Republic France, Lewis-Beck moved from the specifics of such events to develop and test a general theory about political control and public opinion.

His theory was that changing the political control of the economy would cause public opinion to shift in terms of who was held accountable for the economy. In France, during times of unified political control of the top offices, the president is dominant, and thus according to Lewis-Beck's theory the president should be held accountable for economic outcomes. However, during periods of divided control, Lewis-Beck's theory leads to the expectation that the prime minister, because of his or her control of economic management during such periods, should be held accountable for economic outcomes. Through careful analysis of time-series data on political control and economic accountability, Lewis-Beck found that his theory was indeed supported.

Although the results of this study are important for advancing our understanding of French politics, the theoretical contribution made by Lewis-Beck was much greater because he couched it in general terms and without proper nouns. We also can use this logic to move from an understanding of a specific event to general theories that explain variation across multiple events. For example, although it might be tempting to think that every U.S. presidential election is entirely unique – with different candidates (proper names) and different historical circumstances – the better scientific theory does *not* explain only the outcome of the 2008 U.S. presidential election, but of U.S. presidential elections in general. That is, instead of asking "Why did Bush beat Kerry in the 2004 election?" we should ask either "What causes incumbent success rates in U.S. presidential elections?" or "What causes Republican candidates to fare better or worse than Democratic candidates in U.S. presidential elections?"

2.4 EXAMINE PREVIOUS RESEARCH

Once you have identified an area in which you want to conduct research, it is often useful to look at what other work has been done that is related to your areas of interest. As we discussed in Chapter 1, part of taking a scientific approach is to be skeptical of research findings, whether they are our own or those of other researchers. By taking a skeptical look at the

[5] The G-7, now the G-8 with the inclusion of Russia, is an annual summit meeting of the heads of government from the world's most powerful nations.

research of others, we can develop new research ideas of our own and thus develop new theories.

We therefore suggest looking at research that seems interesting to you and, as you examine what has been done, keep the following list of questions in mind:

- What (if any) other causes of the dependent variable did the previous researchers miss?
- Can their theory be applied elsewhere?
- If we believe their findings, are there further implications?
- How might this theory work at different levels of aggregation (micro$\Longleftrightarrow$macro)?

2.4.1   What Did the Previous Researchers Miss?

Any time that we read the work of others, the first thing that we should do is break down their theory or theories in terms of the independent and dependent variables that they claim are causally related to each other.[6] Once we have done this, we should think about whether the causal arguments that other researchers have advanced seem reasonable. (In Chapter 3 we present a detailed four-step process for doing this.) We should also be in the habit of coming up with other independent variables that we think might be causally related to the same dependent variable. Going through this type of mental exercise can lead to new theories that are worth pursuing.

2.4.2   Can Their Theory Be Applied Elsewhere?

When we read about the empirical research that others have conducted, we should be sure that we understand which specific cases they were studying when they tested their theory. We should then proceed with a mental exercise in which we think about what we might find if we applied the same theory to other cases. In doing so, we will probably identify some cases for which we expect to get the same results, as well as other cases for which we might have different expectations. Of course, we would have to carry out our own empirical research to know whether our speculation along these lines is correct, but replicating research can lead to interesting findings. The most useful theoretical development comes when we can identify systematic patterns in the types of cases that will fit and those that will not fit the

---

[6] We cannot overstate the importance of this endeavor. We understand that this can be a difficult task for a beginning student, but it gets easier with practice. A good way to start this process is to look at the figures or tables in an article and ask yourself, "What is the dependent variable here?"

established theory. These systematic patterns are additional variables that determine whether a theory will work across an expanded set of cases. In this way we can think about developing new theories that will subsume the original established theory.

2.4.3 If We Believe Their Findings, Are There Further Implications?

Beginning researchers often find themselves intimidated when they read convincing accounts of the research carried out by more established scholars. After all, how can we ever expect to produce such innovative theories and find such convincingly supportive results from extensive empirical tests? Instead of being intimidated by such works, we need to learn to view them as opportunities – opportunities to carry their logic further and think about what other implications might be out there. If, for example, another researcher has produced a convincing theory about how voters behave, we could ask how might this new understanding alter the behavior of strategic politicians who understand that voters behave in this fashion?

One of the best examples of this type of research extension in political science comes from our previous example of John Mueller's research on rallies in presidential popularity. Because Mueller had found such convincingly supportive evidence of this "rally 'round the flag effect" in his empirical testing, other researchers were able to think through the strategic consequences of this phenomenon. This led to a new body of research on a phenomenon called "diversionary use of force." The idea of this new research is that, because strategic politicians will be aware that international conflicts temporarily increase presidential popularity, they will choose to generate international conflicts at times when they need such a boost.

2.4.4 How Might This Theory Work at Different Levels of Aggregation (Micro ⟺ Macro)?

As a final way to use the research of others to generate new theories we suggest considering how a theory might work differently at varying levels of aggregation. In political science research, the lowest level of aggregation is usually at the level of individual people in studies of public opinion. As we saw in Subsection 2.4.3, when we find a trend in terms of individual-level behavior, we can develop new theoretical insights by thinking about how strategic politicians might take advantage of such trends. Sometimes it is possible to gain these insights by simply changing the level of aggregation. As we have seen, political scientists have often studied trends in public opinion by examining data measured at the national level over time. This type of study is referred to as the study of macro politics. When we find trends in public opinion at higher (macro) levels of aggregation, it is always an interesting thought exercise to consider what types of patterns of individual-level or "micro-" level behavior are driving these aggregate-level findings.

As an example of this, return to the rally 'round the flag example and change the level of aggregation. We have evidence that, when there are international conflicts, public opinion toward the president becomes more positive. What types of individual-level forces might be driving this observed aggregate-level trend? It might be the case that there is a uniform shift across all types of individuals in their feelings about the president. It might also be the case that the shift is less uniform. Perhaps individuals who dislike the president's policy positions on domestic events are willing to put these differences aside in the face of international conflicts, whereas the opinions of the people who were already supporters of the president remain unchanged. Thinking about the individual-level dynamics that drive aggregate observations can be a fruitful source of new causal theories.

2.5 THINK FORMALLY ABOUT THE CAUSES THAT LEAD TO VARIATION IN YOUR DEPENDENT VARIABLE

Thus far in this book we have discussed thinking about the political world in an organized, systematic fashion. By now, we hope that you are starting to think about politics in terms of independent variables and dependent variables and are developing theories about the causal relationships between them. The theories that we have considered thus far have come from thinking rigorously about the phenomena that we want to explain and deducing plausible causal explanations. One extension of this type of rigorous thinking is labeled "**formal theory**" or "**rational choice**."[7]

The formal-theory approach to social science phenomena starts out with a fairly basic set of assumptions about human behavior and then uses game theory and other mathematical tools to build models of phenomena of interest. We can summarize these assumptions about human behavior by saying that formal theorists assume that all individuals are **rational utility maximizers** – that they attempt to maximize their self-interest. Individuals are faced with a variety of choices in political interactions, and those choices carry with them different consequences – some desirable, others

[7] The terms "formal theory" and "rational choice" have been used fairly interchangeably to describe the application of game theory and other formal mathematical tools to puzzles of human behavior. We have a slight preference for the term "formal theory" because it is a more overarching term describing the enterprise of using these tools, whereas "rational choice" describes the most critical assumption that this approach makes.

undesirable. By thinking through the incentives faced by individuals, users of this approach begin with the strategic foundations of the decisions that individuals face. Formal theorists then deduce theoretical expectations of what individuals will do given their preferences and the strategic environment that they confront.

That sounds like a mouthful, we know. Let's begin with a simple example: If human beings are self-interested, then (by definition) members of a legislature are self-interested. This assumption suggests that members will place a high premium on reelection. Why is that? Because, first and foremost, a politician must be in office if she is going to achieve her political goals. And from this simple deduction flows a whole set of hypotheses about congressional organization and behavior.[8]

This approach to studying politics is a mathematically rigorous attempt to think through what it would be like to be in the place of different actors involved in a situation in which they have to choose how to act. In essence, formal theory is a lot like the saying that we should not judge a person until we have walked a mile in his or her shoes. We use the tools of formal theory to try to put ourselves in the position of imagining that we are in someone else's shoes and thinking about the different choices that he or she has to make. In the following subsections we introduce the basic tools for doing this by using an **expected utility** approach and then provide a famous example of how researchers used this framework to develop theories about why people vote.

2.5.1   Utility and Expected Utility

Think about the choice that you have made to read this chapter of this book. What are your expected benefits and what are the costs that you expect to incur? One benefit may be that you are genuinely curious about how we build theories of politics. Another expected benefit may be that your professor is likely to test you on this material, and you expect that you will perform better if you have read this chapter. There are, no doubt, also costs to reading this book. What else might you be doing with your time? This is the way that formal theorists approach the world.

Formal theorists think about the world in terms of the outcome of a collection of individual-level decisions about what to do. In thinking about an individual's choices of actions, formal theorists put everything in terms of **utility**. Utility is an intentionally vague quantity. The utility from a particular action is equal to the sum of all benefits minus the sum of all costs from that action. If we consider an action Y, we can summarize the

---

[8] See Mayhew (1974) and Fiorina (1989).

utility from Y for individual i with the following formula:

$$U_i(Y) = \sum B_i(Y) - \sum C_i(Y),$$

where $U_i(Y)$ is the utility for individual i from action Y, $\sum B_i(Y)$ is the sum of the benefits B_i from action Y for individual i, and $\sum C_i(Y)$ is the sum of the costs C_i from action Y for individual i. When choosing among a set of possible actions (including the decisions not to act), a rational individual will choose that action that maximizes their utility. To put this formally,

given a set of choices $Y = Y_1, Y_2, Y_3, \dots, Y_n$,

individual i will choose Y_a such that $U_i(Y_a) > U_i(Y_b) \; \forall \; b \neq a$,

which translates into, "given a set of choices of action Y_1 through Y_n, individual i will choose that action (Y_a) such that the utility to individual i from that action is greater than the utility to individual i from any action (Y_b) for all ($\forall$) actions b not equal to a." In more straightforward terms, we could translate this into the individual choosing that action which he deems best for himself.

At this point, it is reasonable to look around the real world and think about exceptions. Is this really the way that the world works? What about altruism? During the summer of 2006, the world's second-richest man, Warren Buffet, agreed to donate more than 30 billion dollars to the Bill and Melinda Gates Foundation. Could this possibly have been rational utility-maximizing behavior? What about suicide bombers? The answer to these types of questions shows both the flexibility and a potential problem of the concept of utility. Note that, in the preceding formulae, there is always a subscripted i under each of the referenced utility components, (U_i, B_i, C_i). This is because different individuals have *different* evaluations of the benefits (B_i) and costs (C_i) associated with a particular action. When the critic of this approach says, "How can this possibly be utility-maximizing behavior?" the formal theorist responds, "Because this is just an individual with an unusual utility structure."

Think of it another way. Criticizing formal theory because it takes preferences as "given" – that is, as predetermined, rather than the focus of inquiry – strikes us as beside the point. Other parts of political science can and should study preference formation; think about political psychology and the study of public opinion. What formal theory does, and does well, is to say, "Okay, once an individual has her preferences – regardless of where they came from – how do those preferences interact with strategic opportunities and incentives to produce political outcomes?" Because formal theory takes those preferences as given does not mean that the preference-formation process is unimportant. It merely means that formal theory is here to explain a different portion of social reality.

From a scientific perspective, this is fairly unsettling. As we discussed in Chapter 1, we want to build scientific knowledge based on real-world observation. How do we observe people's utilities? Although we can ask people questions about what they like and don't like, and even their perceptions of costs and benefits, we can never truly observe utilities. Instead, the assumption of utility maximization is just that – an assumption. This assumption is, however, a fairly robust assumption, and we can do a lot if we are willing to make it and move forward while keeping the potential problems in the back of our minds.

Another potentially troubling aspect of the rational-actor utility-maximizing assumption that you may have thought of is the assumption of **complete information**. In other words, what if we don't know exactly what the costs and benefits will be from a particular action? In the preceding formulae, we were operating under the assumption of complete information, for which we knew exactly what would be the costs, benefits, and thus the utility from each possible action. When we relax this assumption, we move our discussion from utility to expected utility. This is a pretty straightforward transformation in which we put expectations in front of all utilities. So, under **incomplete information**, for an individual action Y,

$$E[U_i(Y)] = \sum E[B_i(Y)] - \sum E[C_i(Y)],$$

and a rational actor will maximize his expected utility thus:

given a set of choices $Y = Y_1, Y_2, Y_3, \ldots, Y_n,$

individual i will choose Y_a such that $E[U_i(Y_a)] > E[U_i(Y_b)] \forall b \neq a.$

2.5.2 The Puzzle of Turnout

One of the oldest and enduring applications of formal theory to politics is known as the "paradox of voting." William Riker and Peter Ordeshook set out the core arguments surrounding this application in their influential 1968 article in the *American Political Science Review* titled "A Theory of the Calculus of Voting." Their paper was written to weigh in on a lively debate over the rationality of voting. In Riker and Ordeshook's notation (with subscripts added), the expected utility of voting was summarized as

$$R_i = (B_i P_i) - C_i,$$

where R_i is the reward that an individual receives from voting, B_i is the differential benefit that an individual voter receives "from the success of his more preferred candidate over his less preferred one" (Riker and Ordeshook 1968, p. 25), P_i is the probability that that voter will cast the deciding vote that makes her preferred candidate the winner, and C_i is the sum of the costs that the voter incurs from voting.[9] If R_i is positive, the individual votes; otherwise, she abstains.

We'll work our way through the right-hand side of this formula and think about the likely values of each term in this equation for an individual eligible voter in a U.S. presidential election. The term B_i is likely to be greater than zero for most eligible voters in most U.S. presidential elections. The reasons for this vary widely from policy preferences to gut feelings about the relative character traits of the different candidates. Note, however, that the B_i term is multiplied by the P_i term. What is the likely value of P_i? Most observers of elections would argue that P_i is extremely small and effectively equal to zero for every voter in most elections. In the case of a U.S. presidential election, for one vote to be decisive, that voter must live in a state in which the popular vote total would be *exactly* tied, and this must be a presidential election for which that particular state would swing the outcome in the Electoral College to either candidate. Because P_i is effectively equal to zero, the entire term $(B_i P_i)$ is effectively equal to zero.

What about the costs of voting, C_i? Voting takes time for all voters. Even if a voter lives right next door to the polling place, she has to take some time to walk next door, perhaps stand in a line, and cast her ballot. The well-worn phrase "time is money" certainly applies here. Even if the voter in question is not working at the time that she votes, she could be doing something other than voting. Thus it is pretty clear that C_i is greater than zero. If C_i is greater than zero and $(B_i P_i)$ is effectively equal to zero, then R_i must be negative. How then, do we explain the millions of people that vote in U.S. presidential elections, or, indeed, elections around the world? Is this evidence that people are truly not rational? Or, perhaps, is it evidence that millions of people systematically overestimate P_i? Influential political economy scholars, including Anthony Downs and Gordon Tullock, posed these questions in the early years of formal theoretical analyses of politics.

Riker and Ordeshook's answer was that there must be some other benefit to voting that is not captured by the term $(B_i P_i)$. They proposed that the voting equation should be

$$R_i = (B_i P_i) - C_i + D_i,$$

[9] For simplicity in this example, consider an election in which there are only two candidates competing. Adding more candidates makes the calculation of B_i more complicated, but does not change the basic result of this model.

where D_i is the satisfaction that individuals feel from participating in the democratic process, regardless of the impact of their participation on the final outcome of the election. Riker and Ordeshook argued that D_i could be made up of a variety of different efficacious feelings about the political system, ranging from fulfilling one's duties as a citizen to standing up and being counted.

Think of the contribution that Riker and Ordeshook made to political science, and that, more broadly, formal theory makes to political science, in the following way: Riker and Ordeshook's theory leads us to wonder why any individual will vote. And yet, empirically, we notice that close to half of the adult population votes in any given presidential election in recent history. What formal theory accomplishes for us is that it helps us to focus in on exactly *why* people do bother, rather than to assert, normatively, that people *should*.[10]

2.6 THINK ABOUT THE INSTITUTIONS: THE RULES USUALLY MATTER

One rich source for theoretical insights comes from thinking about institutional arrangements and the influence that they have in shaping political behavior and outcomes. In other words, take some time to think about the rules under which the political game is played. To fully understand these rules and their impact, we need to think through some counterfactual scenarios in which we imagine how outcomes would be altered if there were different rules in place. This type of exercise can lead to some valuable theoretical insights. In the subsections that follow, we consider two examples of thinking about the impact of institutions.

2.6.1 Legislative Rules

Considering the rules of the political game has yielded theoretical insights into the study of legislatures and other governmental decision-making

---

[10] Of course, Riker and Ordeshook did not have the final word in 1968. In fact, the debate over the rationality of turnout has been at the core of the debate over the usefulness of formal theory in general. In their 1994 book titled *Pathologies of Rational Choice Theory*, Donald Green and Ian Shapiro made the first point of attack in their critique of the role that formal theory plays in political science. One of Green and Shapiro's major criticisms of this part of political science was that the linkages between formal theory and empirical hypothesis tests were too weak. In reaction to these and other critics, the National Science Foundation launched a new program titled "Empirical Implications of Theoretical Models" (EITM) that was designed to strengthen the linkage between formal theory and empirical hypothesis tests.

bodies. This has typically involved thinking about the **preference orderings** of expected utility-maximizing actors. For example, let's imagine a legislature made up of three individual members, X, Y, and Z.[11] The task in front of X, Y, and Z is to choose between three alternatives A, B, and C. The preferences orderings for these three rational individuals are as follows:

$$X : ABC,$$

$$Y : BCA,$$

$$Z : CAB.$$

An additional assumption that is made under these circumstances is that the preferences of rational individuals are **transitive**. This means that if individual X likes A better than B and B better than C, then, for X's preferences to be transitive, he or she must also like A better than C. Why is this an important assumption to make? Consider the alternative. What if X liked A better than B and B better than C, but liked C better than A? Under these circumstances, it would be impossible to discuss what X wants in a meaningful fashion because X's preferences would produce an infinite cycle. To put this another way, no matter which of the three choices X chose, there would always be some other choice that X prefers. Under these circumstances, X could not make a rational choice.

In this scenario, what would the group prefer? This is not an easy question to answer. If they each voted for their first choice, each alternative would receive one vote. If these three individuals vote between pairs of alternatives, and they vote according to their preferences, we would observe the following results:

$$A \text{ vs. } B, X\&Z \text{ vs. } Y, A \text{ wins;}$$

$$B \text{ vs. } C, X\&Y \text{ vs. } Z, B \text{ wins;}$$

$$C \text{ vs. } A, Y\&Z \text{ vs. } X, C \text{ wins.}$$

Which of these three alternatives does the group collectively prefer? This is an impossible question to answer because the group's preferences cycle across the three alternatives. Another way of describing this group's preferences is to say that they are **intransitive** (despite the fact that, as you can see, each individual's preferences are transitive).

[11] We know that, in practice, legislatures tend to have many more members. Starting with this type of miniature-scaled legislature makes formal considerations much easier to carry out. Once we have arrived at conclusions based on calculations made on such a small scale, it is important to consider whether the conclusions that we have drawn would apply to more realistically larger-scaled scenarios.

This result should be fairly troubling to people who are concerned with the fairness of democratic elections. One of the often-stated goals of elections is to "let the people speak." Yet, as we have just seen, it is possible that, even when the people involved are all rational actors, their collective preferences may not be rational. Under such circumstances, a lot of the normative concepts concerning the role of elections simply break down. This finding is at the heart of Arrow's theorem, which was developed by Kenneth Arrow in his 1951 book titled *Social Choice and Individual Values*. At the time of its publication, political scientists largely ignored this book. As formal theory became more popular in political science, Arrow's mathematical approach to these issues became increasingly recognized. In 1982 William Riker popularized Arrow's theorem in his book *Liberalism Against Populism*, in which he presented a more accessible version of Arrow's theorem and bolstered a number of Arrow's claims through mathematical expositions.

2.6.2   The Rules Matter!

Continuing to work with our example of three individuals, X, Y, and Z, with the previously described preferences, now imagine that the three individuals will choose among the alternatives in two different rounds of votes between pairs of choices. In the first round of voting, two of the alternatives will be pitted against each other. In the second round of voting, the alternative that won the first vote will be pitted against the alternative that was not among the choices in the first round. The winner of the second round of voting is the overall winning choice.

In our initial consideration of this scenario, we will assume that X, Y, and Z will vote according to their preferences. What if X got to decide on the order in which the alternatives got chosen? We know that X's preference ordering is ABC. Can X set things up so that A will win? What if X made the following rules:

1st round: B vs. C;

2nd round: 1st round winner vs. A.

What would happen under these rules? We know that both X and Y prefer B to C, so B would win the first round and then would be paired against A in the second round. We also know that X and Z prefer A to B, so alternative A would win and X would be happy with this outcome.

Does voting like this occur in the real world? Actually, the answer is "yes." This form of pairwise voting among alternatives is the way that legislatures typically conduct their voting. If we think of individuals X, Y, and Z as being members of a legislature, we can see that whoever controls the ordering of the voting (the rules) has substantial power. To explore these issues further, let's examine the situation of individual Y. Remember that Y's preference ordering is BCA. So Y would be particularly unhappy about the outcome of the voting according to X's rules, because it resulted in Y's least-favorite outcome. But remember that, for our initial consideration, we assumed that X, Y, and Z will vote according to their preferences. If we relax this assumption, what might Y do? In the first round of voting, Y could cast a **strategic vote** for C against B. If both X and Z continued to vote (sincerely) according to their preferences, then C would win the first round. Because we know that both X and Z prefer C to A, C would win the second round and would be the chosen alternative. Under these circumstances, Y would be better off because Y prefers alternative C to A.

From the perspective of members of a legislature, it is clearly better to control the rules than to vote strategically to try to obtain a better outcome. When legislators face reelection, one of the common tactics of their opponents is to point to specific votes in which the incumbent appears to have voted contrary to the preferences of his constituents. It would seem reasonable to expect that legislator Y comes from a district with the same or similar preferences to those of Y. By casting a strategic vote for C over B, Y was able to obtain a better outcome but created an opportunity for an electoral challenger to tell voters that Y had voted against the preferences of his district.

In *Congressmen in Committees*, Richard Fenno's classic study of the U.S. House of Representatives, one of the findings was that the Rules Committee – along with the Ways and Means and the Appropriations Committees – was one of the most requested committee assignments from the individual members of Congress. At first glance, the latter two committees make sense as prominent committees and, indeed, receive much attention in the popular media. By contrast, the Rules Committee very rarely gets any media attention. Members of Congress certainly understand and appreciate the fact that the rules matter, and formal theoretical thought exercises like the preceding one help us to see why this is the case.

2.7 EXTENSIONS

These examples truly represent just the beginning of the uses of formal theory in political science. We have not even introduced two of the more important aspects of formal theory – spatial models and game theory – that are beyond the scope of this discussion. In ways that mirror applications in microeconomics, political scientists have used spatial models to study phenomena such as the placement of political parties along the ideological spectrum, much as economists have used spatial models to study the location of firms in a market. Likewise, game theory utilizes a highly structured sequence of moves by different players to show how any particular actor's utility depends not only on her own choices, but also on the choices made by the other actors. It is easy to see hints about how game theory works in the preceding simple three-actor, two-stage voting examples: X's best vote in the first stage likely depends on which alternative Y and Z choose to support, and vice versa. Game theory, then, highlights how the strategic choices made in politics are interdependent.

2.8 HOW DO I KNOW IF I HAVE A "GOOD" THEORY?

Once you have gone through some or all of the suggested courses of action for building a theory, a reasonable question to ask is, "How do I know if I have a 'good' theory?" Unfortunately there is not a single succinct way of answering this question. Instead, we suggest that you answer a set of questions about your theory and consider your honest answers to these questions as you try to evaluate the overall quality of our theory. You will notice that some of these questions come directly from the "rules of the road" that we developed in Chapter 1:

- Is your theory causal?
- Can you test your theory on data that you have not yet observed?
- How general is your theory?
- How parsimonious is your theory?
- How new is your theory?
- How nonobvious is your theory?

2.8.1 Is Your Theory Causal?

Remember that our first rule of the road to scientific knowledge about politics is "Make your theories causal." If your answer to the question "Is your theory causal?" is anything other than "yes," then you need to go back to the drawing board until the answer is an emphatic "yes."

As scientists studying politics, we want to know why things happen the way that they happen. As such, we will not be satisfied with mere correlations and we demand causal explanations. We know from Chapter 1 that one way initially to evaluate a particular theory is to think about the causal explanation behind it. The causal explanation behind a theory is the answer to the question "Why do you think that this independent variable is causally related to this dependent variable?" If the answer is reasonable, then you can answer this first question with a "yes."

2.8.2   Can You Test Your Theory on Data That You Have Not Yet Observed?

Our second rule of the road is "Don't let data alone drive your theories," which we restated in a slightly longer form as "Try to develop theories before examining the data on which you will perform your tests." If you have derived your theory from considering a set of empirical data, you need to be careful not to have observed all of the data on which you can test your theory. This can be a somewhat gray area, and only you know whether your theory is entirely data driven and whether you observed all of your testing data before you developed your theory.

2.8.3   How General Is Your Theory?

We could rephrase this question for evaluating your theory as "How widely does your theory apply?" To the extent that your theory is not limited to one particular time period or to one particular spatial unit, it is more general. Answers to this question vary along a continuum – it's not the end of the world to have a fairly specific theory, but, all else being equal, a more general theory is more desirable.

2.8.4   How Parsimonious Is Your Theory?

As with the question in the preceding subsection, answers to this question also vary along a continuum. In fact, it is often the case that we face a trade-off between parsimony and generality. In other words, to make a theory more general, we often have to give up parsimony, and to make a theory more parsimonious, we often have to give up generality. The important thing with both of these desirable aspects of a theory is that we have them in mind as we evaluate our theory. If we can make our theory more general or more parsimonious and without sacrifice, we should do so.

2.8.5   How New Is Your Theory?

At first it might seem that this is a pretty straightforward question to answer. The problem is that we cannot know about all of the work that has been done before our own work in any particular area of research. It also is often the case that we may think our theory is really new, and luckily we have not been able to find any other work that has put forward the same theory on the same political phenomenon. But then we discover a similar theory on a related phenomenon. There is no simple answer to this question. Rather, our scholarly peers usually answer this question of newness for us when they evaluate our work.

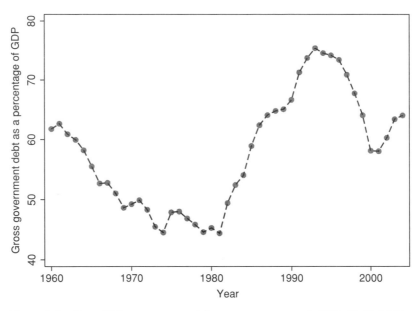

Figure 2.3. Gross U.S. government debt as a percentage of GDP, 1960–2004.

2.8.6   How Nonobvious Is Your Theory?

As with the question "How new is your theory?" the question "How nonobvious is your theory?" is best answered by our scholarly peers. If, when they are presented with your theory, they hit themselves in the head and say, "Wow, I never thought about it like that, but it makes a lot of sense!" then you have scored very well on this question.

Both of these last two questions illustrate an important part of the role of theory development in any science. It makes sense to think about theories as being like products and scientific fields as being very much like markets in which these products are bought and sold. Like other entrepreneurs in the marketplace, scientific entrepreneurs will succeed to the extent that their theories (products) are new and exciting (nonobvious). But, what makes a theory "new and exciting" is very much dependent on what has come before it.

2.9   CONCLUSION

We have presented a series of different strategies for developing theories of politics. Each of these strategies involves some type of thought exercise in which we arrange and rearrange our knowledge about the political world in hopes that doing so will lead to new causal theories. You have, we're certain, noticed that there is no simple formula for generating a new theory

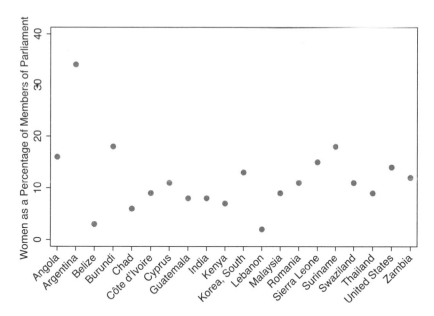

Figure 2.4. Women as a percentage of members of parliament, 2004.

and hopefully, as a result, appreciate our description of theory building as an "art" in the chapter's title. Theoretical developments come from many places and being critically immersed in the ongoing literature that studies your phenomenon of choice is a good place to start.

CONCEPTS INTRODUCED IN THIS CHAPTER

complete information	rational utility maximizers
cross-sectional measure	spatial dimension
expected utility	strategic vote
formal theory	time dimension
incomplete information	time-series measure
intransitive	transitive
preference orderings	utility
rational choice	

EXERCISES

1. Figure 2.3 shows gross U.S. government debt as a percentage of GDP from 1960 to 2004. Can you think of a theory about what causes this variable to be higher or lower?

2. Figure 2.4 shows the percentage of a nation's members of parliament who were women for 20 randomly selected nations in 2004. Can you think of a theory about what causes this variable to be higher or lower?

3. Think about a political event with which you are familiar and follow these instructions:

    (a) Write a short description of the event.

    (b) What is your understanding of why this event happened the way that it happened?

    (c) *Moving from local to global*: Reformulate your answer to part (b) into a general causal theory without proper nouns.

4. Find a political science journal article of interest to you, and of which your instructor approves, answer the questions, and follow the instructions:

    (a) What is the main dependent variable in the article?

    (b) What is the main independent variable in the article?

    (c) Briefly describe the causal theory that connects the independent and dependent variables.

    (d) Can you think of another independent variable that is not mentioned in the article that might be causally related to the dependent variable? Briefly explain why that variable might be causally related to the dependent variable.

5. Imagine that the way in which the U.S. House of Representatives is elected was changed from the current single-member district system to a system of national proportional representation in which any party that obtained at least 3% of the vote nationally would get a proportionate share of the seats in the House. How many and what types of parties would you expect to see represented in the House of Representatives under this different electoral system? What theories of politics can you come up with from thinking about this hypothetical scenario?

6. *Applying formal theory to something in which you are interested*. Think about something in the political world that you would like to better understand. Try to think about the individual-level decisions that play a role in deciding the outcome of this phenomenon. What are the expected benefits and costs that the individual who is making this decision must weigh?

3 Evaluating Causal Relationships

OVERVIEW

Modern political science fundamentally revolves around establishing whether there are *causal relationships* between important concepts. This is rarely straightforward and serves as the basis for almost all scientific controversies. How do we know, for example, if economic development causes democratization, or if democratization causes economic development, or both, or neither? To speak more generally, if we wish to know whether some $X \rightarrow Y$, we need to cross four causal hurdles: (1) Is there a credible causal mechanism that connects X to Y? (2) Can we eliminate the possibility that Y causes X? (3) Is there covariation between X and Y? (4) Is there some Z related to both X and Y that makes the observed relationship between X and Y spurious? Many people, especially those in the media, make the mistake that crossing just the third causal hurdle – observing that X and Y covary – is tantamount to crossing all four. In short, finding a relationship is not the same as finding a *causal* relationship, and causality is what we care about as political scientists.

I would rather discover one causal law than be King of Persia.
  – Democritus (quoted in Pearl 2000)

3.1 CAUSALITY AND EVERYDAY LANGUAGE

Like that of most sciences, the discipline of political science fundamentally revolves around evaluating causal claims. Our theories – which may be right or may be wrong – typically specify that some independent variable causes some dependent variable. We then endeavor to find appropriate empirical evidence to evaluate the degree to which this theory is or is not supported. But how do we go about evaluating causal claims? In this chapter and the next, we discuss some principles for doing this. We focus on the logic of causality and on several criteria for establishing with some confidence the degree to which a causal connection exists between two variables. Then, in Chapter 4, we discuss various ways to design research that help us to investigate causal claims. As we pursue answers to questions about causal relationships, keep our "rules of the road" from Chapter 1 in your mind, in particular the admonition to consider only empirical evidence along the way.

It is important to recognize a distinction between the nature of most scientific theories and the way the world seems to be ordered. Most of our theories are limited to descriptions of relationships between a *single* cause (the independent variable) and a *single* effect (the dependent variable). Such theories, in this sense, are very simplistic representations of reality, and necessarily so. In fact, as we noted at the end of Chapter 1, theories of this sort are laudable in one respect: They are parsimonious, the equivalent of bite-sized, digestible pieces of information. We cannot emphasize strongly enough that almost all of our theories about social and political phenomena are **bivariate** – that is, involving just two variables.

But social reality is *not* bivariate; it is **multivariate**, in the sense that any interesting dependent variable is caused by more than one factor. So although our theories describe the proposed relationship between some cause and some effect, we always have to keep in the forefront of our minds that the phenomenon we are trying to explain surely has many other possible causes. And when it comes time to design research to test our theoretical ideas – which is the topic of Chapter 4 – we have to try to account for, or "control for," those other causes. If we don't, then our causal inferences about whether our pet theory is right – whether X causes Y – may very well be wrong.[1] In this chapter we lay out some practical principles for demonstrating that, indeed, some X does cause Y. You also can apply these criteria when evaluating the causal claims made by others – be they a journalist, a candidate for office, a political scientist, a fellow classmate, a friend, or just about anyone else.

Nearly everyone, nearly every day, uses the language of causality – some of the time formally, but far more often in a very informal manner. Whenever we speak of how some event changes the course of subsequent events, we invoke causal reasoning. Even the word "because" implies that a causal process is in operation.[2] Yet, despite the ubiquitous

---

[1] Throughout this book, in the text as well as in the figures, we will use arrows as a shorthand for "causality." For example, the text "$X \rightarrow Y$" should be read as "X causes Y." Oftentimes, especially in figures, these arrows will have question marks over them, indicating that the existence of a causal connection between the concepts is uncertain.

[2] This example was suggested to us by Brady (2002).

use of the words "because," "affects," "impacts," "causes," and "causality," the meanings of these words are not exactly clear. Philosophers of science have long had vigorous debates over competing formulations of "causality."[3]

Although our goal here is not to wade too deeply into these debates, there is one feature of the discussions about causality that deserves brief mention. Most of the philosophy of science debates originate from the world of the physical sciences. The notions of causality that come to mind in these disciplines are mostly **deterministic** – that is, if some cause occurs, then the effect will occur *with certainty*. In contrast, though, the world of human interactions is **probabilistic** – increases in X are associated with increases (or decreases) in the probability of Y occurring, but those probabilities are not certainties. Whereas physical laws like Newton's laws of motion are deterministic – think of the law of gravity here – social science more closely resembles probabilistic causation like that in Darwin's theory of natural selection, in which random mutations make an organism more or less fit to survive and reproduce.[4] However, in reviewing three prominent attempts within the philosophy of science to elaborate on the probabilistic nature of causality, the philosopher Wesley Salmon (1993, p. 137) notes that "In the vast philosophical literature on causality [probabilistic notions of causality] are largely ignored." But in political science, our conceptions of causality must be probabilistic in nature. When we theorize, for example, that an individual's level of wealth causes her opinions on optimal tax policy, we do not at all mean that *every* wealthy person will want lower taxes, and *every* poor person will prefer higher taxes. Consider what would happen if we found a single rich person who favors high taxes or a single poor person who favors low taxes. One case alone does not decrease our confidence in the theory. In political science there will always be exceptions because human beings are not deterministic robots whose behaviors conform to lawlike statements. In other sciences in which the subjects of study are more robotic, it may make more sense to speak of laws that describe behavior. Consider the study of planetary orbits, in which scientists can precisely predict the movement of celestial bodies hundreds of years in advance. The political world, in contrast, is extremely difficult to predict. As a result, most of the time we are happy to be able to make probabilistic statements about causal relationships.

---

[3] You can find an excellent account of the vigor of these debates in a 2003 book by David Edmonds and John Eidinow titled *Wittgenstein's Poker: The Story of a Ten Minute Argument Between Two Great Philosophers.*

[4] We borrow the helpful comparison of probabilistic social science to Darwinian natural selection from Brady (2004).

What all of this boils down to is that the entire notion of what it means for something "to cause" something else is far from a settled matter. Should social scientists abandon all hope of finding causal connections? Not at all. What it means is that we should proceed cautiously and with an open mind, rather than in some hyperformulaic fashion.

3.2 FOUR HURDLES ALONG THE ROUTE TO ESTABLISHING CAUSAL RELATIONSHIPS

If we wish to investigate whether some independent variable, which we will call X, "causes" some dependent variable, which we will call Y, what procedures must we follow before we can express our degree of confidence that a causal relationship does or does not exist? Finding some sort of covariation (or, equivalently, correlation) between X and Y is not sufficient for such a conclusion.

We encourage you to bear in mind that establishing causal relationships between variables is not at all akin to hunting for DNA evidence like some episode from a television crime drama. Social reality does not lend itself to such simple, cut-and-dried answers. In light of the preceding discussion about the nature of causality itself, consider what follows to be guidelines as to what constitutes "best practice" in political science. With any theory about a causal relationship between X and Y, we should carefully consider the answers to the following four questions:

1. Is there a credible causal mechanism that connects X to Y?
2. Could Y cause X?
3. Is there covariation between X and Y?
4. Is there some **confounding variable** Z that is related to both X and Y and makes the observed association between X and Y **spurious**?

First, we must consider whether it is credible to claim that X *could* cause Y. To do this, we need to go through a thought exercise in which we evaluate the mechanics of how X would cause Y. In other words, what is it specifically about having more (or less) of X that will in all probability lead to more (or less) of Y? In effect, this hurdle represents an effort to answer the "how" and "why" questions about causal relationships. The more outlandish these mechanics would have to be, the less confident we are that our theory has cleared this first hurdle. Failure to clear this first hurdle is a very serious matter; the result being that either our theory needs to be thrown out altogether, or we need to revise it after some careful rethinking of the underlying mechanisms through which it works. It is worth proceeding to the second question only once we have a "yes" answer to this question.

Second, and perhaps with greater difficulty, we must ask whether it is possible (or even likely) that Y might cause X. As you will learn from the discussion of the various strategies for assessing causal connections in Chapter 4, this poses thorny problems for some forms of social science research, but is less problematic for others. Occasionally, this causal hurdle can be crossed logically. For example, when considering whether a person's gender (X) causes him or her to have particular attitudes about abortion policy (Y), it is a rock-solid certainty that the reverse-causal scenario can be dismissed: A person's attitudes about abortion does not "cause" them to be male or female. If our theory does not clear this particular hurdle, the race is not lost. Under these circumstances, we should proceed to the next question, while keeping in mind the possibility that our causal arrow might be reversed.

Throughout our consideration of the first two causal hurdles, we were concerned with only two variables, X and Y. The third causal hurdle can involve a third variable Z, and the fourth hurdle always does. Often it is the case that there are several Z variables.

For the third causal hurdle, we must consider whether X and Y covary (or, equivalently, whether they are correlated or associated). Generally speaking, for X to cause Y, there must be some form of measurable association between X and Y, such as "more of X is associated with more of Y," or "more of X is associated with less of Y." Demonstrating a simple bivariate connection between two variables is a straightforward matter, and we will cover it in Chapter 8. Of course, you may be familiar with the dictum "Correlation does not prove causality," and we wholeheartedly agree. It is worth noting, though, that correlation is normally an essential component of causality. But be careful. It is possible for a causal relationship to exist between X and Y even if there is no bivariate association between X and Y. Thus, even if we fail to clear this hurdle, we should not throw out our causal claim entirely. Instead, we should consider the possibility that there exists some confounding variable Z that we need to "control for" before we see a relationship between X and Y. Whether or not we find a bivariate relationship between X and Y, we should proceed to our fourth and final hurdle.

Fourth, in establishing causal connections between X and Y, we must face up to the reality that, as we noted at the outset of this chapter, we live in a world in which most of the interesting dependent variables are caused by more than one – often many more than one – independent variable. What problems does this pose for social science? It means that, when trying to establish whether a particular X causes a particular Y, we need to "control for" the effects of other causes of Y (and we call those other effects Z). If we fail to control for the effects of Z, we are quite likely to misunderstand the relationship between X and Y and make the wrong inference about whether X causes Y. This is the most serious mistake a social scientist can make. If we find that X and Y are correlated, but that, when we control for the effects of Z on both X and Y, the association between X and Y disappears, then the relationship between X and Y is said to be spurious.

3.2.1 Putting It All Together – Adding Up the Answers to Our Four Questions

As we have just seen, the process for evaluating a theoretical claim that X causes Y is a complicated process. Taken one at a time, each of the four questions in the introduction to this section can be difficult to answer with great clarity. But the challenge of evaluating a claim that X causes Y involves summing across all four of these questions to determine our overall confidence about whether X causes Y. To understand this, think about the analogy that we have been using by calling these questions "hurdles." In track events that feature hurdles, runners must do their best to try to clear each hurdle as they make their way toward the finish line. Occasionally even the most experienced hurdler will knock over a hurdle. Although this slows them down and diminishes their chances of winning the race, all is not lost. If we think about putting a theory through the four hurdles posed by the preceding questions, there is no doubt our confidence will be greatest when we are able to answer all four questions the right way ("yes," "no," "yes," "no") and without reservation. As we described in the introduction to this section, failure to clear the first hurdle should make us stop and rethink our theory. This is also the case if we find our relationship to be spurious. For the second and third hurdles, however, failure to clear them completely does not mean that we should discard the causal claim in question. Figure 3.1 provides a summary of this process. In the subsections that follow, we will go through the process described in Figure 3.1 with a series of examples.

3.2.2 Identifying Causal Claims Is an Essential Thinking Skill

We want to emphasize that the logic just presented does not apply merely to political science research examples. Whenever you see a story in the news, or hear a speech by a candidate for public office, or, yes, read a research article in a political science class, it is almost always the case that some form of causal claim is embedded in the story, speech, or article. Sometimes those causal claims are explicit – indented and italicized so that you just can't miss them. Quite often, though, they are harder to spot, and most of the time not because the speaker or writer is trying to confuse you.

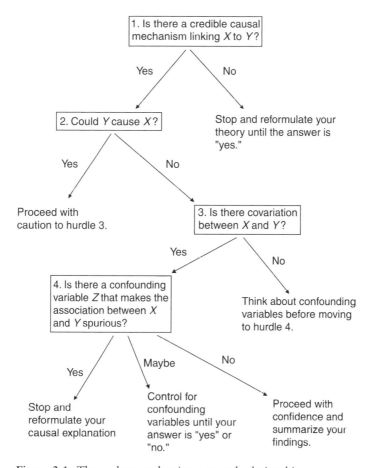

Figure 3.1. The path to evaluating a causal relationship.

What we want to emphasize is that spotting and identifying causal claims is a thinking skill. It does not come naturally to most people, but it can be practiced.

Take a common example from a political campaign: A candidate for president or prime minister who is running for reelection asserts that the voters should give him or her another term in office because the national economy is performing well. (Or, if economic performance is poor, the challenger will claim that the voters should replace the poor economic management team of the incumbent with the challenger's party.) There are perhaps two related causal claims embedded in a candidate's appeal to be reelected on the basis of the economy's performance. First, the candidate may be saying that the economic performance is better than it would be if the voters had chosen the other candidate in the last election. Second, the incumbent may be claiming that economic performance will be better in the future if he or she is reelected than it will be if the opposing candidate wins.

Because the second claim is about an unpredictable future, let's set it aside for the moment; it is interesting speculation, but there's no doubt that it is just speculation. Focus, then, on the first claim: that the economy is performing well because of the administration's economic policies. Is such a causal claim credible? For us to make such a judgment, we need to focus on our four causal hurdles. To start, we need to evaluate whether there is a credible causal mechanism that connects X (the administration and its policies) with Y (economic performance). Thinking through the mechanics of how this causal relationship would work is pretty straightforward. Presidents and prime ministers have a wide array of economic policy-making tools at their disposal. It seems pretty reasonable that the use of these tools could cause the economy to fare better or worse. *The answer to the first question is "yes."* Second, is it possible that Y causes X? This would mean that the current economy caused the administration's economic policies. In this case, we would need to figure out whether policy enactments did or did not precede good economic performance. Because there are so many different policies being enacted at various points in time, this would be a difficult question to answer. To be conservative, let's say that *the answer to the second question is "yes."* To answer our third question we need to figure out whether X (the administration and its policies) is associated with Y (economic performance). Presumably it is, and presumably this relationship is such that the economic performance improved after the administration's policies were put in place – right? – or else the candidate would not be making the claim. But, if we wanted to evaluate such a claim, we would have to choose an indicator of economic performance and make a comparison across time. For now, let's say that *the answer the third question is "yes."* So far, the politician's claim of a causal relationship is doing pretty well (because our answers are "yes," "yes," and "yes"). But the fourth causal hurdle is where the candidate (and we) can get tripped up. Is there some other force, Z, that is related to both X and Y and renders the relationship between X and Y spurious? Think about this one: Can we think of any other reasons, besides administration policies, why the economy might be performing well? Of course we can. It would be patently silly to assert that the *sole cause* of strong economic performance is government policy. Innovation in the private sector (Z), for example, might (by happenstance) coincide with government policy changes (X) and be strongly related to prosperity (Y). Without some further analysis, we have ample reason to be skeptical of such a candidate's claim that the economy is prosperous because of the administration's sound policies. Unfortunately for the politician, *the answer to the fourth question is "maybe."* We're going to have to see some more evidence before we, as scientists, are going to believe her causal claim.

We could rather easily think of a host of other factors that might fit the description of a confounding variable. But let's be careful before we dismiss the politician as a charlatan. Does this mean that the candidate is wrong, and that we know that administration policies did *not* cause prosperity? Absolutely not. All we have done in this simple thinking exercise is to recognize that the dependent variable of interest (Y), the health of the economy, is certainly a function of many things, one of which may or may not be the administration's economic policies (X). To know that the administration produced the prosperity, we would need to *control for* other possible causes of prosperity, and we haven't done that. Therefore we should conclude that it is possible that the candidate's claim is appropriate. But it has not yet been empirically supported, because alternative explanations have not yet been ruled out. Identifying the underlying causal claim, in this case, helps us to be skeptical of the self-interested claims of political actors. A candidate's job, of course, is not to evaluate causal claims carefully; it is to get votes. But evaluating the credibility of a candidate's often-implicit causal claims is important if we, the voters, do not want to be led astray by vote-hungry politicians.

An important part of taking a scientific approach to the study of politics is that we turn the same skeptical logic loose on scholarly claims about causal relationships. Before we can evaluate a causal theory, we need to consider how well the available evidence answers each of the four questions about X, Y, and Z. Once we have answered each of these four questions, one at a time, we then think about the overall level of confidence that we have in the claim that X causes Y.

3.2.3 What Are the Consequences of Failing to Control for Other Possible Causes?

When it comes to any causal claim, as we have just noted, the fourth causal hurdle often trips us up, and not just for evaluating political rhetoric or stories in the news media. This is true for scrutinizing scientific research as well. In fact, a substantial portion of disagreements between scholars boils down to this fourth causal hurdle. When one scholar is evaluating another's work, perhaps the most frequent objection is that the researcher "failed to control for" some potentially important cause of the dependent variable.

What happens when we fail to control for some plausible other cause of our dependent variable of interest? Quite simply, it means that we have failed to cross our fourth causal hurdle. *So long as a credible case can be made that some uncontrolled-for Z might be related to both X and Y, we cannot conclude with full confidence that X indeed causes Y.* Because the main goal of science is to establish whether causal connections between variables exist, then failing to control for other causes of *Y* is a potentially serious problem.

One of the themes of this book is that statistical analysis should not be disconnected from issues of research design – such as controlling for as many causes of the dependent variable as possible. When we discuss multiple regression (in Chapters 10 and 11), which is the most common statistical technique that political scientists use in their research, the entire point of those chapters is to learn how to control for other possible causes of the dependent variable. We will see that failures of research design, such as failing to control for all relevant causes of the dependent variable, have statistical implications, and the implications are always bad. Failures of research design produce problems for statistical analysis, but hold this thought. What is important to realize for now is that good research design will make statistical analysis more credible, whereas poor research design will make it harder for any statistical analysis to be conclusive about causal connections.

3.3 WHY IS STUDYING CAUSALITY SO IMPORTANT? THREE EXAMPLES FROM POLITICAL SCIENCE

Our emphasis on causal connections should be clear. We turn now to several active controversies within the discipline of political science, showing how debates about causality lie at the heart of precisely the kinds of controversies that got you (and most of us) interested in politics in the first place.

3.3.1 Life Satisfaction and Democratic Stability

One of the enduring controversies in political science is the relationship between *life satisfaction in the mass public* and *the stability of democratic institutions*. Life satisfaction, of course, can mean many different things, but for the current discussion let us consider it as varying along a continuum, from the public's being highly unsatisfied with day-to-day life to being highly satisfied. What, if anything, is the causal connection between the two concepts?

Political scientist Ronald Inglehart (1988) argues that life satisfaction (*X*) *causes* democratic system stability (*Y*). If we think through the first of the four questions for establishing causal relationships, we can see that there is a credible causal mechanism that connects *X* to *Y* – if people in a democratic nation are more satisfied with their lives, they will be less likely to want to overthrow their government. *The answer to our first question is "yes."* Moving on to our second question: Is it possible that democratic stability (*Y*) is what causes life satisfaction (*X*)? Certainly it is. It is very easy to conceive of a causal mechanism in which citizens take careful note of the political system when they consider how happy they are and that citizens living in stable democracies are apt to look back on a history of government stability – that is, a recent history without violent revolutions – and feel a sense of safety and happiness as a result. *The answer to our second question is "yes."* We now turn to the third question. Using an impressive amount of data from a wide variety of developed democracies, Inglehart and his colleagues have shown that there is, indeed, an association between average life satisfaction in the public and the length of uninterrupted democratic governance. That is, countries with higher average levels of life satisfaction have enjoyed longer uninterrupted periods of democratic stability. Conversely, countries with lower levels of life satisfaction have had shorter periods of democratic stability and more revolutionary upheaval. *The answer to our third question is "yes."* With respect to the fourth question, it is easy to imagine a myriad of other factors (Z's) that lead to democratic stability, and whether Inglehart has done an adequate job of controlling for those other factors is the subject of considerable scholarly debate. *The answer to our fourth question is "maybe."* Inglehart's theory has satisfactorily answered questions 1 and 3, but it is the answers to questions 2 and 4 that have given skeptics substantial reasons to doubt his causal claim.

3.3.2   School Choice and Student Achievement

In recent years, during which there has been considerable concern about the performance of public elementary and secondary schools, the possibility of the government issuing vouchers to allow families to send children to private schools has become highly controversial. Setting the normative issues aside about whether "school choice" is either inherently desirable or instead something that will by its nature drain the public schools, there is lurking in the background an important empirical and causal issue: Does the type of school a child attends (X) affect student performance (Y)? It can be argued that, as researchers cannot demonstrate that school-choice programs improve student performance, the programs lose a substantial portion of their appeal.

Clearly, the first question establishing causal relationships is easy enough to answer, because a credible (if not airtight) argument can be made that children will receive an education that better prepares them for standardized tests in private schools, which typically have smaller class sizes and fewer layers of bureaucracy. *The answer to our first question is "yes."* In this example, the second hurdle is pretty easy to clear – how could test-score results (Y) *cause* the type of school (X)? *The answer to our second question is "no."*

Let's move to the third question of whether there is covariation between X and Y. At first glance, this would seem like an entirely straightforward matter. Find a city or state where there is a school-choice program; compare the scores on standardized tests between students in the public school with those in the private school; then draw a conclusion. Is this comparison useful? Suppose we were to compare scores on a standardized math test among eighth-graders in Metropolis, USA, some of whom went to private schools by way of a school-choice program and others who remained in Metropolis's public schools. And suppose we find that, indeed, the average math test score among students who participate in the choice program is higher than that of those who remained in the public school. In this hypothetical case, *the answer to our third question is "yes."* Our theory is looking pretty good. So far, all of the answers have supported it. Does this mean that the choice program *caused* their test scores to be higher?

It is a tempting conclusion to leap to, isn't it? It sounds like a classic case of comparing apples to apples, so to speak. But let's try to stick to our four questions. We have already, in our hypothetical example, conceded that the type of school (X) is associated with test scores (Y).

The fourth question is the only one remaining, and it is, in this case, a difficult question to answer. Can you think of another cause (Z) that is related to whether or not a student enrolls in the choice program (X) that will also be related to the standardized test score? Yes. In this case, the level of parental involvement (Z) could surely affect both X and Y and might make the association that we see between X and Y spurious. Parents who are actively involved in their child's education (Z) are more likely to be aware of a school-choice program in their district and are more likely to pursue that option (X). Similarly, parents with high levels of involvement in their child's education (Z) are more likely to have children who perform well on standardized tests (Y); such parents read to their children more, help them with homework, and stress the importance of education in a child's life.

In this case, the Z variable we have identified produces what is called a **selection effect** – a situation in which a systematic force causes only a nonrandom subset of eligible targets to participate in a program. In any substantive area in which we are trying to evaluate the effectiveness of a government policy, it is critical to compare participants in the program with nonparticipants in a rigorous fashion. If we find systematic differences between participants and nonparticipants – as we surely would in a school-choice program – then it becomes *exceedingly crucial* to try to control for those forces when evaluating the program's effectiveness. In the school-choice example considered here, what seemed like a simple apples-to-apples

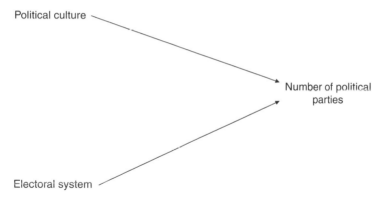

Figure 3.2. Theoretical causes of the number of parties in legislatures.

comparison really turned out to be an apples-to-giraffes comparison. At the very least, *the answer to our fourth question is "maybe."*[5]

Let's be extremely careful here. Does this mean that school-choice programs do not help to improve student performance on tests? Not at all. What our four questions do is remind us that, sometimes, the temptingly easy conclusion needs additional scrutiny before we embrace it. In Chapter 4, we will talk about some research designs that can help to ameliorate situations precisely like this one.

3.3.3 Electoral Systems and the Number of Political Parties

Political science has a long tradition of examining the impact of institutional arrangements on political outcomes. One prominent example of this type of research has focused on the influence of electoral systems on the number of political parties in legislatures. Figure 3.2 depicts a theoretical model of the number of parties that will be represented in a legislature. The first theory is that, the more societal divisions there are that shape a political culture, the more political parties there will be in the legislature. The second theory on which we focus in this subsection is that, if we hold constant the political culture of the area that the legislature represents, the more disproportional the electoral system is in translating votes into seats (X) and fewer political parties will be represented in the legislature (Y).

The term "disproportional" in this theory is expressed in terms of the translation of votes into seats for political parties. A perfectly proportional system would be one in which the percentage of votes cast for each party was *exactly* equal to the percentage of seats awarded to that party in the

---

[5] In addition to parental involvement, there are other possible selection mechanisms at work. A private school involved in a school-choice program, for example, might choose to use test scores as a criterion for admission.

legislature as a result of the election. In practice, perfectly proportional electoral systems are never found; in fact electoral systems differ substantially in terms of how close they come to this ideal. Turning to our four hurdles, the causal mechanism behind the theory of electoral systems and the number of parties is driven by the organizational incentives politicians face when deciding whether to form new political parties or work within established parties to contest elections. Disproportionate electoral systems tend to reward the largest parties and greatly penalize the smaller parties in terms of translating votes into seats. Thus, the more disproportionate the electoral system, the greater will be the tendency for politicians who are competing for legislative seats to band together, resulting in fewer political parties in the legislature. If you believe this, then *the answer to our first question is "yes."*

To better understand this theory of the influence of electoral institutions, consider the U.S. House of Representatives. A quick review of the history of party membership in the U.S. House indicates that, with few exceptions, two political parties have held all or most of the seats. According to this theory, this is the case *because* the U.S. House of Representatives is elected by use of a set of rules that produce disproportionate outcomes in terms of the translation of votes to seats. That system is known as a "single-member district plurality" system. The entire country is divided into electoral districts, and on election day whichever candidate receives the most votes (a plurality) is elected to represent that district. When the votes and seats are tallied up at the national level, results tend disproportionately to favor the parties with the most votes. For example, in the 1992 U.S. House elections, Democratic Party candidates received 49.95% of the votes cast and 59.31% of the seats. In that same election, Republican Party candidates received 44.75% of the votes cast and 40.46% of the seats; all other parties together received 5.3% of the votes cast and only one seat (or 0.2% of the available seats).

One of the most proportional electoral systems in history was that of the Weimar Republic in Germany between World War I and World War II. Under the Weimar Republic electoral system, Germany was divided into 13 electoral regions, and seats in the national legislature were awarded to any party that managed to get 60,000 or more votes in any one of the electoral regions. Given that the number of voters who turned out in Weimar Republic elections was never less than 28 million, politicians had very little legal incentive to band together to contest elections. Consistent with the theory, the Reichstag had many different political parties throughout the time of the Weimar Republic. Some scholars have suggested that, because the politicians were divided into so many different political parties in the legislature, they were unable to band together to counter the

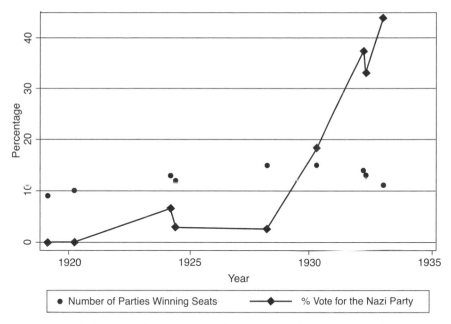

Figure 3.3. Nazi vote and the number of parties winning seats in Weimar Republic elections, 1919–1933.

rising strength and popularity of the Nazi Party. The Nazi Party, in contrast with many of the other parties in Germany at the time, was willing and able to hold together its politicians through coercive means. Figure 3.3 shows the number of parties in the Reichstag and the percentage of votes for the Nazi Party across the period of the Weimar Republic.

In the aftermath of World War II, the constitution of West Germany was designed with the Weimar Republic experience very much in mind. Although the electoral system continued to be a form of proportional representation, one major change was that parties that got less than 5% of the vote nationally were not given seats in the national legislature.[6] If we look at Figure 3.4, we can see an interesting pattern. In the first election after World War II, 11 political parties won seats in the Bundestag. After this, though, fewer and fewer political parties were represented, with only four parties in the Bundestag throughout the 1960s and 1970s. In the 1980s, the political culture of what was then West Germany began to change. The Green Party cleared the 5% threshold and was represented in the Bundesrat. In 1990 East and West Germany were reunified. In each of the elections since then,

[6] The West German electoral system, which is now the electoral system for reunified Germany, is one of the most complicated electoral systems in the world. It is possible for a party to gain seats despite failing to clear the 5% threshold provided that they win district-level seats. For a nice overview of this system, we recommend Gallagher, Laver, and Mair (2006).

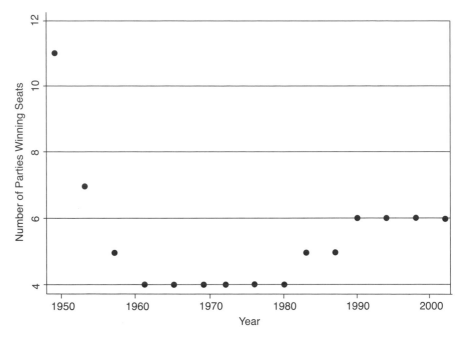

Figure 3.4. Number of parties winning seats in German Bundestag elections, 1949–2002.

six parties have been represented in the Bundesrat. The additional party is the Party of Democratic Socialism, which is a left-wing party created out of the remains of the East German Communist Party.

Consider the evidence from Germany in terms of our four questions. In the preceding subsections, we have a reasonably credible mechanism (incentives faced by office-seeking politicians) of how X (type of electoral system) causes Y (the number of political parties), and thus we answer our first question. We do not have any evidence from this case that the number of political parties *caused* the electoral system so we can be confident that *the answer to our second question is "no."* Figures 3.3 and 3.4 certainly seem to indicate that there was covariation between the electoral system and the number of parties.[7] When the more disproportionate electoral system of post–World War II Germany was put into effect, the number of political parties went down substantially. On the basis of this evidence we can conclude preliminarily that *the answer to our third question is "yes."* We have not yet conducted an extensive search for confounding variables (Z) that may be related to both the electoral system (X) and the number of political parties (Y). But it is difficult to imagine such a variable. So, on the basis of our consideration of our theories so far, *the answer to our fourth question is "no."* Taken together, this theory has done very well as

---

[7] Beginning in Chapter 8 we will discuss more systematic ways in which to use statistical techniques to evaluate empirical evidence of relationships between variables.

we have subjected it to the four causal hurdles. But, as we will learn later, we should base our answer to question 3 on more evidence than what we have examined thus far.

3.4 WHY IS STUDYING CAUSALITY SO IMPORTANT? THREE EXAMPLES FROM EVERYDAY LIFE

Causal claims are not limited to social science research like those previously discussed. There are times when causal claims in politics, the news, or just everyday life are downright humorous. Learning the intellectual habit of sifting through an argument to find the embedded causal argument can be useful.

3.4.1 Alcohol Consumption and Income

When you're in the checkout line at the grocery store, do you ever pick up the tabloids and scan them for the latest news about alien abductions and celebrity breakups? If so, you might remember this gem in the tabloid magazine *Weekly World News* of May 14, 2002, under the screaming headline "Want to be loaded? Then get loaded!":

> Do you want to be rich and successful, like Donald Trump, Bill Gates or Oprah Winfrey? Then belly up to the bar and drink your way to wealth! . . . when it comes to raking in the dough, boozers leave teetotalers in the dust, with all but the heaviest drinkers earning more.

Perhaps it's easy to believe that such a claim would appear in a tabloid magazine. At least, in this case, the causal claim is right there in the title of the article. Think about it for a moment: Given the fact that the consumers of tabloids do not have a bevy of data at their disposal about both alcohol consumption and adult earnings, what kind of evaluation can we make about such a causal claim? Think about our causal hurdles. Perhaps – perhaps! – we can cross the third hurdle by finding that it is true that alcohol consumption (X) is associated with higher earnings (Y). What about our second hurdle? Is it possible that earnings cause alcohol consumption? It is, at least in the sense that individuals with higher incomes have more discretionary dollars to spend on anything – including alcohol – that they like, and that, in contrast, people with lower levels of income have a natural ceiling on how much they can spend on alcohol. So maybe the causal arrow runs the other way after all, though not in the pernicious way that the tabloid suggests. The fourth causal hurdle – trying to think of possible confounding variables that might be related to both X and Y – is also simple in this case: People who work in corporate America and have business dinners with clients are more likely to consume alcohol, and they are also apt to make higher salaries than those who are not in the corporate world. But, most egregiously, the first causal hurdle trips us up. As much as avid producers and consumers of alcoholic beverages might like to convince people that higher levels of drinking will translate to higher income, can you think of a *credible* causal mechanism that connects alcohol consumption to income?

Treatment Choice and Breast Cancer Survival

In 2006 the National Breast Cancer Foundation forecast that 211,000 women and 1600 men in the United States would be told by their doctors that they have breast cancer. One of the most painful situations that some patients have to face occurs when they have to choose a treatment option to pursue.

Two treatment strategies strike different balances between the desirability of aggressively treating the cancer and keeping the procedures as minimally invasive as possible. The first strategy, called a radical mastectomy, represents an effort to try to purge the entire body of cancer by removing the entire breast. In effect, this strategy acknowledges that the breast can produce cancer, so the choice is to remove it. Because of this, it is maximally invasive to a patient's body, and, understandably, few patients find it appealing. The second strategy, called a lumpectomy, is a more localized surgery in which the cancerous tumor is removed from the patient's breast, but as much of the breast as possible is left intact. Certainly this treatment is less invasive, less aggressive, and is less distasteful to most breast cancer patients. It also carries with it the risk that some cancer cells might be missed during the surgery and, as a result, left behind in the body.

Which treatment option should a patient choose? Obviously, patients might consider a myriad of factors when faced with such a choice, but among them might be the expected survival rates for each treatment option. They might expect that patients who choose radical mastectomies, on average, live longer than patients who choose lumpectomies, for the simple fact that the lumpectomy procedure carries with it the risk that some cancer cells will be missed and left behind in the breast tissue, a risk that the radical mastectomy, by its very nature, avoids.

Perplexingly, there tends to be *no association* between breast cancer treatment choice (X) and posttreatment longevity (Y). That is, patients who go through both procedures have roughly the same 1-year and 5-year survival rates. (This is to say, the third causal hurdle has not been crossed.) Does this mean that radical mastectomies are unnecessarily invasive and should not be considered a good treatment option?

Again, consider the rest of our causal hurdles. From the preceding discussion of treatments, it is pretty clear that we can clear the first hurdle – there is a credible causal mechanism between X and Y. The second hurdle, that longevity (Y) might cause treatment (X), is obviously not possible. But the fourth causal hurdle is crucial for evaluating this relationship. Can we imagine any factors (Z) that might be related to both treatment choice (X) and longevity (Y)? Certainly we can. Not all cancers are detected at the same stage of advancement. Some are caught early, whereas others are detected only when the cancer has spread considerably. Thus the severity of cancer at detection (Z) might affect both treatment choice and longevity. Patients whose cancers are diagnosed in early stages (Z), when the tumors are small, may be more likely to choose lumpectomies (X) and are more likely to survive (Y). Conversely, patients whose cancer is spotted in advanced stages (Z) may have almost no choice but to get the more radical treatment (X), and their prospects for long-term survival (Y) are less bright.

Like the school-choice example discussed earlier, this is a case in which a third variable – severity of the disease when it is detected – operates as a selection mechanism that makes the comparison between individuals with different values of the independent variable – treatment – extremely difficult to compare. Although it might be tempting simply to examine the bivariate relationship between treatment and survival rates and conclude that the treatments don't produce different results, that conclusion might be exactly wrong. Why? Because the patients who get radical mastectomies are systematically different from those who get lumpectomies. Simple comparisons in such a case can produce incorrect inferences about causal effects.[8]

Note that this is one of those somewhat unusual situations in which we believe that X may indeed cause Y *in spite of the fact that we did not successfully clear the third causal hurdle* – that is, that there is no bivariate association between X and Y. This supports our view that once a theory has successfully cleared the first hurdle (meaning that there is a credible causal mechanism) it should be put through all of the remaining three causal hurdles.

3.4.3 Explicit Lyrics and Teen Sexual Behavior

What is the role of popular culture in determining teen behavior? Is it the case that the explicit sexual content that saturates so much of today's

---

[8] It should be obvious that we are not oncologists with particular expertise in this very sensitive area. We are not in any way advocating or disparaging a particular treatment for breast cancer. Rather, we think it's important to show how thinking rigorously about causality can lead us to look past surface relationships and dig deeper to find better answers.

culture causes teenagers (especially) to be sexually active at an earlier age? Or is it the case that popular culture is merely a mirror, reflecting back to us who we truly are? A study reported by the Associated Press in 2006, titled "Sexual lyrics prompt teens to have sex," takes a rather clear position on this issue:

> Teens whose iPods are full of music with raunchy, sexual lyrics start having sex sooner than those who prefer other songs, a study found.... Teens who said they listened to lots of music with degrading sexual messages were almost twice as likely to start having intercourse or other sexual activities within the following two years as were teens who listened to little or no sexually degrading music. Among heavy listeners, 51 percent started having sex within two years, versus 29 percent of those who said they listened to little or no sexually degrading music.

So the third causal hurdle – whether X (music listening) and Y (sexual behavior) are related – has been been cleared. And, for the moment, let's dismiss the reverse-causal scenario (question 2) that a teen's sexual behavior causes them to listen to particular kinds of music.

But focus on the fourth causal question. Surely explicit lyrics cannot be the sole factor that causes teens to be sexually active. (And it's worth noting that no person in the article makes the claim that it is the only cause.) Are there other factors that might be related to both music-listening habits and sexual behaviors? According to the article, the research "tried to account for other factors that could affect teens' sexual behavior, including parental permissiveness, and still found explicit lyrics had a strong influence." Surely, parental permissiveness (Z) could be related to both music listening (X) and sexual behavior (Y), and the finding that the X–Y connection survived such a control is helpful. But are there *still other* possible causes in addition to parental permissiveness? Certainly, and critics mentioned in the article are quick to point them out. Could peer pressure (Z) be related to both X and Y? Absolutely. What about self-esteem? Again, yes. Failing to account for those possible causes – and any others that you might think of that can be related to both X and Y – can cause us to make the wrong inference about whether exposure to lyrics causes sexual behavior.

With respect to the first question – the existence of a credible causal mechanism – the article quotes a psychologist who sees a logical connection:

> The brain's impulse-control center undergoes "major construction" during the teen years at the same time that an interest in sex starts to blossom.... Add sexually arousing lyrics and "it's not that surprising that a kid with a heavier diet of that...would be at greater risk for sexual behavior."

Other psychologists might disagree, of course. But the failure to control for all other confounding variables that might be related to the independent and dependent variables is more than enough ammunition to allow a savvy record-company executive to cast doubts on such a study.

3.5 WRAPPING UP

Learning the thinking skills required to evaluate causal claims as conclusively as possible requires practice. They are intellectual habits that, like a good knife, will sharpen with use.

Translating these thinking skills into actively designing new research that helps to address causal questions is the subject of Chapter 4. All of the "research designs" that you will learn in that chapter are strongly linked to issues of evaluating causal claims. Keeping the lessons of this chapter in mind as we move forward is essential to making you a better consumer of information, as well as edging you forward toward being a producer of research.

CONCEPTS INTRODUCED IN THIS CHAPTER

bivariate	probabilistic
confounding variable	selection effect
deterministic	spurious
multivariate	

EXERCISES

1. Think back to a history class in which you learned about the "causes" of a particular historical event (for instance, the Great Depression, the French Revolution, or World War I). How well does each causal claim perform when you try to answer the four questions for establishing causal relationships?

2. Go to your local newspaper's web site (if it has one; if not, pick the web site of any media outlet you visit frequently). In the site's "Search" box, type the words "research cause" (without quotes). (*Hint:* You may need to limit the search time frame, depending on the site you visit.) From the search results, find two articles that make claims about causal relationships. Print them out, and include a brief synopsis of the causal claim embedded in the article.

3. For each of the following examples, imagine that some researcher has found the reported pattern of covariation between X and Y. Can you think of a variable Z that might make the relationship between X and Y spurious?

   (a) The more firefighters (X) that go to a house fire, the greater property damage that occurs (Y).

(b) The more money spent by an incumbent member of Congress's campaign (X), the lower their percentage of vote (Y).

(c) The more children in a community that participate in a Head Start program (X), the greater percentage of students that demonstrate kindergarten readiness (Y).

(d) The higher the salaries of Presbyterian ministers (X), the higher the price of rum in Havana (Y).

4. For each of the following pairs of independent and dependent variables, write about both a probabilistic and a deterministic relationship to describe the likely relationship:

(a) A person's education (X) and voter turnout (Y).

(b) A nation's economic health (X) and political revolution (Y).

(c) Candidate height (X) and election outcome (Y).

5. Take a look at the codebook for the data set "BES 2005 Subset" and write about your answers to the following items:

(a) Develop a causal theory about the relationship between an independent variable (X) and a dependent variable (Y) from this data set. Is it the credible causal mechanism that connects X to Y? Explain your answer.

(b) Could Y cause X? Explain your answer.

(c) What other variables (Z) would you like to control for in your tests of this theory?

4 Research Design

OVERVIEW

Given our focus on causality, what research strategies do political scientists use to investigate causal relationships? Generally speaking, the controlled experiment is the foundation for scientific research. And some political scientists use experiments in their work. However, owing to the nature of our subject matter, most political scientists adopt one of two types of "observational" research designs that are intended to mimic experiments. The cross-sectional observational study focuses on variation across individual units (like people or countries). The time-series observational study focuses on variation in aggregate quantities (like presidential popularity) over time. What is an "experiment" and why is it so useful? How do observational studies try to mimic experimental designs? Most important, what are the strengths and weaknesses of each of these three research designs in establishing causal relationships between concepts? That is, how does each one help us to get across the four causal hurdles identified in Chapter 3? Relatedly, we introduce issues relating to the selection of samples of cases to study in which we are not able to study the entire population of cases to which our theory applies. This is a subject that will feature prominently in many of the subsequent chapters.

4.1 COMPARISON AS THE KEY TO ESTABLISHING CAUSAL RELATIONSHIPS

So far, you have learned that political scientists care about causal relationships. You have learned that most phenomena we are interested in explaining have multiple causes, but our theories typically deal with only one of them while ignoring the others. In some of the research examples in the previous chapters, we have noted that the multivariate nature of the world can make our first glances misleading. In the breast cancer example, at first it did not appear that any kind of relationship (let alone a causal relationship) existed between treatment choice and patient longevity. In the school-choice example, it first appeared that a relationship (and perhaps a causal one) did exist between participation in the program and test scores. But, we argued, in both cases those first glances were potentially quite misleading.

Why? Because what appeared to be the straightforward comparisons between two groups – patients who chose one treatment compared with patients who chose another, or eighth-graders in one school compared with eighth-graders in another school – ended up being far from simple. On some very important factors, our different groupings for our independent variable X were far from equal. That is, patients who chose different treatment options (X) had differing levels of the disease when it was discovered (Z), which also affected their longevity (Y). And students in different school programs (X) had parents who had systematically different levels of involvement in their childrens' education (Z), which also affected test scores (Y). As convincing as those bivariate comparisons might have been, they would likely be misleading.

Comparisons are at the heart of science. If we are evaluating a theory about the relationship between some X and some Y, the scientist's job is to do everything possible to make sure that no other influences (Z) interfere with the comparisons that we will rely on to make our inferences about a possible causal relationship between X and Y.

The obstacles to causal inference that we described in Chapter 3 are substantial, but surmountable. We don't know whether, in reality, X causes Y. We may be armed with a theory that suggests that X does, indeed, cause Y, but theories can be (and often are) wrong or incomplete. So how do scientists generally, and political scientists in particular, go about testing whether X causes Y? There are several strategies, or **research designs**, that researchers can use toward that end. The goal of all types of research designs are to help us evaluate how well a theory fares as it makes its way over the four causal hurdles – that is, to answer as conclusively as is possible the question about whether X causes Y. In the next two sections we focus on the two strategies that political scientists use most commonly and effectively: experiments and observational studies.

4.2 EXPERIMENTAL RESEARCH DESIGNS

Suppose that you were the CEO of a pharmaceutical company, and your scientific team tells you that they have just discovered a new drug that will help lower blood pressure. The pharmacists tell you that they have successfully tested the drug on rats and developed a dosage regimen that they expect will be effective on people. However, the drug has yet to be tested on people.

And it is important to add here that the causal claim has a particular directional component to it; that is, increased (not decreased) amounts of the drug are alleged to lower (not raise) blood pressure.

How would researchers in the physical sciences and medicine evaluate whether this new and promising drug works on humans? Note the focus on causality here. In more "causal" language, how can we find out whether taking the drug (X) will *cause* patients to have lower blood pressure (Y)? As the introduction to this chapter highlights, we will need a comparison of some kind, and we will want that comparison to isolate any potentially different effects that the drug has on a patient's blood pressure. It is very important, and not at all surprising, to realize that patients may have high or low blood pressure for a variety of reasons (Z's) that have nothing to do with our new drug – varying exercise habits, varying diets, and varying genetic predispositions can all cause blood pressure to be high or low. So how can we establish whether, among these other influences (Z), our new drug (X) also causes a patient's blood pressure (Y) to fall?

The standard answer to this question in the physical and medical sciences is that we would need to conduct an **experiment**. Because the word "experiment" has such common usage, its scientific meaning is frequently misunderstood. An experiment is *not* simply any kind of analysis that is quantitative in nature; neither is it exclusively the domain of laboratories and white-coated scientists with pocket protectors. We define an experiment as follows: An experiment is a research design in which the researcher both controls and randomly assigns values of the independent variable to the participants.

Notice the twin components of the definition of the experiment: That the researcher both *controls* values of the independent variable – or X, as we have called it – as well as *randomly assigns* those values to the participants in the experiment. Together, these two features form a complete definition of an experiment, which means that there are no other essential features of an experiment beside these two.

What does it mean to say that a researcher "controls" the value of the independent variable that the participants receive? It means, most importantly, that the values of the independent variable that the participants receive are *not* determined either by the participants themselves or by nature. In our example of our blood-pressure drug, this requirement means that we cannot compare people who, by their own choice, already take the drug with those who do not (in this case the choice of whether or not to take the drug is a Z variable that may exert an influence on Y separate from X). It means that we, the researchers, have to decide which of our experimental participants will take the drug and which ones will not.

But the definition of an experiment has one other essential component as well: We, the researchers, must not only control the values of the independent variable, but *we must also assign those values to participants randomly*. In the context of our drug-testing example, this means that we must toss coins, draw numbers out of a hat, use a random-number generator, or some other such mechanism to ensure that our participants are divided into a **treatment group** (who will receive our drug) and a **control group** (who will not receive the drug, but will instead presumably receive a placebo).

What's the big deal here? Why is randomly assigning subjects to treatment groups important? What scientific benefits arise from the random assignment of people to treatment groups? To see why this is so crucial, recall that we have emphasized that all science is about comparisons and also that every interesting phenomenon worth exploring – every interesting dependent variable – is caused by many factors, not just one. Random assignment to treatment groups ensures that the comparison we make between the treatment group and the control group is as pure as possible and that some other cause of the dependent variable (Z) will not pollute that comparison. By first taking a group of participants and then randomly splitting them into two groups on the basis of a coin flip, what we have ensured is that the participants will not be systematically different from one another. Indeed, in the **aggregate** – and provided that the participant pool is reasonably large – randomly assigning participants to treatment groups ensures that the groups, as a whole, are *identical*. If the two groups are identical, save for the coin flip, then we can be certain that any differences we observe in the groups must be because of the independent variable that we have assigned to them.

Return to our drug-trial example. An experiment involving our new blood-pressure drug would involve finding a group of people – however obtained – and then randomly assigning them to receive either the new drug or a placebo. We fully realize that there are other causes of low and high blood pressure and that our experiment does not negate those factors. In fact, our experiment will have nothing whatsoever to say about those other causes. What it *will* do, and do well, is to determine whether our drug has an effect on blood pressure.

Contrast the comparison that results from an experiment with a comparison that arises from a nonexperiment. (Be patient. We'll talk all about nonexperimental designs in the next section.) Suppose that the makers of a particular brand of aspirin wanted to test the claim that people who take their aspirin have lower blood pressure than people who don't take their

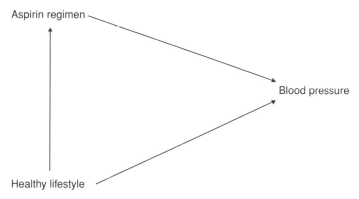

Figure 4.1. The possibly confounding effects of a healthy lifestyle on the aspirin–blood-pressure relationship.

aspirin. Let's even assume that they conduct a random-sample survey of adults, and that people answer the survey truthfully about their aspirin intake and blood pressure. If there is an elevated rate of high blood pressure in the nonaspirin group compared with that of the aspirin takers, does that mean that aspirin *caused* – see that word again – people to have lower blood pressure? No.[1] Why not? Because aspirin-takers and non-aspirin-takers might be *systematically different*. What does that mean? People who take a daily aspirin are more likely to be more health conscious than non-aspirin-takers. In this instance, the level of health consciousness could be an important Z variable. These individuals likely exercise more and eat a healthier diet. Both of these things, of course, are probably associated with lower blood pressure. What this means is that the comparison between aspirin-takers and non-aspirin-takers is potentially misleading because it is confounded by other factors like diet and exercise. So is the lower blood pressure the result of the aspirin, or is it the result of the better diet and increased exercise that aspirin-takers also benefit from? Because this particular nonexperimental research design does not answer that question, it does not clear our fourth causal hurdle. It is impossible to know whether it was the aspirin that caused the lower blood pressure. In this nonexperimental design just described, because there are other factors that influence blood pressure – and, critically, because these factors are also related to whether or not people take aspirin – it is very difficult to say conclusively that the independent variable (aspirin intake) causes the dependent variable (blood pressure). Figure 4.1 shows this graphically.

Here is where experiments differ so drastically from any other kind of research design. What experimental research designs accomplish by way

---

[1] Technically, of course, aspirin may or may not cause changes in blood pressure. But even if it does, the evidence just described does not prove it.

of random assignment to treatment groups, then, is to decontaminate the comparison between the treatment and control group of all other influences. Before any stimulus (like a drug or placebo) is administered, all of the participants are in the same pool. Researchers divide them by using some random factor like a coin flip, and that difference is the only difference between the two groups.

Think of it another way. The way that the confounding variables in Figure 4.1 are correlated with the independent variable is highly improbable in an experiment. Why? Because if X is determined by randomness, like a coin flip, then (by the very definition of randomness) it is exceedingly unlikely to be correlated with anything (including confounding variables Z). When researchers control and assign values of X randomly, the comparison between the different groups will not be affected by the fact that other factors certainly do cause Y, the dependent variable.

Connect this back to our discussion from Chapter 3 about how researchers attempt to establish whether some X causes Y. As we will see, experiments are not the only method that help researchers cross the four causal hurdles, but they are uniquely capable in accomplishing that task. Consider each hurdle in turn. First, we should evaluate whether there is a credible causal mechanism before we decide to run the experiment. It is worth noting that the crossing of this causal hurdle is neither easier nor harder in experiments than in nonexperiments. Coming up with a credible causal scenario that links X to Y heightens our dependence on theory, not on data or research design.

Second, in an experiment, it is impossible for Y to cause X – the second causal hurdle – for two reasons. First, assigning X occurs in time before Y is measured, which makes it impossible for Y to cause X. In addition, as previously noted, if X is generated by randomness alone, then nothing (including Y) can cause it.

Establishing, third, whether X and Y are correlated is easily done in any research design (as we will see in Chapter 8). What about our fourth causal hurdle? Is there some Z that is related to both X and Y that makes the association between X and Y spurious? Experiments are uniquely well equipped to help us answer this question definitively. An experiment does not, in any way, eliminate the possibility that a variety of other variables (that we call Z) might also affect Y (as well as X). What the experiment does, through the process of randomly assigning subjects to different values of X, is to equate the treatment and control groups on all possible factors. On every possible variable, whether or not it is related to X, or to Y, or to both, or to neither, the treatment and control groups should, in theory, be identical. That makes the comparison between the two values of X

unpolluted by any possible Z variables because we expect the groups to be equivalent on all values of Z.

In our example of the new drug and blood pressure, by experimentally assigning our participants to treatment (drug) and control (placebo) groups, we do not deny that diet and exercise, for example, might affect blood pressure; we merely neutralize those influences. How? Say that some of our participants are triathletes, who likely have low blood pressure, and others are couch potatoes, who likely have high blood pressure. Randomly assigning all participants – triathletes and couch potatoes alike – to the drug and placebo groups will neutralize the effects of their exercise (or lack thereof) on the aggregate blood-pressure statistics for the two groups. Why? Because, by randomly assigning all participants to the drug or the placebo group, we would expect, on average, half of the triathletes to be in the drug group and half in the placebo group. Likewise, we would expect half of our couch potatoes to be in the treatment group, and half in the placebo group. Thus, when the treatment and control groups' rates of high blood pressure are compared, the effects of different amounts of exercise will not mislead us into thinking that the drug does (or does not) have an effect.

Remarkably, the experimental ability to control for the effects of outside variables (Z) applies to *all* possible confounding variables, regardless of whether we, the researchers, are aware of them. Let's make the example downright preposterous. Let's say that, 20 years from now, another team of scientists discovers that having attached (as opposed to detached) earlobes causes people to have low blood pressure. Does that possibility threaten the inference that we draw from our experiment about our drug and blood pressure today? No, not at all. Why not? Because, whether or not we are aware of it, the random assignment of participants to treatment groups means that, whether we are paying attention to it or not, we would expect our treatment and control groups to have equal numbers of people with attached earlobes, and for both groups to have equal numbers of people with detached earlobes. The key element of an experimental research design – randomly assigning subjects to different values of X, the independent variable – controls for every Z in the universe, whether or not we are aware of that Z.

Together, all of this means that experiments bring with them a particularly strong confidence in the causal inferences drawn from the analysis. In scientific parlance, this is called **internal validity**. If a research design produces high levels of confidence in the conclusions about causality, it is said to have high internal validity. Conversely, research designs that do not allow for particularly definitive conclusions about whether X causes Y are said to have low degrees of internal validity.

4.2.1   "Random Assignment" versus "Random Sampling"

It is critical that you do not confuse the experimental process of randomly assigning people to treatment groups, on the one hand, with the process of randomly sampling people for participation, on the other hand. They are entirely different, and in fact have nothing more in common than that six-letter word "random." They are, however, quite often confused for one another. **Random assignment to treatment groups** occurs when the participants for an experiment are assigned randomly to one of several possible values of X, the independent variable; importantly, this definition says nothing at all about how the subjects were selected for participation. But **random sampling** is, at its very heart, about how researchers select people for participation in a study – they are selected at random, that is, every member of the underlying population has an equal probability of being selected. (This is common in survey research, for example.) Mixing up these two critical concepts will produce a good bit of confusion.

4.2.2   Are There Drawbacks to Experimental Research Designs?

Experiments, as we have seen, have a unique ability to get social scientists across our hurdles needed to establish whether X causes Y. But that does not mean they are without their disadvantages. Many of these disadvantages are related to the differences between medical and physical sciences, on the one hand, and the social sciences, on the other. We now discuss four such drawbacks to experimentation.

First, especially in the social sciences, not every independent variable (X) is controllable and subject to experimental manipulation. Suppose, for example, that we wish to study the effects of gender on political participation. Do men contribute more money, vote more, volunteer more in campaigns, than women? There are a variety of nonexperimental ways to study this relationship, but it is impossible to experimentally manipulate a subject's gender. Recall that the definition of an experiment is that the researcher both controls and randomly assigns the values of the independent variable. In this case, the presumed cause (the independent variable) is a person's gender. Compared with drugs versus placebos, assigning a participant's gender is another matter entirely. It is, to put it mildly, impossible. People show up at an experiment either male or female, and it is not within the experimenter's power to "randomly assign" a participant to be male or female.

This is true in many, many political science examples. There are simply myriads of substantive problems that are impossible to study in an experimental fashion. How does a person's partisanship (X) affect his issue opinions (Y)? How does a person's income level (X) affect her campaign contributions (Y)? How does a country's level of democratization (X) affect its openness to international trade (Y)? How does the level of military spending in India (X) affect the level of military spending in Pakistan (Y) – and, for that matter, vice versa? How does media coverage (X) in an election campaign influence voters' priorities (Y)? In each of these examples that intrigues social scientists, the independent variable is simply not subject to experimental manipulation. Social scientists cannot, in any meaningful sense, "assign" people a party identification or an income, "assign" a country a level of democratization or level of military spending, or "assign" a campaign-specific, long-term amount of media coverage. These variables simply exist in nature, and we cannot control exposure to them and randomly assign different values to different cases (that is, individual people or countries).

A second potential disadvantage of experimental research designs is that experiments often suffer from low degrees of **external validity**. We have noted that the key strength of experiments is that they typically have high levels of internal validity. That is, we can be quite confident that the conclusions about causality reached in the analysis are not confounded by other variables. External validity, in a sense, is the other side of the coin, as it represents the degree to which we can be confident that the results of our analysis apply not only to the participants in the study, but also to the population more broadly construed. Recall that there is nothing whatsoever in our definition of an experiment that describes how researchers recruit or select people to participate in the experiment. To reiterate: *It is absolutely not the case that experiments require a random sample of the target population.* Indeed, it is extremely rare for experiments to draw a random sample from a population.[2] In drug-trial experiments, for example, it is common to place advertisements in newspapers or on the radio to invite participation, usually involving some form of compensation to the participants. Clearly, people who see and respond to advertisements like this are not a random sample of the population of interest, which is typically thought of as all potential recipients of the drug. Similarly, when professors "recruit" people from their (or their colleagues') classes, the

---

[2] Since 1990 or so, however, there has been a growing movement in the field of survey research – which has always used random samples of the population – to use computers in the interviewing process that includes experimental randomization of variations in survey questions, in a technique called a "survey experiment." Such designs are intended to reap the benefits of both random assignment to treatment groups, and hence have high internal validity, as well as the benefits of a random sample, and hence have high external validity. See Piazza, Sniderman, and Tetlock (1990) and Sniderman and Piazza (1993).

participants are not a random sample of *any* population.[3] The participant pool in this case represents what we would call a **sample of convenience**, which is to say, "this is more or less the group of people we could beg, coerce, entice, or cajole to participate."

With a sample of convenience, it is simply unclear how, if at all, the results of the experiment generalize to a broader population. As we will learn in Chapter 7, this is a critical issue in the social sciences. Because most experiments make use of such samples of convenience, with any single experiment, it is difficult to know whether the results of that analysis are in any way typical of what we would find in a different sample. With experimental designs, then, scientists learn about how their results apply to a broader population through the process of **replication**, in which researchers implement the same procedures repeatedly in identical form to see if the relationships hold in a consistent fashion.

Experimental research designs, at times, can be plagued with a third disadvantage, namely that they carry special ethical dilemmas for the researcher. Ethical issues about the treatment of human participants occur frequently with medical experiments, of course. If we wished to study experimentally the effects of different types of cancer treatments on survival rates, this would require obtaining a sample of patients with cancer and then randomly assigning the patients to differing treatment regimens. This is typically not considered acceptable medical practice. In such high-stakes medical situations, most individuals value making these decisions themselves, in consultation with their doctor, and would not relinquish the important decisions about their treatment to a random-number generator.

Ethical situations arise less frequently, and typically less dramatically, in social science experimentation, but they do arise on occasion. During the behavioral revolution in psychology in the 1960s, several famous experiments conducted at universities produced vigorous ethical debates. Psychologist Stanley Milgram conducted experiments on how easily he could make individuals obey an authority figure. In this case, the dependent variable was the willingness of the participant to administer what he believed to be a shock to another participant, who was in fact an employee of Milgram's. (The ruse was that Milgram told the participant that he was testing how negative reinforcement – electric shocks – affected the "learning" of the "student.") The independent variable was the degree to which

---

[3] Think about that for a moment. Experiments in undergraduate psychology or political science classes are not a random sample of 18- to-22 year olds, or even a random sample of undergraduate students, or even a random sample of students from your college or university. Your psychology class is populated with people more interested in the social sciences than in the physical sciences or engineering or the humanities.

Milgram conveyed his status as an authority figure. In other words, the X that Milgram manipulated was the degree to which he presented himself as an authority who must be obeyed. For some participants, Milgram wore a white lab coat and informed them that he was a professor at Yale University. For others, he dressed more casually and never mentioned his institutional affiliation. The dependent variable, then, was how strong the (fake) shocks would be before the subject simply refused to go on. At the highest extreme, the instrument that delivered the "shock" said "450 volts, XXX." The results of the experiment were fascinating because, to his surprise, Milgram found that the great majority of his participants were willing to administer even these extreme shocks to the "learners." But scientific review boards consider such experiments unethical today, because the experiment created a great degree of emotional distress among the true participants.

A fourth potential drawback of experimental research designs is that, when interpreting the results of an experiment, we sometimes make mistakes of emphasis. If an experiment produces a finding that some X does indeed cause Y, that does not mean that that particular X is the most prominent cause of Y. As we have emphasized repeatedly, a variety of independent variables are causally related to every interesting dependent variable in the social sciences. Experimental research designs often do not help to sort out which causes of the dependent variable have the largest effects and which ones have smaller effects.

4.3 OBSERVATIONAL STUDIES (IN TWO FLAVORS)

Taken together, the drawbacks of experiments mean that, for any given political science research situation, implementing an experiment often proves to be unworkable, and sometimes downright impossible. As a result, experimentation is not the most common research design used by political science researchers. In some subfields, such as political psychology – which, as the name implies, studies the cognitive and emotional underpinnings of political decision making – experimentation is quite common. And it is becoming more common in the study of public opinion and electoral competition. But the experiment, for many researchers and for varying reasons, remains a tool that is not applicable to many of the phenomena that we seek to study.

Does this mean that researchers have to shrug their shoulders and abandon their search for causal connections before they even begin? Not at all. But what options do scholars have when they cannot control exposure to different values of the independent variables? In such cases, the only choice is to take the world as it already exists and make the comparison between either individual units – like people, political parties, or countries – or between an aggregated quantity that varies over time. These represent two variants of what is most commonly called an **observational study**. Observational studies are not experiments, but they seek to emulate them. They are known as observational studies because, unlike the controlled and somewhat artificial nature of most experiments, in these research designs, researchers simply take reality as it is and "observe" it, attempting to sort out causal connections without the benefit of randomly assigning participants to treatment groups. Instead, different values of the independent variable already exist in the world, and what scientists do is observe them and then evaluate their theoretical claims by putting them through the same four causal hurdles to discover whether X causes Y.

This leads to the definition of an observational study: An observational study is a research design in which the researcher does *not* have control over values of the independent variable, which occur naturally. However, it is necessary that there be some degree of variability on the independent variable between cases, as well as variation in the dependent variable.

Because there is no random assignment to treatment groups, as in experiments, some scholars claim that it is impossible to speak of causality in observational studies, and therefore sometimes refer to them as **correlational studies**. Along with most political scientists, we do not share this view. Certainly experiments produce higher degrees of confidence about causal matters than do observational studies. However, in observational studies, if sufficient attention is paid to accounting for all of the other possible causes of the dependent variable that are suggested by current understanding, then we can make informed evaluations of their confidence that the independent variable does cause the dependent variable.

Observational studies, as this discussion implies, face exactly the same four causal hurdles as do experiments. (Recall that those hurdles are present in any research design.) So how, in observational studies, do we cross these hurdles? The first causal hurdle – focusing on a credible mechanism connecting X and Y – is identical in experimental and observational studies.

In an observational study, however, crossing the second causal hurdle – can we rule out the possibility that Y causes X? – can sometimes be problematic. For example, do countries with higher levels of economic development (X) have, as a consequence, more stable democratic regimes (Y)? Crossing the second causal hurdle, in this case, is a rather dicey matter. It is clearly plausible that having a stable democratic government makes economic prosperity more likely, which is the reverse-causal scenario. After all, investors are probably more comfortable taking risks with their money in democratic regimes than in autocratic ones. Those risks, in turn, likely produce greater degrees of economic prosperity. It is possible, of course, that X and Y are mutually reinforcing – that is, X causes Y and Y causes X.

The third hurdle – do X and Y covary – is no more difficult for an observational study than for an experiment. (The techniques for examining relationships between two variables are straightforward, and you will learn them in Chapter 8.) But, unlike in an experimental setting, if we fail to find covariation between X and Y in an observational setting, we should still proceed to the fourth hurdle because the possibility remains that we will find covariation between and X and Y when we control for some variable Z (think back to the breast cancer example).

The most pointed comparison between experiments and observational studies, though, occurs with respect to the fourth causal hurdle. The near-magic that happens in experiments because of random assignment to treatment groups – which enables researchers to know that no other factors interfere in the relationship between X and Y – is not present in an observational study. So, in an observational study, the comparison between groups with different values of the independent variable may very well be polluted by other factors, interfering with our ability to make conclusive statements about whether X causes Y.

Within observational studies, there are two pure types – **cross-sectional observational studies**, which focus on variation between **spatial units** for a single **time unit**, and **time-series observational studies**, which focus on variation within a single spatial unit over multiple time units. There are, in addition, hybrid designs, but for sake of simplicity we will focus on the pure types.[4] Before we get into the two types of observational studies, we need to provide a brief introduction to observational data.

4.3.1 Datum, Data, Data Set

The word **"data"** is one of the most grammatically misused words in the English language. Why? Because most people use this word as though it were a singular word when it is, in fact, plural. Any time you read "the data is," you have found a grammatical error. Instead, when describing data, the phrasing should be "the data are." Get used to it: You are now one of the foot soldiers in the crusade to get people to use this word appropriately. It will be a long and uphill battle.

The singular form of the word data is **"datum."** Together, a collection of datum produces data or a "data set." We define observational data sets by the variables that they contain and the spatial and time units over which they are measured. Political scientists use data measured on a variety of

---

[4] The classic statements of observational studies appeared in 1963 in Donald Campbell and Julian Stanley's seminal work *Experimental and Quasi-experimental Designs for Research.*

Table 4.1. Example of cross-sectional data		
Nation	Government debt as a percentage of GNP	Unemployment rate
Finland	6.6	2.6
Denmark	5.7	1.6
United States	27.5	5.6
Spain	13.9	3.2
Sweden	15.9	2.7
Belgium	45.0	2.4
Japan	11.2	1.4
New Zealand	44.6	0.5
Ireland	63.8	5.9
Italy	42.5	4.7
Portugal	6.6	2.1
Norway	28.1	1.7
Netherlands	23.6	2.1
Germany	6.7	0.9
Canada	26.9	6.3
Greece	18.4	2.1
France	8.7	2.8
Switzerland	8.2	0.0
United Kingdom	53.6	3.1
Australia	23.8	2.6

different spatial units. For instance, in survey research, the spatial unit is the individual survey respondent. In comparative U.S. state government studies, the spatial unit is the U.S. state. In international relations, the spatial unit is often the nation. Commonly studied time units are months, quarters, and years. It is also common to refer to the spatial and time units that define data sets as the **data set dimensions**.

Two of the most common types of data sets correspond directly to the two types of observational studies that we just introduced. For cross-section quasi-experiments, researchers analyze cross-sectional data to determine whether the third causal hurdle has been cleared. For instance, Table 4.1 presents a cross-sectional data set in which the time unit is the year 1972 and the spatial unit is nations. These data could be used to test the theory that unemployment percentage (X) $\rightarrow$ government debt as a percentage of gross national product (Y).

For time-series observational studies, time-series data are analyzed to determine whether the third causal hurdle has been cleared. These data contain measures of X and Y across time for a single spatial unit. For instance, Table 4.2 displays a time-series data set in which the spatial unit is the United States and the time unit is months. We could use these data to

Table 4.2. Example of time-series data		
Month	Presidential approval	Inflation
2002.01	83.7	1.14
2002.02	82.0	1.14
2002.03	79.8	1.48
2002.04	76.2	1.64
2002.05	76.3	1.18
2002.06	73.4	1.07
2002.07	71.6	1.46
2002.08	66.5	1.80
2002.09	67.2	1.51
2002.10	65.3	2.03
2002.11	65.5	2.20
2002.12	62.8	2.38

test the theory that inflation $(X) \rightarrow$ presidential approval (Y). In a data set, researchers analyze only those data or **data points** that contain measured values for both the independent variable (X) and the dependent variable (Y) to determine whether the third causal hurdle has been cleared.

4.3.2 Cross-Sectional Observational Studies

As the name implies, a cross-sectional observational study examines a cross section of social reality, focusing on variation between *individual spatial units* – again, like citizens, elected officials, voting districts, or countries – and explaining the variation in the dependent variable across them.

For example, what, if anything, is the connection between the preferences of the voters from a district (X) and a representative's voting behavior (Y)? In a cross-sectional observational study, the strategy that a researcher would pursue in answering this question involves comparing the aggregated preferences of voters from a variety of districts (X) with the voting records of the representatives (Y). Such an analysis, of course, would have to be observational, instead of experimental, because this particular X is not at all subject to experimental manipulation. Such an analysis might take place within the confines of a single legislative session, for a variety of practical purposes (such as the absence of turnover in seats, which is an obviously complicating factor).

Bear in mind, of course, that observational studies have to cross the same four casual hurdles as do experiments. And we have noted that, unlike experiments, with their random assignment to treatment groups, observational studies will often get stuck on our fourth hurdle. That might indeed be the case here. Assuming the other three hurdles can be cleared, consider the possibility that there are confounding variables that cause Y and are also correlated with X, which make the X–Y connection spurious. (Can you think of any such factors?) How do cross-sectional observational studies deal with this critical issue? The answer is that, in most cases, this can be accomplished through a series of rather straightforward statistical controls. In particular, in Chapter 10, you will learn the most common social science research tool for "controlling for" other possible causes of Y, namely the multivariate regression model. What you will learn there is that multivariate regression can allow researchers to see how, if at all, controlling for another variable (like Z) affects the relationship between X and Y.

4.3.3   Time-Series Observational Studies

The other major variant of observational studies is the time-series observational study, which has, at its heart, a comparison over time within a single spatial unit. Unlike in the cross-sectional variety, which examines relationships between variables across individual units typically at a single time point, in the time-series observational study, political scientists typically examine the variation within one spatial unit over time.[5]

For example, how, if at all, do changes in media coverage about the economy (X) affect public concern about the economy (Y)?[6] To be a bit more specific, when the media spend more time talking about the potential problem of inflation, does the public show more concern about inflation, and when the media spend less time on the subject of inflation, does public concern about inflation wane? We can measure these variables in aggregate terms that vary over time. For example, how many stories about inflation make it onto the nightly news in a given month? It is almost certain that that quantity will not be the same each and every month. And how much concern does the public show (through opinion polls, for example) about inflation in a given month? Again, the percentage of people who identify inflation as a pressing problem will almost certainly vary from month to month.

Of course, as with its cross-sectional cousin, the time-series observational study will require us to focus hard on that fourth causal hurdle. Are there any other variables (Z) that are related to the varying volume of news coverage about inflation (X) and public concern about inflation (Y)? (The third exercise at the end of this chapter will ask for your thoughts on this subject.) If we can identify any other possible causes of why the public is

---

[5] The spatial units analyzed in time-series observational studies are usually aggregated.

[6] See Iyengar and Kinder (1987).

sometimes more concerned about inflation, and why they are sometimes less concerned about it, then we will need to control for those factors in our analysis.

4.3.4   The Major Difficulty with Observational Studies

We noted that experimental research designs carry some drawbacks with them. So, too, do observational studies. Here, we focus only on one, but it is a big one. As the preceding examples demonstrate, when we need to control for the other possible causes of Y to cross the fourth causal hurdle, we need to control for *all of them*, not just one.[7] But how do we know whether we have controlled for all of the other possible causes of Y? In many cases, we don't know that for certain. We need to try, of course, to control statistically for all other possible causes that we can, which involves carefully considering the previous research on the subject and gathering as much data on those other causes as is possible. But in many cases, we will simply be unable to do this perfectly.

What all of this means, in our view, is that observational analysis must be a bit more tentative in its pronouncements about causality. Indeed, if we have done the very best we can to control for as many causes of Y, then the most sensible conclusion we can reach, in many cases, is that X causes Y. But in practice, our conclusions are rarely definitive, and subsequent research can modify them. That can be frustrating, we know, for students to come to grips with – and it can be frustrating for researchers, too. But the fact that conclusive answers are difficult to come by should only make us work harder to identify other causes of Y.

4.4   SUMMARY

For almost every phenomenon of interest to political scientists, there is more than one form of research design that they could implement to address questions of causal relationships. Before starting a project, researchers need to decide whether to use experimental or observational methods; and if they opt for the latter, as is common, they have to decide what type of observational study to use. And sometimes researchers choose more than one type of design.

Different research designs help shed light on different questions. Focus, for the moment, on a simple matter like preferences for a more liberal

---

[7] As we will see in Chapter 10, technically we need to control only for the factors that might affect Y and are also related to X. In practice, though, that is a very difficult distinction to make.

or conservative government policy. Cross-sectional and time-series approaches are both useful in this respect. They simply address different types of substantive questions. Cross-sectional approaches look to see why some other individuals prefer more liberal government policies, and why some individuals prefer more conservative government policies. That is a perfectly worthwhile undertaking for a political scientist: What causes some people to be liberals and others to be conservatives? But consider the time-series approach, which focuses on why the public as an aggregated whole prefers a more liberal or a more conservative government at different points in time. That is simply a different question. Neither approach is inherently better or worse than the other, but they both shed light on different aspects of social reality. Which design researchers should choose depends on what type of question they intend to ask and answer.

CONCEPTS INTRODUCED IN THIS CHAPTER

aggregate	observational study
control group	random assignment to treatment
correlational studies	groups
cross-sectional observational studies	random sampling
data	replication
data points	research designs
data set dimensions	sample of convenience
datum	spatial units
experiment	time units
external validity	time-series observational studies
internal validity	treatment group

EXERCISES

1. Consider the following proposed relationships between an independent and a dependent variable. In each case, would it be realistic for a researcher to perform an experiment to test the theory? If yes, briefly describe what would be randomly assigned in the experiment; if not, briefly explain why not.

    (a) An individual's level of religiosity (X) and his or her preferences for different political candidates (Y)
    (b) Exposure to negative political news (X) and political apathy (Y)
    (c) Military service (X) and attitudes toward foreign policy (Y)
    (d) A speaker's personal characteristics (X) and persuasiveness (Y)

2. Consider the relationship between education level (X) and voting turnout (Y). How would the design of a cross-sectional observational study differ from that of a time-series observational study?

3. In the section on time-series observational studies, we introduced the idea of how varying levels of media coverage of inflation (X) might cause variation in public concern about inflation (Y). Can you think of any relevant Z variables that we will need to control for, statistically, in such an analysis, to be confident that the relationship between X and Y is causal?

4. In the previous chapter (specifically, Sections 3.3 and 3.4), we gave examples of research problems. For each of these examples, identify the spatial unit(s) and time unit(s). For each, say whether the study was an experiment, a cross-sectional observational study, or a time-series observational study.

5. Table 4.1 presents data for a test of a theory by use of a cross-sectional observational study. If this same theory were tested by use of a time-series observational study, what would the data table look like?

6. Compare the two designs for testing the preceding theory. Across the two forms of observational studies, what are the Z variables for which you want to control?

7. Table 4.2 presents data for a test of a theory by use of a time-series observational study. If this same theory were tested by use of a cross-sectional observational study, what would the data table look like?

8. Compare the two designs for testing the preceding theory. Across the two forms of observational studies, what are the Z variables for which you want to control?

5 Measurement

OVERVIEW

Although what political scientists care about is discovering whether causal relationships exist between concepts, what we *actually* examine is statistical associations between variables. Therefore it is critical that we have a clear understanding of the concepts that we care about so we can measure them in a valid and reliable way. In this chapter we focus on several examples from the political science literature, such as the concept of political tolerance. We know that political tolerance and intolerance is a "real" thing – that it exists to varying degrees in the hearts and minds of people. But how do we go about measuring it? What are the implications of poor measurement?

I know it when I see it.
> – Associate Justice of the United States Supreme Court Potter Stewart, in an attempt to define "obscenity" in a concurring opinion in *Jacobellis v. Ohio* (1964)

These go to eleven.
> – Nigel Tufnel (played by Christopher Guest), describing the volume knob on his amplifier, in the movie *This Is Spinal Tap*

5.1 WHY MEASUREMENT MATTERS

We have emphasized the role of theory in political science. That is, we care about causal relationships between concepts that interest us as political scientists. At this point, you are hopefully starting to develop theories of your own about politics. If these original theories are in line with the rules of the road that we laid out in Chapter 1, they will be causal, general, and parsimonious. They may even be elegant and clever.

But at this point, it is worth pausing and thinking about what a theory really *is* and *is not*. To help us in this process, take a look back at Figure 1.2. A theory, as we have said, is merely a conjecture about the possible causal relationship between two or more concepts. As scientists, we must always resist the temptation to view our theories as somehow supported until we have evaluated evidence from the real world, and until we have done everything we can with empirical evidence to evaluate how well our theory does through the four causal hurdles we identified in Chapter 3. In other words, we cannot evaluate a theory until we have gone through the rest of the process depicted in Figure 1.2. This chapter deals with **operationalization,** or the movement of variables from the rather abstract conceptual level to the very real measured level. We can conduct hypothesis tests and make reasonable evaluations of our theories only after we have gone carefully through this important process with all of our variables.

If our theories are statements about relationships *between concepts*, when we look for evidence to test our theories, we are immediately confronted with the reality that we do not actually *observe* those concepts. Many of the concepts that we care about in political science, as we will see shortly, are inherently elusive and downright impossible to observe empirically in a direct way, and sometimes incredibly difficult to measure quantitatively.

In this chapter, we describe the problem of measurement and the importance of measuring the concepts we are interested in as precisely as possible. During this process, you will learn some thinking skills about evaluating the measurement strategies of scholarship that you read, as well as learn about creating measures of your own.

We begin with a section on measurement in the social sciences generally. We focus on examples from economics and psychology, two social sciences that are at rather different levels of agreement about the measurement of their major variables. In political science, we have a complete range of variables in terms of the levels of agreement about their measurement. In the remaining sections we discuss the core concepts of measurement and give some examples from political science research. Throughout our discussion of measurement, we focus on the measurements of variables that take on a numeric range of values we feel comfortable treating the way that we normally treat numeric values. In Chapter 6 we will discuss this further and focus on some variable types that can take different types of nonnumeric values.

5.2   SOCIAL SCIENCE MEASUREMENT: THE VARYING CHALLENGES OF QUANTIFYING HUMANITY

Measurement is a "problem" in all sciences – from the physical sciences of physics and chemistry to the social sciences of economics, political science, psychology, and the rest. But in the physical sciences, the problem of measurement is often reduced to a problem of instrumentation, in which scientists develop well-specified protocols for measuring, say, the amount of gas released in a chemical reaction or the amount of light given off by a star. The social sciences, by contrast, are younger sciences, and scientific consensus on how to measure our important concepts is rare. Perhaps more crucial, though, is the fact that the social sciences deal with an inherently difficult-to-predict subject matter: human beings.

The problem of measurement exists in all of the social sciences. It would be wrong, though, to say that it is equally problematic in all of the social science disciplines. Some disciplines pay little heed to issues of measurement, whereas others are mired nearly constantly in measurement controversies and difficulties.

Consider the subject matter in much research in economics: dollars (or euros, or yen, or what have you). If the concept of interest is "economic output" (or "GDP"), which is commonly defined as the total sum of goods and services produced by labor and property in a given time period, then it is a relatively straightforward matter to obtain an empirical observation that is consistent with the concept of interest.[1] Such measures will not be controversial among the vast majority of scholars. To the contrary, once economists agree on a measure of economic output, they can move on to the next (and more interesting) step in the scientific process – to argue about what forces *cause* greater or less growth in economic output. (That's where the agreement among economists ends.)

Not every concept in economics is measured with such ease, however. Many economists are concerned with poverty: Why are some individuals poor whereas others are not? What forces cause poverty to rise or fall over time? Despite the fact that we all know that poverty is a very real thing, measuring who is poor and who is not poor turns out to be a bit tricky. The federal government defines the concept of poverty as "a set of income cutoffs adjusted for household size, the age of the head of the household, and the number of children under age 18."[2] The intent of the cutoffs is to describe "minimally decent levels of consumption."[3] There are difficulties

---

[1] For details about how the federal government measures GDP, see http://www.bea.gov.

[2] See http://www.census.gov/hhes/www/poverty/poverty.html.

[3] Note a problem right off the bat: What is "minimally decent"? Do you suspect that what qualified as "minimally decent" in 1950 or 1975 would be considered "minimally decent"

in obtaining empirical observations of poverty, though. Among them, consider the reality that most Western democracies (including the United States) have welfare states that provide transfer payments – in the form of cash payments, food stamps, or services like subsidized health care – to their citizens below some income threshold. Such programs, of course, are designed to minimize or eliminate the problems that afflict the poor. When economists seek to measure a person's income level to determine whether or not he is poor, should they use a "pretransfer" definition of income – a person's or family's income level *before* receiving any transfer payments from the government – or a "posttransfer" definition? Either choice carries some negative consequences. Choosing a pretransfer definition of income gives a sense of how much the private sector of the economy is failing. On the other hand, a posttransfer definition gives a sense of how much welfare-state programs are falling short and how people are actually living. As the Baby Boom generation in the United States continues to age, though, more and more people are retiring from work. Using a pretransfer measure of poverty means that researchers will not consider Social Security payments – this country's largest source of transfer payments by far – and therefore the (pretransfer) poverty rate should grow rather steadily over the next few decades, regardless of the health of the overall economy. This might not accurately represent what we mean by "poverty" (Danziger and Gottschalk 1983).

If, owing to their subject matter, economists rarely (but occasionally) have measurement obstacles, the opposite end of the spectrum would be the discipline of psychology. The subject matter of psychology – human behavior, cognition, and emotion – is rife with concepts that are extremely difficult to measure. Consider a few examples. We all know that the concept of "depression" is a real thing; some individuals are depressed, and others are not. Some individuals who are depressed today will not be depressed as time passes, and some who are not depressed today will become depressed. Yet how is it possible to assess scientifically whether a person is or is not depressed?[4] Why does it matter if we measure depression accurately? Recall the scientific stakes described at the beginning of this chapter: If we don't measure depression well, how can we know whether remedies like clinical

---

today? This immediately raises issues of how sensible it is to compare the poverty rates from the past with those of today. If the floor of what is considered minimally decent continues to rise, then the comparison is problematic at best, and meaningless at worst.

[4] Since 1952, the American Psychological Association has published the *Diagnostic and Statistical Manual of Mental Disorders*, now in its fourth edition (called DSM-IV), which diagnoses depression by focusing on four sets of symptoms that indicate depression: mood, behavioral symptoms such as withdrawal, cognitive symptoms such as concentration, and somatic symptoms such as insomnia.

therapy or chemical antidepressants are effective?[5] Psychology deals with a variety of other concepts that are notoriously slippery, such as the clinical focus on "anxiety," or the social–psychological focus on concepts such as "stereotyping" or "prejudice" (which are also of concern to political scientists).

Political science, in our view, lies somewhere between the extremes of economics and psychology in terms of how frequently we encounter serious measurement problems. Some subfields in political science operate relatively free of measurement problems. The study of political economy – which examines the relationship between the economy and political forces such as government policy, elections, and consumer confidence – has much the same feel as economics, for obvious reasons. Other subfields encounter measurement problems regularly. The subfield of political psychology – which studies the way that individual citizens interact with the political world – shares much of the same subject matter as social psychology, and hence, because of its focus on the attitudes and feelings of people, it shares much of social psychology's measurement troubles.

Consider the following list of critically important concepts in the discipline of political science that have sticky measurement issues:

- **Judicial activism:** In the United States, the role of the judiciary in the policy-making process has always been controversial. Some view the federal courts as the protectors of important civil liberties, whereas others view the courts as a threat to democracy, because judges are not elected. How is it possible to identify an "activist judge" or an "activist decision"?[6]
- **Congressional roll-call liberalism:** With each successive session of the U.S. Congress, commentators often compare the level of liberalism and conservatism of the present Congress with that of its most recent predecessors. How do we know if the Congress is becoming more or less liberal over time (Poole and Rosenthal 1997)?
- **Political legitimacy:** How can analysts distinguish between a "legitimate" and an "illegitimate" government? The key conceptual issue is more or less "how citizens evaluate governmental authority" (Weatherford 1992). Some view it positively, others quite negatively. Is

---

[5] In fact, the effectiveness of clinical "talk" therapy is a matter of some contention among psychologists. See "Married with Problems? Therapy May Not Help," *The New York Times*, April 19, 2005.

[6] In this particular case, there could even be a disagreement over the conceptual definition of "activist." What a conservative and a liberal would consider to be "activist" might produce no agreement at all. See "Activist, Schmactivist," *The New York Times*, August 15, 2004, for a journalistic account of this issue.

legitimacy something that can objectively be determined, or is it an inherently subjective property among citizens?

- **Political sophistication:** Some citizens know more about politics and are better able to process political information than other citizens who seem to know little and care less about political affairs. How do we distinguish politically sophisticated citizens from the politically unsophisticated ones? Moreover, how can we tell if a society's level of political sophistication is rising or falling over time (Luskin 1987)?

- **Social capital:** Some societies are characterized by relatively high levels of interconnectedness, with dense networks of relationships that make the population cohesive. Other societies, in contrast, are characterized by high degrees of isolation and distrustfulness. How can we measure what social scientists call *social capital* in a way that enables us to compare one society's level of connectedness with another's or one society's level of connectedness at varying points in time (Putnam 2000)?

In Sections 5.4 and 5.5, we describe the measurement controversies surrounding two other concepts that are important to political science – democracy and political tolerance. But first, in the next section, we describe some key issues that political scientists need to grapple with when measuring their concepts of interest.

5.3 PROBLEMS IN MEASURING CONCEPTS OF INTEREST

We can summarize the problems of measuring concepts of interest in preparation for hypothesis testing as follows: First, you need to make sure that you have conceptual clarity. Next, settle on a reasonable level of measurement. Finally, ensure that your measure is both valid and reliable. After you repeat this process for each variable in your theory, you are ready to test your hypothesis.

Unfortunately, there is no clear map to follow as we go through these steps with our variables. Some variables are very easy to measure, whereas others, because of the nature of what we are trying to measure, will always be elusive. As we will see, debates over issues of measurement are at the core of many interesting fields of study in political science.

5.3.1 Conceptual Clarity

The first step in measuring any phenomenon of interest to political scientists is to have a clear sense of what the concept is that we are trying to measure. In some cases, like the ones we subsequently discuss, this is an exceedingly revealing and difficult task. It requires considerably disciplined thought to ferret out precisely what we mean by the concepts about which we are theorizing. But even in some seemingly easy examples, this is more difficult than might appear at first glance.

Consider a survey in which we needed to measure a person's *income*. That would seem easy enough. Once we draw our sample of adults, why not just ask each respondent, "What is your income?" and offer a range of values, perhaps in increments of $10,000 or so, on which respondents could place themselves. What could be the problem with such a measure? Imagine a 19-year-old college student whose parents are very wealthy, but who has never worked herself, answering such a question. How much income has that person earned in the last year? Zero. In such a circumstance, this is the true answer to such a question. But it is not a particularly *valid* measure of her income. We likely want a measure of income that reflects the fact that her parents earn a good deal of money, which affords her the luxury of not having to work her way through school as many other students do. That measure should place the daughter of wealthy parents ahead of a relatively poor student who works 40 hours a week and carries a full load just to pay her tuition. Therefore, we might reconsider our seemingly simple question and ask instead, "What is the total amount of income earned in the most recently completed tax year by you and any other adults in your household, including all sources of income?" This measure puts the nonworking child of wealthy parents ahead of the student from the less-well-off family. And, for most social science purposes, this is the measure of "income" that we would find most theoretically useful.[7]

At this point, it is worth highlighting that the *best* measure of income – as well as that of most other concepts – depends on what our theoretical objectives are. The best measure of something as simple as a respondent's income depends on what we intend to relate that measure to in our hypothesis testing.

5.3.2 Reliability

An operational measure of a concept is said to be **reliable** to the extent that it is repeatable or consistent; that is, applying the same measurement rules to the same case or observation will produce identical results. An unreliable measure, by contrast, would produce inconsistent results for the same observation. For obvious reasons, all scientists want their measures to be reliable.

---

[7] The same issues would arise in assessing the income of retired people who no longer participate in the workforce.

Perhaps the most simple example to help you understand this is your bathroom scale. Say you step up on the scale one morning and the scale tells you that you weigh 150 pounds. You step down off the scale and it returns to zero. But have you ever *not* trusted that scale reading, and thought to yourself, "Maybe if I hop back up on the scale, I'll get a number I like better?" That is a reliability check. If you (immediately) step back on the scale, and it tells you that you now weigh 146 pounds, your scale is unreliable, because repeated measures of the same case – your body at that particular point in time – produced different results.

To take our bathroom scale example to the extreme, we should not confuse over-time variability with unreliability. If you wake up 1 week later and weigh 157 instead of 150 that does not necessarily mean that your scale is unreliable (though that might be true). Perhaps you substituted french fries for salads at dinner in the intervening week, and perhaps you exercised less vigorously or less often.

Reliability is often an important issue when scholars need to code events or text for quantitative analysis. For example, if a researcher was trying to code the text of news coverage that was favorable or unfavorable toward a candidate for office, he would develop some specific coding rules to apply to the text – in effect, to count certain references as either "pro" or "con" with respect to the candidate. Suppose that, for the coding, the researcher employs a group of students to code the text – a practice that is common in political research. A *reliable* set of coding rules would imply that, when one student applies the rules to the text, the results would be the same as when another student takes the rules and applies them to the same text. An *unreliable* set of coding rules would imply the opposite, namely, that when two different coders try to apply the same rules to the same news articles, they reach different conclusions.[8] The same issues arise when one codes things such as events by using newspaper coverage.[9]

5.3.3 Measurement Bias and Reliability

One of the concerns that comes up with any measurement technique is **measurement bias,** which is the systematic overreporting or underreporting of values for a variable. Although measurement bias is a serious problem for anyone who wants to know the "true" values of variables for particular cases, it is less of a problem than you might think for theory-testing

---

[8] Of course, it is possible that the coding *scheme* is perfectly reliable, but the *coders themselves* are not.

[9] There are a variety of tools for assessing reliability, many of which are beyond the scope of this discussion.

purposes. To better understand this, imagine that we have to choose between two different operationalizations of the same variable. Operationalization A is biased but reliable, and Operationalization B is unbiased but unreliable. For theory-testing purposes we would greatly prefer the biased but reliable Operationalization A!

You will be better able to see why this is the case once you have an understanding of statistical hypothesis testing from Chapters 8 and beyond. For now, though, keep in mind that as we test our theories we are looking for general patterns between two variables. For instance, with *higher* values of X do we tend to see *higher* values of Y, or with *higher* values of X do we tend to see *lower* values of Y? If the measurement of X was biased upward, the same general pattern of association with Y would be visible. But if the measurement of X was unreliable, it would obscure the underlying relationship between X and Y.

5.3.4 Validity

The most important feature of a measure is that it is **valid**. A valid measure accurately represents the concept that it is supposed to measure, whereas an invalid measure measures something other than what was originally intended. All of this might sound a bit circular, we realize.

Perhaps it is useful to think of some important concepts that represent thorny measurement examples in the social sciences. In both social psychology and political science, the study of the concept of *prejudice* has been particularly important. Among individuals, the level of prejudice can vary, from vanishingly small amounts to very high levels. Measuring prejudice can be important in social–psychological terms, so we can try to determine what factors cause some people to be prejudiced whereas others do not. In political science, in particular, we are often interested in what the attitudinal and behavioral consequences of prejudice might be. Assuming that some form of truth serum is unavailable, how can we obtain a quantitative measure of prejudice that can tell us who harbors large amounts of prejudice, who harbors some, and who harbors none? It would be easy enough to ask respondents to a survey if they were prejudiced or not. For example, we could ask respondents: "With respect to people who have a different race or ethnicity than you, would you say that you are extremely prejudiced, somewhat prejudiced, mildly prejudiced, or not at all prejudiced toward them?" But we would have clear reasons to doubt the validity of their answers – whether their measured responses accurately reflected their true levels of prejudice.

There are a variety of ways to assess a measure's validity, though it is critical to note that all of them are theoretical and subject to large degrees of disagreement. There is no simple formula to check for a measure's validity on a scale of 0 to 100, unfortunately. Instead, we rely on several overlapping ways to determine a measure's validity. First, and most simply, we can examine a measure's **face validity**. When examining a measurement strategy, we can first ask whether or not, on its face, the measure appears to be measuring what it purports to be measuring. This is face validity. Second, and a bit more advanced, we can scrutinize a measure's **content validity**. What is the concept to be measured? What are all of the essential elements to that concept and the features that define it? And have you excluded all of the things that are not it? For example, the concept of democracy surely contains the element of "elections," but it also must incorporate more than mere elections, because elections are held in places like North Korea, which we know to be nondemocratic. What else must be in a valid measure of democracy? (More on this notion later on.) Basically, content validation is a rigorous process that forces the researcher to come up with a list of all of the critical elements that, as a group, define the concept we wish to measure. Finally, we can examine a measure's **construct validity**: the degree to which the measure is related to other measures that theory requires them to be related to. That is, if we have a theory that connects democratization and economic development, then a measure of democracy that is related to a measure of economic development (as our theory requires) serves simultaneously to confirm the theory and also to validate the measure of democracy. Of course, one difficulty with this approach is what happens when the expected association is not present. Is it because our measure of democracy is invalid or because the theory is misguided? There is no conclusive way to tell.

5.3.5 The Relationship between Validity and Reliability

What is the connection between validity and reliability? Is it possible to have a valid but unreliable measure? And is it possible to have a reliable but invalid measure? With respect to the second question, some scientific debate exists; there are some who believe that it is possible to have a reliable but invalid measure. In our view, that is possible in abstract terms. But because we are interested in measuring concepts in the interest of evaluating causal theories, we believe that, in all practical terms, any conceivable measures that are reliable but invalid will not be useful in evaluating causal theories.

Similarly, it is theoretically possible to have valid but unreliable measures. But those measures also will be problematic for evaluating causal theories, because we will have no confidence in the hypothesis tests that we conduct. We present the relationship between reliability and validity in Figure 5.1, where we show that, if a measure is unreliable, there is little

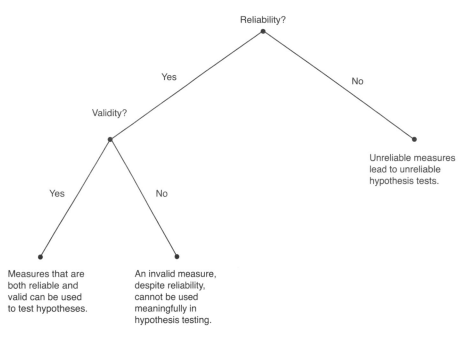

Figure 5.1. Reliability, validity, and hypothesis testing.

point in evaluating its validity. Once we have established that a measure is reliable, we can assess its validity, and only reliable and valid measures are useful for evaluating causal theories.

5.4   CONTROVERSY 1: MEASURING DEMOCRACY

Although we might be tempted to think of democracy as being similar to pregnancy – that is, a country either *is* or *is not* a democracy much the same way that a woman either *is* or *is not* pregnant – on a bit of additional thought, we are probably better off thinking of democracy as a *continuum*.[10] That is, there can be varying degrees to which a government is democratic. Furthermore, within democracies, some countries are more democratic than others, and a country can become more or less democratic as time passes.

But defining a continuum that ranges from democracy, on one end, to totalitarianism, on the other end, is not at all easy. We might be tempted to resort to the Potter Stewart "I know it when I see it" definition. As political scientists, of course, this is not an option. We have to begin by asking ourselves, what do we mean by democracy? What are the core elements

[10] This position, though, is controversial within political science. For an interesting discussion about whether researchers should measure democracy as a binary concept or a continuous one, see Elkins (2000).

that make a government more or less democratic? Political philosopher Robert Dahl (1971) persuasively argued that there are two core attributes to a democracy: "contestation" and "participation." That is, according to Dahl, democracies have competitive elections to choose leaders and broadly inclusive rules for and rates of participation.

Several groups of political scientists have attempted to measure democracy systematically in recent decades.[11] The best known – though by no means universally accepted – of these is the Polity IV measure.[12] The project measures democracy with annual scores ranging from -10 (strongly autocratic) to $+10$ (strongly democratic) for every country on Earth from 1800 to 2004.[13] In these researchers' operationalization, democracy has four components:

1. Regulation of executive recruitment
2. Competitiveness of executive recruitment
3. Openness of executive recruitment
4. Constraints on chief executive

For each of these dimensions, experts rate each country on a particular scale. For example, the first criterion, "regulation of executive recruitment," allows for the following possible values:

- $+3$ = regular competition between recognized groups
- $+2$ = transitional competition
- $+1$ = factional or restricted patterns of competition
- 0 = no competition

Countries that have regular elections between groups that are more than ethnic rivals will have higher scores. By similar procedures, the scholars associated with the project score the other dimensions that comprise their democracy scale.

Figure 5.2 presents the Polity score for Pakistan from 1947 (when India and Pakistan were partitioned) through 2003.[14] Remember that higher scores represent points in time when Pakistan was more democratic, and lower scores represent times when Pakistan was more autocratic. There has

---

[11] For a useful review and comparison of these various measures, see Munck and Verkuilen (2002).

[12] The project's web site, which provides access to a vast array of country-specific over-time data, is http://www.cidcm.umd.edu/inscr/polity.

[13] They derive the scores on this scale from two separate 10-point scales, one for democracy and the other for autocracy. A country's Polity score for that year is its democracy score minus its autocracy score; thus, a country that received a 10 on the democracy scale and a 0 on the autocracy scale would have a net Polity score of 10 for that year.

[14] Source: http://www.cidcm.umd.edu/inscr/polity/pak2.htm.

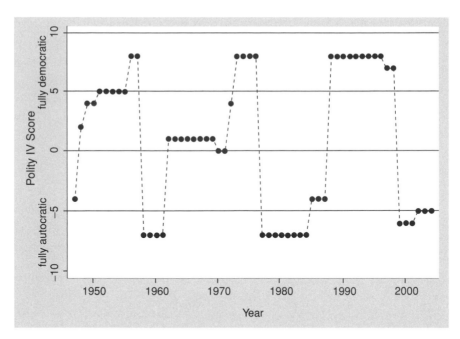

Figure 5.2. Polity IV score for Pakistan.

been, as you can see, enormous variation in the democratic experience in Pakistan, which has been ruled by the military for over half of the country's existence. In fact, Pakistan's president in 2003, Pervez Musharraf, seized power in a military coup in October 1999. The steep decline in the most recent portion of the trend line represents the severe restrictions by Islamic political parties that the Musharraf regime has imposed since cooperating with the U.S. War on Terror.

The Polity measure is rich in historical detail, as is obvious from Figure 5.2. The coding rules are transparent and clear, and the amount of raw information that goes into a country's score for any given year is impressive. And yet it is fair to criticize the Polity measure for including only one part of Dahl's definition of democracy. The Polity measure contains rich information about what Dahl calls "contestation" – whether a country has broadly open contests to decide on its leadership. But the measure is much less rich when it comes to gauging a country's level of what Dahl calls "participation" – the degree to which citizens are engaged in political processes and activities. This may be understandable, in part, because of the impressive time scope of the study. After all, in 1800 (when the Polity time series begins), very few countries had broad electoral participation. Since the end of World War II, broadly democratic participation has spread rapidly across the globe. But if the world is becoming a more democratic place, owing to expansion of suffrage, our measures of democracy ought to incorporate that reality. The Polity IV measure, despite its considerable strengths, does not fully encompass what it means, conceptually, to be more or less democratic.

5.5 CONTROVERSY 2: MEASURING POLITICAL TOLERANCE

We know that some continuum exists in which, on the one end, some individuals are extremely "tolerant" and, on the other end, other individuals are extremely "intolerant." In other words, political tolerance and intolerance, at the conceptual level, are real things. Some individuals have more tolerance and others have less. It is easy to imagine why political scientists would be interested in political tolerance and intolerance. Are there systematic factors that cause some people to be tolerant and others to be intolerant?

Measuring political tolerance, on the other hand, is far from easy. Tolerance is not like cholesterol, for which a simple blood test can tell us how much of the good and how much of the bad we have inside of us. The naive approach to measuring political tolerance – conducting a survey and asking people directly "Are you tolerant or intolerant?" – seems silly right off the bat. Any such survey question would surely produce extremely high rates of "tolerance," because presumably very few people – even intolerant people – think of themselves as intolerant. Even those who are aware of their own intolerance are unlikely to admit that fact to a pollster. Given this situation, how have political scientists tackled this problem?

During the 1950s, when the spread of Soviet communism represented the biggest threat to America, Samuel Stouffer (1955) conducted a series of opinion surveys to measure how people reacted to the Red Scare. He asked national samples of Americans whether they would be willing to extend certain civil liberties – like being allowed to teach in a public school, to be free from having phones tapped, and the like – to certain unpopular groups like communists, socialists, and atheists. He found that a variety of people were, by these measures, intolerant; they were not willing to grant these civil liberties to members of those groups. The precise amount of intolerance varied, depending on the target group and the activity mentioned in the scenarios, but intolerance was substantial – at least 70% of respondents gave the intolerant response. Stouffer found that the best predictor of an individual's level of tolerance was how much formal education he or she had received; people with more education emerged as more tolerant, and people with less education were less tolerant. In the 1970s, when the Red Scare was subsiding somewhat, a new group of researchers asked the identical questions to a new sample of Americans. They found that the levels of intolerance had dropped considerably over the 20-odd years – in only one scenario did intolerance exceed 60% and in the majority of scenarios it was below 50% – leading some to speculate that political intolerance was waning.

However, also in the late 1970s, a different group of researchers led by political scientist John Sullivan questioned the *validity* of the Stouffer measures and hence questioned the conclusions that Stouffer reached. The concept of political tolerance, wrote Sullivan, Pierson, and Marcus (1979), "presupposes opposition." That is, unless a survey respondent actively opposed communists, socialists, and atheists, the issue of tolerance or intolerance simply does not arise. By way of example, consider asking such questions of an atheist. Is an atheist who agrees that atheists should be allowed to teach in public schools politically tolerant? Sullivan and his colleagues thought not.

They proposed a new set of survey-based questions that were, in their view, more consistent with a conceptual understanding of tolerance. If, as they defined it, tolerance presupposes opposition, then researchers need to *find out* whom the survey respondent opposes; *assuming* that the respondent might oppose a particular group is not a good idea. They identified a variety of groups active in politics at the time – including racist groups, both pro- and anti-abortion groups, and even the Symbianise Liberation Army – and asked respondents which one they disliked the most. They followed this up with questions that looked very much like the Stouffer items, only directed at *the respondent's own* disliked groups instead of the ones Stouffer had picked out for them.

Among other findings, two stood out. First, the levels of intolerance were strikingly high. As many as 66% of Americans were willing to forbid members of their least-liked group from holding rallies, and fully 71% were willing to have the government ban the group altogether. Second, under this new conceptualization and measurement of tolerance, they found that an individual's perception of the threatening nature of the target group, and not their level of education, was the primary predictor of intolerance. In other words, individuals who found their target group to be particularly threatening were most likely to be intolerant, whereas those who found their most-disliked group to be less threatening were more tolerant. Education did not directly affect tolerance either way. In this sense, measuring an important concept differently produced rather different substantive findings about causes and effects.[15]

---

[15] But see Gibson 1992.

It is important that you see the connection to valid measurement here. Sullivan and his colleagues argued that Stouffer's survey questions were not valid measures of tolerance because the question wording did not accurately capture what it meant, in the abstract, to be intolerant (specifically, opposition). Creating measures of tolerance and intolerance that more truthfully mirrored the concept of interest produced significantly different findings about the persistence of intolerance, as well as about the factors that cause individuals to be tolerant or intolerant.

5.6 ARE THERE CONSEQUENCES TO POOR MEASUREMENT?

What happens when we fail to measure the key concepts in our theory in a way that is both valid and reliable? Refer back to Figure 1.2, which highlights the distinction between the abstract concepts of theoretical interest and the variables we observe in the real world. If the variables that we observe in the real world do not do a good job of mirroring the abstract concepts, then that affects our ability to evaluate conclusively a theory's empirical support. That is, how can we know if our theory is supported if we have done a poor job measuring the key concepts that we observe? If our empirical analysis is based on measures that do not capture the essence of the abstract concepts in our theory, then we are unlikely to have any confidence in the findings themselves.

5.7 CONCLUSIONS

How we measure the concepts that we care about matters. As we can see from the preceding examples, different measurement strategies can and sometimes do produce different conclusions about causal relationships.

One of the take-home points of this chapter should be that measurement cannot take place in a theoretical vacuum. The *theoretical purpose* of the scholarly enterprise must inform the process of how we measure what we measure. For example, recall our previous discussion about the various ways to measure poverty. How we want to measure this concept depends on what our objective is. In the process of measuring poverty, if our theoretical aim is to evaluate the effectiveness of different policies at combating poverty, we would have different measurement issues than would scholars whose theoretical aim is to study how being poor influences a person's political attitudes. In the former case, we would give strong consideration to pretransfer measures of poverty, whereas in the latter example, posttransfer measures would likely be more applicable.

CONCEPTS INTRODUCED IN THIS CHAPTER

construct validity	measurement bias
content validity	operationalization
face validity	reliable
measurement	valid

EXERCISES

1. Suppose that a researcher wanted to measure the federal government's efforts to make the education of its citizens a priority. The researcher proposed to count the government's budget for education as a percentage of the total GDP and use that as the measure of the government's commitment to education. In terms of validity, what are the strengths and weaknesses of such a measure?

2. Suppose that a researcher wanted to create a measure of media coverage of a candidate for office, and therefore created a set of coding rules to code words in newspaper articles as either "pro" or "con" toward the candidate. Instead of hiring students to implement these rules, however, the researcher used a computer to code the text, by counting the frequency with which certain words were mentioned in a series of articles. What would be the reliability of such a computer-driven measurement strategy, and why?

3. For each of the following concepts, identify whether there would, in measuring the concept, likely be a problem of measurement bias, invalidity, unreliability, or none of the above:

    (a) Measuring the concept of the public's approval of the president by using a series of survey results asking respondents whether they approve or disapprove of the president's job performance.
    (b) Measuring the concept of political corruption as the percentage of politicians in a country in a year who are convicted of corrupt practices.
    (c) Measuring the concept of democracy in each nation of the world by reading their constitution and seeing if it claims that the nation is "democratic."

4. Download a codebook for a political science data set in which you are interested.

    (a) Describe the data set and the purpose for which it was assembled.
    (b) What are the time and space dimensions of the data set?

    Read the details of how one of the variables in which you are interested was coded. Write your answers to the following questions:

    (c) Does this seem like a reliable method of operationalizing this variable? How might the reliability of this operationalization be improved?
    (d) Assess the various elements of the validity for this variable operationalization. How might the validity of this operationalization be improved?

5. If you did not yet do Chapter 3, Exercise 5, do so now. For the theory that you developed, evaluate the measurement of both the independent and dependent variables. Write about the reliability, and the various aspects of validity for each measure. Can you think of a better way to operationalize these variables to test your theory?

6 Descriptive Statistics and Graphs

OVERVIEW

Descriptive statistics and descriptive graphs are what they sound like – they are tools that describe variables. These tools are valuable, because they can summarize a tremendous amount of information in a succinct fashion. In this chapter we discuss some of the most commonly used descriptive statistics and graphs, how we should interpret them, how we should use them, and their limitations.

6.1 KNOW YOUR DATA

In Chapter 5 we discussed the measurement of variables. A lot of thought and effort goes into the measurement of individual variables. Once measurement has been conducted, it is important for the researcher to get a good idea of the types of values that the individual variables take on before moving to testing for causal connections between two or more variables. What do "typical" values for a variable look like? How tightly clustered (or widely dispersed) are the these values?

Before proceeding to test for theorized relationships *between* two or more variables, it is essential to understand the properties and characteristics of each variable. To put it differently, we want to learn something about what the values of each variable "look like." How do we accomplish this? One possibility is to list all of the observed values of a measured variable. For example, the following are the percentages of popular votes for major party candidates that went to the candidate of the party of the sitting president during U.S. presidential elections from 1880 to 2004[1]: 50.22,

---

[1] This measure is constructed so that it is comparable across time. Because independent or third-party candidates have occasionally contested elections, we focus on only those votes for the two major parties. Also, because we want to test the theory of economic voting,

49.846, 50.414, 48.268, 47.76, 53.171, 60.006, 54.483, 54.708, 51.682, 36.119, 58.244, 58.82, 40.841, 62.458, 54.999, 53.774, 52.37, 44.595, 57.764, 49.913, 61.344, 49.596, 61.789, 48.948, 44.697, 59.17, 53.902, 46.545, 54.736, 50.265, 51.2. We can see from this example that, once we get beyond a small number of observations, a listing of values becomes unwieldy. We will get lost in the trees and have no idea of the overall shape of the forest. For this reason, we turn to descriptive statistics and descriptive graphs, to take what would be a large amount of information and reduce it to bite-size chunks that summarize that information.

Descriptive statistics and graphs are useful tools for helping researchers to get to know their data before they move to testing causal hypotheses. They are also sometimes helpful when writing about one's research. You have to make the decision of whether or not to present descriptive statistics and/or graphs in the body of a paper on a case-by-case basis. It is scientifically important, however, that this information be made available to consumers of your research in some way.[2]

One major way to distinguish among variables is the **measurement metric**. A variable's measurement metric is the type of values that the variable takes on, and we discuss this in detail in the next section by describing three different variable types. We then explain that, despite the imperfect nature of the distinctions among these three variable types, we are forced to choose between two broad classifications of variables – categorical or continuous – when we describe them. The rest of this chapter discusses strategies for describing categorical and continuous variables.

6.2   WHAT IS THE VARIABLE'S MEASUREMENT METRIC?

There are no hard and fast rules for describing variables, but a major initial juncture that we encounter involves the metric in which we measure each variable. Remember from Chapter 1 that we can think of each variable in terms of its label and its values. The label is the description of the variable – such as "Gender of survey respondent" – and its values are the denominations in which the variable occurs – such as "Male" or "Female." For treatment in most statistical analyses, we are forced to divide our variables into two types according to the metric in which the values of the variable occur: categorical or continuous. In reality, variables come in at

---

we need to have a measure of support for incumbents. In elections in which the sitting president is not running for reelection, there is still reason to expect that their party will be held accountable for economic performances.

[2] Many researchers will present this information in an appendix unless there is something particularly noteworthy about the characteristics of one or more of their variables.

least three different metric types, and there are a lot of variables that do not neatly fit into just one of these classifications. To help you to better understand each of these variable types, we will go through each with an example. All of the examples that we are using in these initial descriptions come from survey research, but the same basic principles of measurement metric hold regardless of the type of data being analyzed.

6.2.1   Categorical Variables

Categorical variables are variables for which cases have values that are either different or the same as the values for other cases, but about which we cannot make any universally holding ranking distinctions. If we think consider a variable that we might label "Religious Identification," some values for this variable are "Catholic," "Muslim," "nonreligious," and so on. Although these values are clearly different from each other, we cannot make universally holding ranking distinctions across them. More casually, with categorical variables like this one, it is not possible to rank order the categories from least to greatest: The value "Muslim" is neither greater nor less than "nonreligious" (and so on), for example. Instead, we are left knowing that cases with the same value for this variable are the same, whereas those cases with different values are different. The term "categorical" expresses the essence of this variable type; we can put individual cases into categories based on their values, but we cannot go any further in terms of ranking or otherwise ordering these values.

6.2.2   Ordinal Variables

Like categorical variables, **ordinal variables** are also variables for which cases have values that are either different or the same as the values for other cases. The distinction between ordinal and categorical variables is that we *can* make universally holding ranking distinctions across the variable values for ordinal variables. For instance, consider the variable labeled "Retrospective Family Financial Situation" that has commonly been used as an independent variable in individual-level economic voting studies. In the 2004 National Election Study (NES), researchers created this variable by first asking respondents to answer the following question: "We are interested in how people are getting along financially these days. Would you say that you (and your family living here) are better off or worse off than you were a year ago?" Researchers then asked respondents who answered "Better" or "Worse": "Much [better/worse] or somewhat [better/worse]?" The resulting variable was then coded as follows:

1. much better
2. somewhat better
3. same
4. somewhat worse
5. much worse

This variable is pretty clearly an ordinal variable because as we go from the top to the bottom of the list we are moving from better to worse evaluations of how individuals (and their families with whom they live) have been faring financially in the past year.

As another example, consider the variable labeled "Party Identification." In the 2004 NES researchers created this variable by using each respondent's answer to the question, "Generally speaking, do you usually think of yourself as a Republican, a Democrat, an independent, or what?"[3] which we can code as taking on the following values:

1. Republican
2. Independent
3. Democrat

If all cases that take on the value "Independent" represent individuals whose views lie somewhere between "Republican" and "Democrat," we can call "Party Identification" an ordinal variable. If this is not the case, then this variable is a categorial variable.

6.2.3 Continuous Variables

An important characteristic that ordinal variables *do not* have is **equal unit differences**. A variable has equal unit differences if a one-unit increase in the value of that variable *always* means the same thing. If we return to the examples from the previous section, we can rank order the five categories of Retrospective Family Financial Situation from 1 for the best situation to 5 for the worst situation. But we may not feel very confident working with these assigned values the way that we typically work with numbers. In other words, can we say that the difference between "somewhat worse" and "same" $(4 - 3)$ is the same as the difference between "much worse"

---

[3] Almost all U.S. respondents put themselves into one of the first three categories. For instance, in 2004, 1,128 of the 1,212 respondents (93.1%) to the postelection NES responded that they were a Republican, Democrat, or an independent. For our purposes, we will ignore the "or what" cases. Note that researchers usually present partisan identification across seven values ranging from "Strong Republican" to "Strong Democrat" based on follow-up questions that ask respondents to further characterize their positions.

and "somewhat worse" (5 − 4)? What about saying that the difference between "much worse" and "same" (5 − 3) is twice the difference between "somewhat better" and "much better" (2 − 1)? If the answer to both questions is "yes," then Retrospective Family Financial Situation is a continuous variable.

If we ask the same questions about Party Identification, we should be somewhat skeptical. We can rank order the three categories of Party Identification, but we cannot with great confidence assign "Republican" a value of 1, "Independent" a value of 2, and "Democrat" a value of 3 and work with these values in the way that we typically work with numbers. We cannot say that the difference between an "Independent" and a "Republican" (2 − 1) is the same as the difference between a "Democrat" and an "Independent" (3 − 2) – despite the fact that both 3 − 2 and 2 − 1 = 1. Certainly, we cannot say that the difference between a "Democrat" and a "Republican" (3 − 1) is twice the difference between an "Independent" and a "Republican" (2 − 1) – despite the fact that 2 is twice as big as 1.

The metric in which we measure a variable has equal unit differences if a one-unit increase in the value of that variable indicates the same amount of change across *all values* of that variable. **Continuous variables** are variables that *do* have equal unit differences.[4] Imagine, for instance, a variable labeled "Age in Years." A one-unit increase in this variable *always* indicates an individual who is 1 year older; this is true when we are talking about a case with a value of 21 just as it is when we are talking about a case with a value of 55.

6.2.4   Variable Types and Statistical Analyses

As we saw in the preceding subsections, variables do not always neatly fit into the three categories. When we move to the vast majority of statistical analyses, we must decide between treating each of our variables as though it is categorical or as though it is continuous. For some variables, this is a very straightforward choice. However, for others, this is a very difficult choice. If we treat an ordinal variable as though it is categorical, we are acting as though we know less about the values of this variable than we really know. On the other hand, treating an ordinal variable as though it is a continuous variable means that we are assuming that it has equal unit differences. Either way, it is critical that we be aware of our decisions. We

---

[4] We sometimes call these variables "interval variables." A further distinction you will encounter with continuous variables is whether they have a substantively meaningful zero point. We usually describe variables that have this characteristic as "ratio" variables.

Table 6.1. Frequency table for religious identification in the 2004 NES		
Category	Number of cases	Percent
Protestant	672	56.14
Catholic	292	24.39
Jewish	35	2.92
Other	17	1.42
None	181	15.12

can always repeat our analyses under a different assumption and see how robust our conclusions are to our choices.

With all of this in mind, we present separate discussions of the process of describing a variable's **variation** for categorical and continuous variables. A variable's variation is the distribution of values that it takes across the cases for which we measure it. It is important that we have a strong knowledge of the variation in each of our variables before we can translate our theory into hypotheses, assess whether there is covariation between two variables (causal hurdle 3 from Chapter 3), and think about whether or not there might exist a third variable that makes any observed covariation between our independent and dependent variables spurious (hurdle 4). As we just outlined, descriptive statistics and graphs are useful summaries of the variation for individual variables. Another way in which we describe distributions of variables is through measures of **central tendency**. Measures of central tendency tell us about typical values for a particular variable.

6.3 DESCRIBING CATEGORICAL VARIABLES

With categorical variables, we want to understand the frequency with which each value of the variable occurs in our data. The simplest way of seeing this is to produce a frequency table in which the values of the categorical variable are displayed down one column and the frequency with which it occurs (in absolute number of cases and/or in percentage terms) is displayed in another column(s). Table 6.1 shows such a table for the variable "Religious Identification" from the NES survey measured during the 2004 national elections in the United States.

The only measure of central tendency that is appropriate for a categorical variable is the **mode**, which we define as the most frequently occurring value. In Table 6.1, the mode of the distribution is "Protestant," because there are more Protestants than there are members of any other single category.

A typical way in which we present frequency data is in a pie graph such as Figure 6.1. Pie graphs are useful for seeing the percentage of cases that fall into particular categories. Bar graphs, such as Figure 6.2, are another graphical way to illustrate frequencies of categorical variables. It is worth

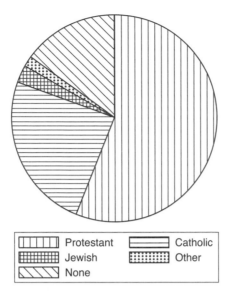

Figure 6.1. Pie graph of religious identification, NES 2004.

noting, however, that most of the information that we are able to gather from these two figures is very clearly and precisely presented in the columns of frequencies and percentages displayed in Table 6.1.

6.4 DESCRIBING CONTINUOUS VARIABLES

The statistics and graphs for describing continuous variables are considerably more complicated than those for categorical variables. This is because

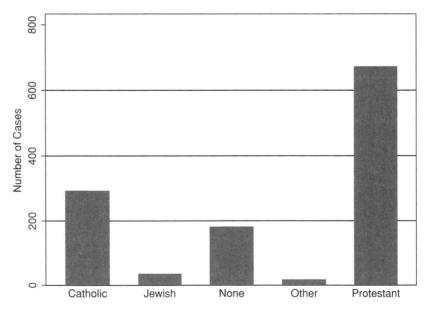

Figure 6.2. Bar graph of religious identification, NES 2004.

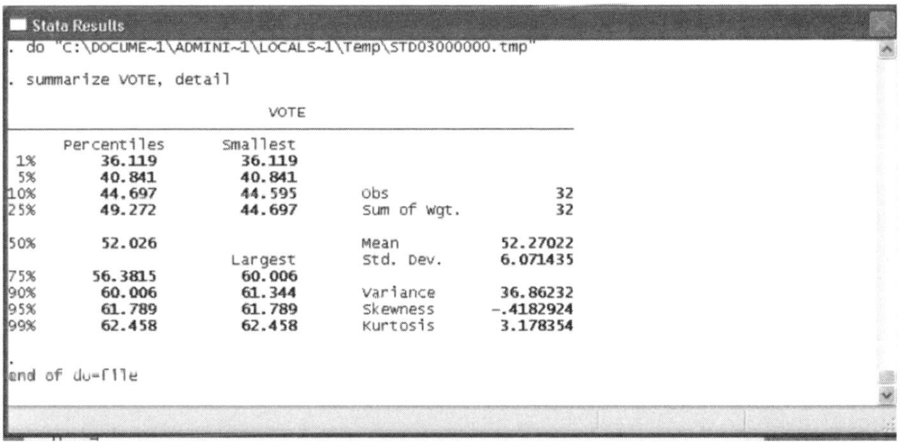

```
Stata Results
. do "C:\DOCUME~1\ADMINI~1\LOCALS~1\Temp\STD03000000.tmp"

. summarize VOTE, detail

                            VOTE
-------------------------------------------------------------
      Percentiles      Smallest
 1%     36.119          36.119
 5%     40.841          40.841
10%     44.697          44.595       Obs                  32
25%     49.272          44.697       Sum of Wgt.          32

50%     52.026                       Mean           52.27022
                        Largest      Std. Dev.      6.071435
75%     56.3815         60.006
90%     60.006          61.344       Variance       36.86232
95%     61.789          61.789       Skewness      -.4182924
99%     62.458          62.458       Kurtosis       3.178354

.
end of do-file
```

Figure 6.3. Example output from Stata's "summarize" command with "detail" option.

continuous variables are more mathematically complex than categorical variables. With continuous variables, we want to know about the central tendency and the spread or variation of the values around the central tendency. With continuous variables we also want to be on the lookout for **outliers**. Outliers are cases for which the value of the variable is extremely high or low relative to the rest of the values for that variable. When we encounter an outlier, we want to make sure that such a case is real and not created by some kind of error.

Most statistical software programs have a command for getting a battery of descriptive statistics on continuous variables. Figure 6.3 shows the output from Stata's "summarize" command with the "detail" option for the percentage of the major party vote won by the incumbent party in every U.S. presidential election between 1880 and 2004. The statistics on the left-hand side (the first three columns on the left) of the computer printout are what we call **rank statistics**, and the statistics on the right-hand side (the two columns on the right-hand side) are known as the **statistical moments.** Although both rank statistics and statistical moments are intended to describe the variation of continuous variables, they do so in slightly different ways and are thus quite useful together for getting a complete picture of the variation for a single variable.

6.4.1 Rank Statistics

The calculation of rank statistics begins with the ranking of the values of a continuous variable from smallest to largest, followed by the identification of crucial junctures along the way. Once we have our cases ranked, the midpoint as we count through our cases is known as the median case.

Remember that earlier in the chapter we defined the variable in Figure 6.3 as the percentage of popular votes for major-party candidates that went to the candidate from the party of the sitting president during U.S. presidential elections from 1880 to 2004. We will call this variable "Incumbent Vote" for short. To calculate rank statistics for this variable, we need to first put the cases in order from the smallest to the largest observed value. This ordering is shown in Table 6.2. With rank statistics we measure the central tendency as the **median value** of the variable. The median value is the value of the case that sits at the exact center of our cases when we rank them from the smallest to the largest observed values. When we have an even number of cases, as we do in Table 6.2, we average the value of the two centermost ranked cases to obtain the median value (in our example we calculate the median as $\frac{51.682+52.37}{2} = 52.026$). This is also known as the value of the variable at the 50% rank. In a similar way, we can talk about the value of the variable at any other percentage rank in which we have an interest. Other ranks that are often of interest are the 25% and 75% ranks, which are also known as the first and third "quartile ranks" for a distribution. The difference between the variable value at the 25% and the 75% ranks is known as the "interquartile range" or "IQR" of the variable. In our example variable, the 25% value is 49.272 and the 75% value is 56.3815. This makes the IQR = $56.3815 - 49.272 = 7.1095$. In the language of rank statistics, the median value for a variable is a measure of its central tendency, whereas the IQR is a measure of the **dispersion**, or spread, of values.

With rank statistics, we also want to look at the smallest and largest values to identify outliers. Remember that we defined outliers at the beginning of this section as "cases for which the value of the variable is extremely high or low relative to the rest of the values for that variable." If we look at the highest values in Table 6.2, we can see that there aren't really any cases that fit this description. Although there are certainly some values that are a lot higher than the median value and the 75% value, they aren't "extremely" higher than the rest of the values. Instead, there seems to be a fairly even progression from the 75% value up to the highest value. The story at the other range of values in Table 6.2 is a little different. We can see that the two lowest values are pretty far from each other and the rest of the low values. The value of 36.119 in 1920 seems to meet our definition of an outlier. The value of 40.841 in 1932 is also a borderline case. Whenever we see outliers, we should begin by checking whether we have measured the values for these cases accurately. Sometimes we find that outliers are the result of errors when entering data. In this case, a check of our data set reveals that the outlier case occurred in 1920 when the incumbent-party candidate received only 36.119% of the votes cast for the two major

Table 6.2. Values of incumbent vote ranked from smallest to largest

Rank	Year	Value
1	1920	36.119
2	1932	40.841
3	1952	44.595
4	1980	44.697
5	1992	46.545
6	1896	47.76
7	1892	48.268
8	1976	48.948
9	1968	49.596
10	1884	49.846
11	1960	49.913
12	1880	50.22
13	2000	50.265
14	1888	50.414
15	2004	51.2
16	1916	51.682
17	1948	52.37
18	1900	53.171
19	1944	53.774
20	1988	53.902
21	1908	54.483
22	1912	54.708
23	1996	54.736
24	1940	54.999
25	1956	57.764
26	1924	58.244
27	1928	58.82
28	1984	59.17
29	1904	60.006
30	1964	61.344
31	1972	61.789
32	1936	62.458

parties. A further check of our data indicates that this was indeed a correct measure of this variable for 1920.[5]

Figure 6.4 presents a box-whisker plot of the rank statistics for our presidential vote variable. This plot displays the distribution of the variable along the vertical dimension. If we start at the center of the box in Figure 6.4, we see the median value (or 50% rank value) of our variable represented as the slight gap in the center of the box. The other two ends of the box show the values of the 25% rank and the 75% rank of our variable. The ends of the whiskers show the lowest and highest nonoutlier values of our variable. Each statistical program has its own rules for dealing with outliers, so it is important to know whether your box-whisker plot is or is not set up to display outliers. These settings are usually adjustable within the statistical program. The calculation of whether an individual case is or is not an outlier in this box-whisker plot is fairly standard. This calculation starts with the IQR for the variable. Any case is defined as an outlier if its value is either 1.5 times the IQR higher than the 75% value or if its value is 1.5 times the IQR lower than the 25% value. For Figure 6.4 we have set things up so that the plot displays the outliers, and we can see one such a value at the bottom of our figure. As we already know from Table 6.2, this is the value of 36.119 from the 1920 election.

[5] An obvious question is "Why was 1920 such a low value?" This was the first presidential election in the aftermath of World War I, during a period when there was a lot of economic and political turmoil. The election in 1932 was at the very beginning of the large economic downturn known as "the Great Depression," so it makes sense that the party of the incumbent president would not have done very well during this election.

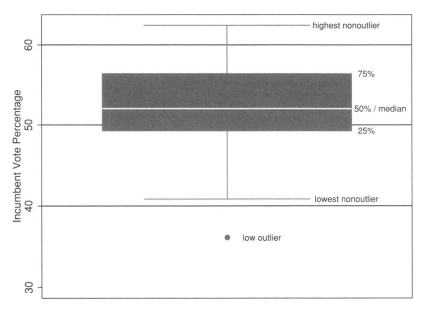

Figure 6.4. Box-whisker plot of incumbent-party presidential vote percentage, 1880–2004.

6.4.2 Moments

The statistical moments of a variable are a set of statistics that describe the central tendency for a single variable and the distribution of values around it. The most familiar of these statistics is known as the **mean value** or "average" value for the variable. For a variable Y, the mean value is depicted and calculated as

$$\bar{Y} = \frac{\sum_{i=1}^{n} Y_i}{n},$$

where $\bar{Y}$, known as "Y-bar," indicates the mean of Y, which is equal to the sum of all values of Y across individual cases of Y, Y_i, divided by the total number of cases[6] n. Although everyone is familiar with mean or average values, not everyone is familiar with the two characteristics of the mean value that make it particularly attractive to people who use statistics. The first is known as the "**zero-sum property**":

$$\sum_{i=1}^{n} (Y_i - \bar{Y}) = 0,$$

---

[6] To understand formulae like this, it is helpful to read through each of the pieces of the formula and translate them into words, as we have done here.

which means the sum of the difference between each Y value, Y_i, and the mean value of Y, $\bar{Y}$, is equal to zero. The second desirable characteristic of the mean value is known as the "**least-squares property**":

$$\sum_{i=1}^{n}(Y_i - \bar{Y})^2 < \sum_{i=1}^{n}(Y_i - c)^2 \ \forall \ c \neq \bar{Y},$$

which means that the sum of the squared differences between each Y value, Y_i, and the mean value of Y, $\bar{Y}$, is less than the sum of the squared differences between each Y value, Y_i, and some value c, for all ($\forall$) c's not equal to ($\neq$) $\bar{Y}$. Because of these two properties, the mean value is also referred to as the **expected value** of a variable. Think of it this way: If someone were to ask you to guess what the value for an individual case is without giving you any more information than the mean value, based on these two properties of the mean, the mean value would be the best guess.

The next statistical moment for a variable is the **variance**. We represent and calculate the variance as follows:

$$\text{var}(Y) = \text{var}_Y = s_Y^2 = \frac{\sum_{i=1}^{n}(Y_i - \bar{Y})^2}{n - 1},$$

which means that the variance of Y is equal to the sum of the squared differences between each Y value, Y_i, and its mean divided by the number of cases minus one.[7] If we look through this formula, what would happen if we had no variation on Y at all ($Y_i = \bar{Y} \ \forall \ i$)? In this case, variance would be equal to zero. But as individual cases are spread further and further from the mean, this calculation would increase. This is the logic of variance: It conveys the spread of the data around the mean. A more intuitive measure of variance is the **standard deviation**:

$$\text{sd}(Y) = \text{sd}_Y = s_Y = \sqrt{\text{var}(Y)} = \sqrt{\frac{\sum_{i=1}^{n}(Y_i - \bar{Y})^2}{n - 1}}.$$

Roughly speaking, this is the average difference between values of Y (Y_i) and the mean of Y ($\bar{Y}$). At first glance, this may not be apparent. But the important thing to understand about this formula is that the purpose of squaring each difference from the mean and then taking the square root of the resulting sum of squared deviations is to keep the negative and positive deviations from canceling each other out.[8]

---

[7] The "minus one" in this equation is an adjustment that is made to account for the number of "degrees of freedom" with which this calculation was made. We will discuss degrees of freedom in Chapter 8.

[8] An alternative method that would produce a very similar calculation would be to calculate the average value of the absolute value of each difference from the mean: $\left(\frac{\sum_{i=1}^{n}|Y_i - \bar{Y}|}{n}\right)$.

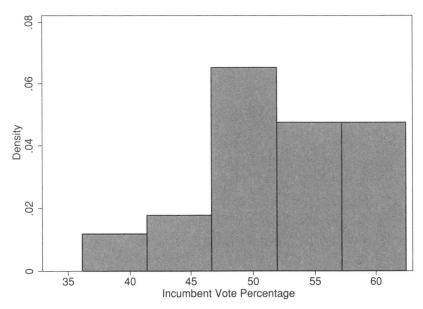

Figure 6.5. Histogram of incumbent-party presidential vote percentage, 1880–2004.

The variance and the standard deviation give us a numerical summary of the distribution of cases around the mean value for a variable.[9] We can also visually depict distributions. The idea of visually depicting distributions is to produce a two-dimensional figure in which the horizontal dimension (*x* axis) displays the values of the variable and the vertical dimension (*y* axis) displays the relative frequency of cases. One of the most popular visual depictions of a variable's distribution is the **histogram**, such as Figure 6.5. One problem with histograms is that we (or the computer program with which we are working) must choose how many rectangular blocks (called "bins") are depicted in our histogram. Changing the number of blocks in a histogram can change our impression of the distribution of the variable being depicted. Figure 6.6 shows the same variable as in Figure 6.5 with 2 and then 10 blocks. Although we generate both of the

---

[9] The **skewness** and the **kurtosis** of a variable convey the further aspects of the distribution of a variable. The skewness calculation indicates the symmetry of the distribution around the mean. If the data are symmetrically distributed around the mean, then this statistic will equal zero. If skewness is negative, this indicates that there are more values below the mean than there are above; if skewness is positive, this indicates that there are more values above the mean than there are below. The kurtosis indicates the steepness of the statistical distribution. Positive kurtosis values indicate very steep distributions, or a concentration of values close to the mean value, whereas negative kurtosis values indicate a flatter distribution, or more cases further from the mean value. Both skewness and kurtosis are measures that equal zero for the normal distribution, which we will discuss in Chapter 7.

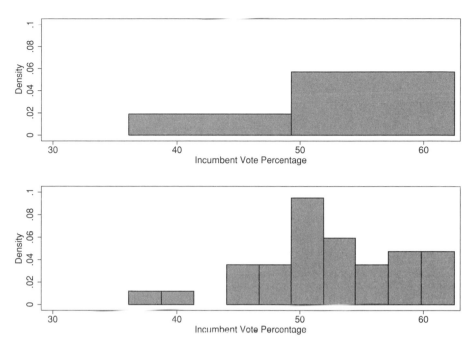

Figure 6.6. Histograms of incumbent-party presidential vote percentage, 1880–2004, depicted with 2 and then 10 blocks.

graphs in Figure 6.6 from the same data, they are fairly different from each other.

Another option is the **kernel density plot,** as in Figure 6.7, which is based on a smoothed calculation of the density of cases across the range of values.

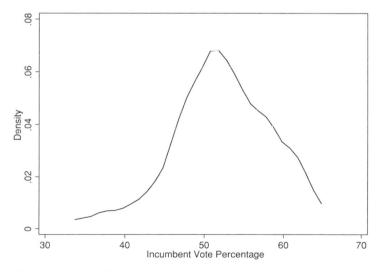

Figure 6.7. Kernel density plot of incumbent-party presidential vote percentage, 1880–2004.

6.5 LIMITATIONS

The tools that we have presented in this chapter are helpful for providing a first look at data, one variable at a time. Taking a look at your data with these tools will help you to better know your data and make fewer mistakes in the long run. It is important, however, to note that we cannot test causal theories with a single variable. After all, as we have noted, a theory is a tentative statement about the possible causal relationship between two variables. Because we have discussed how to describe only a single variable, we have not yet begun to subject our causal theories to appropriate tests.

CONCEPTS INTRODUCED IN THIS CHAPTER

categorical variables	measurement metric
central tendency	mode
continuous variables	ordinal variables
dispersion	outliers
equal unit differences	rank statistics
expected value	skewness
histogram	standard deviation
kernel density plot	statistical moments
kurtosis	variance
least-squares property	variation
mean value	zero-sum property
median value	

EXERCISES

1. *Collecting and describing a categorical variable.* Find data for a categorical variable in which you are interested. Get those data into a format that can be read by the statistical software that you are using. Produce a frequency table and describe what you see.

2. *Collecting and describing a continuous variable.* Find data for a continuous variable in which you are interested. Get those data into a format that can be read by the statistical software that you are using. Produce a table of descriptive statistics and either a histogram or a kernel density plot. Describe what you have found out from doing this.

3. In Table 6.1, why would it be problematic to calculate the mean value of the variable "Religious Identification?"

Table 6.3. Median incomes of the 50 states, 2004–2005			
State	Income	State	Income
Alabama	37,502	Montana	36,202
Alaska	56,398	Nebraska	46,587
Arizona	45,279	Nevada	48,496
Arkansas	36,406	New Hampshire	57,850
California	51,312	New Jersey	60,246
Colorado	51,518	New Mexico	39,916
Connecticut	56,889	New York	46,659
Delaware	50,445	North Carolina	41,820
Florida	42,440	North Dakota	41,362
Georgia	44,140	Ohio	44,349
Hawaii	58,854	Oklahoma	39,292
Idaho	45,009	Oregon	43,262
Illinois	48,008	Pennsylvania	45,941
Indiana	43,091	Rhode Island	49,511
Iowa	45,671	South Carolina	40,107
Kansas	42,233	South Dakota	42,816
Kentucky	36,750	Tennessee	39,376
Louisiana	37,442	Texas	42,102
Maine	43,317	Utah	53,693
Maryland	59,762	Vermont	49,808
Massachusetts	54,888	Virginia	52,383
Michigan	44,801	Washington	51,119
Minnesota	56,098	West Virginia	35,467
Mississippi	34,396	Wisconsin	45,956
Missouri	43,266	Wyoming	45,817

Source: http://www.census.gov/hhes/www/income/income05/statemhi2.html.
Accessed January 11, 2007.

4. *Moving from mathematical formulae to textual statements.* Write a sentence that conveys what is going on in each of the following equations:
   (a) $Y = 3 \ \forall \ X_i = 2$,
   (b) $Y_{\text{total}} = \sum_{i=1}^{n} Y_i = n\bar{Y}$.

5. *Computing means and standard deviations.* Table 6.3 contains the median income for each of the 50 U.S. states for the years 2004–2005. What is the mean of this distribution, and what is its standard deviation? Show all of your work.

7 Statistical Inference

OVERVIEW

As researchers begin to consider possible tests of their theoretical propositions, they must make a series of important decisions. In this chapter we provide a discussion of choices of population and sample and inferences from samples about populations. We introduce this topic by using examples familiar to political science students – namely, the "plus-or-minus" error figures in presidential horse-race polls, showing where such figures come from and how they illustrate the principles of building bridges between samples we know about with certainty and the underlying population of interest.

How dare we speak of the laws of chance? Is not chance the antithesis of all law?
  – Bertrand Russell

7.1 POPULATIONS AND SAMPLES

In Chapter 6, we discussed how to use descriptive statistics to summarize large amounts of information about a single variable. In particular, you learned how to characterize a distribution by computing measures of central tendency (like the mean) and measures of dispersion (like the standard deviation). For example, you can implement these formulae to characterize the distribution of income in the United States, or, for that matter, the scores of a midterm examination your professor may have just handed back.

But it is time to draw a critical distinction between two types of data sets that social scientists might use. The first type is data about the **population** – that is, data for every possible relevant case. In your experience, the example of population data that might come to mind first is that of the U.S.

Census, an attempt by the U.S. government to gather some critical bits of data about the entire U.S. population once every 10 years.[1] It is a relatively rare occurrence that social scientists will make use of data pertaining to the entire population.[2]

The second type of data is drawn from a **sample** – a subset of cases that are drawn from an underlying population. Because of the proliferation of public-opinion polls today, many of you might assume that the word "sample" implies a **random sample**.[3] It does not. Researchers *may* draw a sample of data on the basis of randomness – meaning that each member of the population has an equal probability of being selected in the sample. But samples may also be nonrandom, which we refer to as samples of convenience. The vast majority of all analyses undertaken by social scientists is done on sample data, not population data.

Why make this distinction? Even though the vast majority of social science data sets are based on samples, not the population, it is critical to note that we are not interested in the properties of the sample per se; we are interested in the sample only insofar as it helps us to learn about the underlying population. In effect, we try to build a bridge from what we know about the sample to what we believe, probabilistically, to be true about the broader population. That process is called **statistical inference**, because we use what we *know* to be true about one thing (the sample) to *infer* what is likely to be true about another thing (the population).

There are implications for using sample data to learn about a population. First and foremost is that this process of statistical inference involves, at its core, some degree of uncertainty. That notion is relatively straightforward: Any time that we wish to learn something general based on something specific, we are going to encounter some degree of uncertainty. In this chapter, we discuss this process of statistical inference, including the tools that social scientists use to learn about the population that they are interested in by using samples of data.

---

[1] The Bureau of the Census's web site is http://www.census.gov.

[2] But we try to make inferences about some population of interest, and it is up to the researcher to define explicitly what that population of interest is. Sometimes, as in the case of the U.S. Census, the relevant population – all U.S. residents – is easy to understand. Other times, it is a bit less obvious. Consider a preelection survey, in which the researcher needs to decide whether the population of interest is all adult citizens, or likely voters, or something else.

[3] When we discussed research design in Chapter 4, we distinguished between the experimental notion of random assignment to treatment groups, on the one hand, and random sampling, on the other. See Chapter 4 if you need a refresher on this difference.

7.2 LEARNING ABOUT THE POPULATION FROM A SAMPLE: THE CENTRAL LIMIT THEOREM

The reasons that social scientists rely on sample data instead of on population data – in spite of the fact that we care about the results in the population instead of in the sample – are easy to understand. Consider an election campaign, in which the media, the public, and the politicians involved all want a sense of which candidates the public favors and by how much. Is it practical to take a census in such circumstances? Of course not. The adult population in the United States is approximately 200 million people, and it is an understatement to say that we can't interview each and every one of these individuals. We simply don't have the time or the money to do that. There is a reason why the U.S. government conducts a **census** only once every 10 years.[4]

Of course, anyone familiar with the ubiquitous public-opinion polls knows that scholars and news organizations conduct surveys on a sample of Americans routinely and use the results of these surveys to generalize about the people as a whole. When you think about it, it seems a little audacious to think that you can interview perhaps as few as 1000 people and then use the results of those interviews to generalize to the beliefs and opinions of the entire 200 million. How is that possible?

The answer lies in a fundamental result from statistics called the **central limit theorem**, which Dutch statistician Henk Tijms (2007) calls "the unofficial sovereign of probability theory." Before diving into what the theorem demonstrates, and how it applies to social science research, we need to explore one of the most useful probability distributions in statistics, the **normal distribution**.

7.2.1 The Normal Distribution

To say that a particular distribution is "normal" is *not* to say that it is "typical" or "desirable" or "good." A distribution that is not "normal" is not something odd like the "deviant" or "abnormal" distribution. It is worth emphasizing, as well, that normal distributions are not necessarily common in the real world. Yet, as we will see, they are incredibly useful in the world of statistics.

The normal distribution is often called a "bell curve" in common language. It is shown in Figure 7.1 and has several special properties. First,

---

[4] You might not be aware that, even though the federal government conducts only one census per 10 years, it conducts sample surveys with great frequency in an attempt to measure population characteristics such as economic activity.

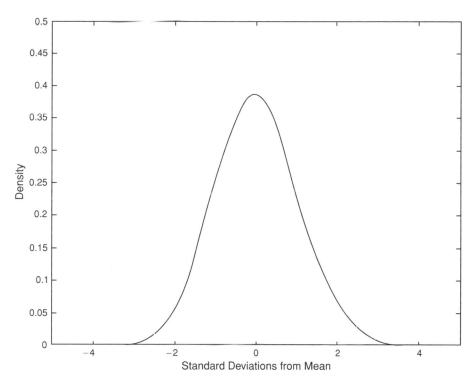

Figure 7.1. The normal probability distribution.

it is symmetrical about its mean,[5] such that the mode, median, and mean are the same. Second, the normal distribution has a predictable area under the curve within specified distances of the mean. Starting from the mean and going one standard deviation in each direction will capture 68% of the area under the curve. Going one additional standard deviation in each direction will capture a shade over 95% of the total area under the curve.[6] And going a third standard deviation in each direction will capture more than 99% of the total area under the curve. This is commonly referred to as the **68–95–99 rule** and is illustrated in Figure 7.2. You should bear in mind that this is a special feature of the normal distribution and does not apply to any other-shaped distribution. What do the normal distribution and the 68–95–99 rule have to do with the process of learning about population characteristics based on a sample?

[5] Equivalently, but a bit more formally, we can characterize the distribution by its mean and variance (or standard deviation) – which implies that its skewness and kurtosis are both equal to zero.

[6] To get exactly 95% of the area under the curve, we would actually go 1.96, not 2, standard deviations in each direction from the mean. Nevertheless, the rule of two is a handy rule of thumb for many statistical calculations.

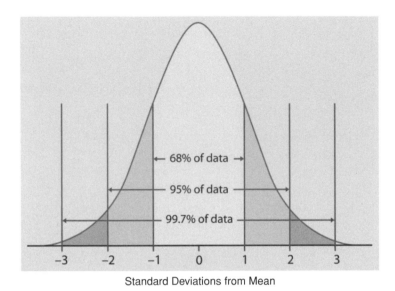

Figure 7.2. The 68–95–99 rule.

A distribution of actual scores in a sample – called a **frequency distribution,** to represent the frequency of each value of a particular variable – on any variable might be shaped normally, or it might not be. Consider the frequency distribution of 600 rolls of a six-sided (and unbiased) die, presented in Figure 7.3. Note something about Figure 7.3 right off the bat: That frequency distribution does not even remotely resemble a normal

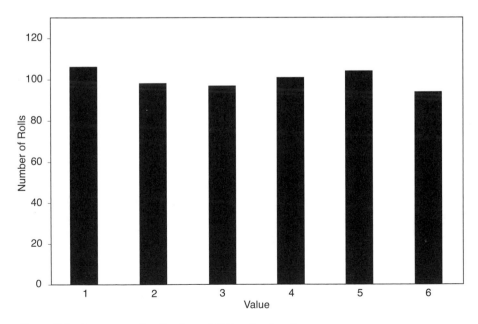

Figure 7.3. Frequency distribution of 600 rolls of a die.

distribution.[7] If we roll a fair six-sided die 600 times, how many 1's, 2's, etc., should we see? On average, 100 each, right? That's *pretty close* to what we see in the figure, but only pretty close. Purely because of chance, we rolled a couple too many 1's, for example, and a couple too few 6's.

What can we say about this sample of 600 rolls of the die? And, more to the point, from these 600 rolls of the die, what can we say about the underlying population of all rolls of a fair six-sided die? Before we answer the second question, which will require some inference, let's answer the first, which we can answer with certainty. We can calculate the mean of these rolls of dice in the straightforward way that we learned in Chapter 6: Add up all of the "scores" – that is, the 1's, 2's, and so on – and divide by the total number of rolls, which in this case is 600. That will lead to the following calculation:

$$\bar{Y} = \frac{\sum_{i=1}^{n} Y_i}{n}$$

$$= \frac{\sum (1 \times 106) + (2 \times 98) + (3 \times 97) + (4 \times 101) + (5 \times 104) + (6 \times 94)}{600} = 3.47.$$

Following the formula for the mean, for our 600 rolls of the die, in the numerator we must add up all of the 1's (106 of them), all of the 2's (98 of them), and so on, and then divide by 600 to produce our result of 3.47.

We can also calculate the standard deviation of this distribution:

$$s_Y = \sqrt{\frac{\sum_{i=1}^{n}(Y_i - \bar{Y})^2}{n-1}} = \sqrt{\frac{1753.40}{599}} = 1.71.$$

Looking at the numerator for the formula for the standard deviation that we learned in Chapter 6, we see that $\sum (Y_i - \bar{Y})^2$ indicates that, for each observation (a 1, 2, 3, 4, 5, or 6) we subtract its value from the mean (3.47), then square that difference, then add up all 600 squared deviations from the mean, which produces a numerator of 1753.40 beneath the square-root sign. Dividing that amount by 599 (that is, $n - 1$), then taking the square root, produces a standard deviation of 1.71.

As we noted, the sample mean is 3.47, but what should we have *expected* the mean to be? If we had exactly 100 rolls of each side of the die, the mean would have been 3.50, so our sample mean is a bit lower than we would have expected. But then again, we can see that we rolled a few "too many" 1's and a few "too few" 6's, so the fact that our mean is a bit below 3.50 makes sense.

What would happen, though, if we rolled that same die another 600 times? What would the mean value of those rolls be? We can't say for

---

[7] In fact, the distribution in the figure very closely resembles a uniform or flat distribution.

certain, of course. Perhaps we would come up with another sample mean of 3.47, or perhaps it would be a bit above 3.50, or perhaps the mean would hit 3.50 on the nose. Suppose that we rolled the die 600 times like this not once, and not twice, but an infinite number of times. Let's be clear: We do not mean *an infinite number of rolls*, we mean *rolling the die 600 times for an infinite number of times*. That distinction is critical. We are imagining that we are taking a sample of 600, not once, but an infinite number of times. We can refer to a hypothetical distribution of sample means, such as this, as a **sampling distribution**. It is hypothetical because scientists almost never actually draw more than one sample from an underlying population at one given point in time.

If we followed this procedure, we could take those sample means and plot them. Some would be above 3.50, some below, some right on it. Here is the key outcome, though: The sampling distribution would be normally shaped, even though the underlying frequency distribution is clearly not normally shaped.

That is the insight of the central limit theorem. If we can envision an infinite number of random samples and plot our sample means to each of these random samples, those sample means would be distributed normally. Furthermore, the mean of the sampling distribution would be equal to the true population mean. The standard deviation of the sampling distribution is

$$\sigma_{\bar{Y}} = \frac{s_Y}{\sqrt{n}},$$

where n is the sample size. The standard deviation of the sampling distribution of sample means, which is known as the **standard error of the mean** (or simply **standard error**), is simply equal to the sample standard deviation divided by the square root of the sample size. In the preceding die-rolling example, the standard error of the mean is

$$\sigma_{\bar{Y}} = \frac{1.71}{\sqrt{600}} = 0.07.$$

Recall that our goal here is to learn what we can about the underlying population based on what we know with certainty about our sample. We know that the mean of our sample of 600 rolls of the die is 3.47 and its standard deviation is 1.71. From those characteristics, we can imagine that, if we rolled that die 600 times an infinite number of times, the resulting sampling distribution would have a standard deviation of 0.07. Our best approximation of the population mean is 3.47, because that is the result that our sample generated.[8] But we realize that our sample of 600 might be different from the true population mean by a little bit, either too high or too low. What we can do, then, is use our knowledge that the sampling distribution is shaped normally and invoke the 68–95–99 rule to create a **confidence interval** about the likely location of the population mean.

How do we do that? First, we choose a degree of confidence that we want to have in our estimate. Although we can choose any confidence range up from just above 0 to just below 100, social scientists traditionally rely on the 95% confidence level. If we follow this tradition – and because our sampling distribution is normal – we would merely start at our mean (3.47) and move *two* standard errors of the mean in each direction to produce the interval that we are approximately 95% confident that the population mean lies within. Why *two* standard errors? Because just over 95% of the area under a normal curve lies within two standard errors of the mean. Again, to be precisely 95% confident, we would move 1.96, not 2, standard errors in each direction. But the rule of thumb of two is commonly used in practice. In other words,

$$\bar{Y} \pm 2 \times \sigma_{\bar{Y}} = 3.47 \pm (2 \times 0.07) = 3.47 \pm 0.14.$$

That means, from our sample, we are 95% confident that the population mean for our rolls of the die lies somewhere on the interval between 3.33 and 3.61.

Is it possible that we're wrong and that the population mean lies outside that interval? Absolutely. Moreover, we know exactly *how* likely. There is a 2.5% chance that the population mean is less than 3.33, and a 2.5% chance that the population mean is greater than 3.61, for a total of a 5% chance that the population mean is not in the interval from 3.33 to 3.61. For a variety of reasons, we might like to have more confidence in our estimate. Say that, instead of being 95% confident, we would be more comfortable with a 99% level of confidence. In that case, we would simply move *three* (instead of two) standard errors in each direction from our sample mean of 3.47, yielding an interval of 3.26–3.68.

Throughout this example we have been helped along by the fact that we knew the underlying characteristics of the data-generating process (a fair die). In the real world, social scientists almost never have this advantage. In the next section we consider such a case.

---

[8] One might imagine that our best guess should be 3.50 because, in theory, a fair die ought to produce such a result.

7.3 EXAMPLE: PRESIDENTIAL APPROVAL RATINGS

On October 5 and 6, 2006, *Newsweek* magazine sponsored a survey in which 1004 randomly selected Americans were interviewed about their political beliefs. Among the questions they were asked was the following item intended to tap into a respondent's evaluation of the president's job performance:

> Do you approve or disapprove of the way George W. Bush is handling his job as president?

This question wording is the industry standard, used for over a half-century by almost all polling organizations.[9] In early October, 2006, 33% of the sample approved of Bush's job performance, 59% disapproved, and 8% were unsure.[10]

Newsweek, of course, is not inherently interested in the opinions of those 1004 Americans who happened to be in the sample, except insofar as they tell us something about the adult population as a whole. But we can use these 1004 responses to do precisely that, using the logic of the central limit theorem and the tools previously described.

To reiterate, we know the properties of our randomly drawn sample of 1004 people with absolute certainty. If we consider the 331 approving responses to be 1's and the remaining 673 responses to be 0's, then we calculate our sample mean, $\bar{Y}$, as follows[11]:

$$\bar{Y} = \frac{\sum_{i=1}^{n} Y_i}{n} = \frac{\sum (331 \times 1) + (673 \times 0)}{1004} = 0.33.$$

We calculate the sample standard deviation, s_Y, in the following way:

$$s_Y = \sqrt{\frac{\sum_{i=1}^{n}(Y_i - \bar{Y})^2}{n - 1}} = \sqrt{\frac{331(1 - 0.33)^2 + 673(0 - 0.33)^2}{1004 - 1}}$$

$$= \sqrt{\frac{221.8756}{1003}} = 0.47.$$

---

[9] The only changes, of course, are for the name of the current president.

[10] The source for the survey was http://www.pollingreport.com/BushJob1.htm, accessed October 8, 2006.

[11] There are a variety of different ways in which to handle mathematically the 8% of "uncertain" responses. In this case, because we are interested in calculating the "approval" rating for this example, it is reasonable to lump the disapproving and unsure answers together. When we make decisions like this in our statistical work, it is very important to communicate exactly what we have done so that the scientific audience can make a reasoned evaluation of our work.

But what can we say about the population as a whole? Obviously, unlike the sample mean, the population mean cannot be known with certainty. But if we imagine that, instead of one sample of 1004 respondents, we had an infinite number of samples of 1004, then the central limit theorem tells us that those sample means would be distributed normally. Our best guess of the population mean, of course, is 0.33, because it is our sample mean. The standard error of the mean is

$$\sigma_{\bar{Y}} = \frac{0.47}{\sqrt{1004}} = 0.015,$$

which is our measure of uncertainty about the population mean. If we use the rule of thumb and calculate the 95% confidence interval by using two standard errors in either direction from the sample mean, we are left with the following interval:

$$\bar{Y} \pm 2 \times \sigma_{\bar{Y}} = 0.33 \pm (2 \times 0.015) = 0.33 \pm 0.03,$$

or between 0.30 and 0.36, which translates into being 95% confident that the population value of Bush approval is between 30% and 36%.

And this is where the "plus-or-minus" figures that we always see in public opinion polls come from.[12] The best guess for the population mean value is the sample mean value, plus or minus two standard errors. So the plus-or-minus figures we are accustomed to seeing are built, typically, on the 95% interval.

7.3.1   What Kind of Sample Was That?

If you read the preceding example carefully, you will have noted that the *Newsweek* poll we described used a *random* sample of 1004 individuals. That means that they used some mechanism (like random-digit telephone dialing) to ensure that all members of the population had an equal probability of being selected for the survey. We want to reiterate the importance of using random samples. The central limit theorem applies *only* to samples that are selected randomly. With a sample of convenience, by contrast, we cannot invoke the central limit theorem to construct a sampling distribution and create a confidence interval.

This lesson is critical: A nonrandomly selected sample of convenience does very little to help us build bridges between the sample and the

---

[12] In practice, most polling firms have their own additional adjustments that they make to these calculations, but they start with this basic logic.

population about which we want to learn. This has all sorts of implications about "polls" that news organizations conduct on their web sites. What do such "surveys" say about the population as a whole? Because their samples are clearly not random samples of the underlying population, the answer is "nothing."

There is a related lesson involved here. The preceding example represents an entirely straightforward connection between a sample (the 1004 people in the survey) and the population (all adults in the United States). Often the link between the sample and the population is less straightforward. Consider, for example, an examination of votes in a country's legislature during a given year. Assuming that it's easy enough to get all of the roll-call voting information for each member of the legislature (which is our sample), we are left with a slightly perplexing question: What is the population of interest? The answer is not obvious, and not all social scientists would agree on the answer. Some might claim that the data don't represent a sample, but a population, because the data set contains the votes of every member of the legislature. Others might claim that the sample is a sample of one year's worth of the legislature since its inception. Others still might say that the sample is one realization of the infinite number of legislatures that could have been happened in that particular year. Suffice it to say that there is no clear scientific consensus, in this example, of what would constitute the "sample" and what would constitute the "population."

7.3.2 A Note on the Effects of Sample Size

As the formula for the confidence interval indicates, the smaller the standard errors, the "tighter" our resulting confidence intervals will be; larger standard errors will produce "wider" confidence intervals. If we are interested in estimating population values, based on our samples, with as much precision as possible, then it is desirable to have tighter instead of wider confidence intervals.

How can we achieve this? From the formula for the standard error of the mean, it is clear through simple algebra that we can get a smaller quotient either by having a smaller numerator or a larger denominator. Because obtaining a smaller numerator – the sample standard deviation – is not something we can do in practice, we can consider whether it is possible to have a larger denominator – a larger sample size.

Larger sample sizes will reduce the size of the standard errors, and smaller sample sizes will increase the size of the standard errors. This, we hope, makes intuitive sense. If we have a large sample, then it should be easier to make inferences about the population of interest; smaller samples should produce less confidence about the population estimate.

In the preceding example, if instead of having our sample of 1004, we had a much larger sample – say, 2500 – our standard errors would have been

$$\sigma_{\bar{Y}} = \frac{0.47}{\sqrt{2500}} = 0.0094,$$

which is less than two-thirds the size of our actual standard errors of 0.015. You can do the math to see that going two standard errors of 0.009 in either direction produces a narrower interval than going two standard errors of 0.015. But note that the cost of reducing our error by about 1.5% in either direction is the addition of nearly another 1500 respondents, and in many cases that reduction in error will not be worth the financial and time costs involved in obtaining all of those extra interviews.

Consider the opposite case. If, instead of interviewing 1004 individuals, we interviewed only 400, then our standard errors would have been

$$\sigma_{\bar{Y}} = \frac{0.47}{\sqrt{400}} = 0.0235,$$

which, when doubled to get our 95% confidence interval, would leave a plus-or-minus 0.047 (or nearly 5%) in each direction.

We could be downright silly and obtain a random sample of only 64 people if we liked. (We're sure that you notice that all of our hypothetical sample sizes are perfect squares.) That would generate some rather wide confidence intervals. The standard error would be

$$\sigma_{\bar{Y}} = \frac{0.47}{\sqrt{64}} = 0.05875,$$

which, when doubled to get the 95% confidence interval, would leave a rather hefty plus-or-minus 0.1175 (or 11.75%) in each direction. In this circumstance, we would guess that Bush approval in the population was 33%, but we would be 95% confident that it was between 21.25% and 44.75% – and that alarmingly wide interval would be just too wide to be particularly informative.

In short, the answer to the question, "How big does my sample need to be?" is another question: "How tight do you want your confidence intervals to be?"

7.4 A LOOK AHEAD: EXAMINING RELATIONSHIPS BETWEEN VARIABLES

Let's take stock for a moment. In this book, we have emphasized that political science research involves evaluating causal explanations, which entails examining the relationships between two or more variables. Yet, in this chapter, all we have done is talk about the process of statistical inference with a *single* variable. This was a necessary tangent, because we had to teach you the logic of statistical inference – that is, how we use samples to learn something about an underlying population.

In Chapter 8, you will learn three different ways to move into the world of bivariate hypothesis testing. We will examine relationships between two variables, typically in a sample, and then make probabilistic assessments of the likelihood that those relationships exist in the population. The logic is identical to what you have just learned; we merely extend it to cover relationships between two variables. After that, in Chapter 9, you will learn one other way to conduct hypothesis tests involving two variables – the bivariate regression model.

CONCEPTS INTRODUCED IN THIS CHAPTER

68–95–99 rule	random sample
census	sample
central limit theorem	sampling distribution
confidence interval	standard error
frequency distribution	standard error of the mean
normal distribution	statistical inference
population	

EXERCISES

1. Go to http://www.pollingreport.com and find a polling statistic that interests you most. Be sure to click on the "full details" option, where available, to get the sample size for the survey item that most interests you. Then calculate the 95% and 99% confidence intervals for the population value of the statistic you have in mind, showing all of your work.

2. For the same survey item, what would happen to the confidence interval if the sample size were cut in half? What would happen instead if it were doubled? Show your work.

3. Are more data always better than less data? Explain your answer.

4. Refer back to Table 6.2, which shows the incumbent vote percentage in U.S. presidential elections. Calculate the standard error of the mean for that distribution, and then construct the 95% confidence interval for the population mean. What does the 95% confidence interval tell us in this particular case?

5. If we take a representative draw of 1000 respondents from the population of the United States for a particular survey question and obtain a 95% confidence margin, how many respondents would you need to draw from the population of Maine to obtain the same interval, assuming that the distribution of responses is the same for both populations?

8 Bivariate Hypothesis Testing

OVERVIEW

Once we have set up a hypothesis test and collected data, how do we evaluate what we have found? In this chapter we provide hands-on discussions of the basic building blocks used to make statistical inferences about the relationship between two variables. We deal with the often-misunderstood topic of "statistical significance" – focusing both on what it is and what it is not – as well as the nature of statistical uncertainty. We introduce three ways to examine relationships between two variables: tabular analysis (crosstabs), difference of means tests, and correlation coefficients. (We will introduce a fourth technique, bivariate regression analysis, in Chapter 9.)

8.1 BIVARIATE HYPOTHESIS TESTS AND ESTABLISHING CAUSAL RELATIONSHIPS

In the preceding chapters we introduced the core concepts of hypothesis testing. In this chapter we discuss the basic mechanics of hypothesis testing with three different examples of bivariate hypothesis testing. It is worth noting that, although this type of analysis was the main form of hypothesis testing in the professional journals up through the 1970s, it is seldom used as the *primary* means of hypothesis testing in the professional journals today.[1] This is the case because these techniques are good at helping us with only

---

[1] By definition, researchers conducting bivariate hypothesis tests are making one of two assumptions about the state of the world. They are assuming either that there are no other variables that are causally related to the dependent variable in question, or that, if there are such omitted variables, they are unrelated to the independent variable in the model. We will have much more to say about omitting independent variables from causal models in Chapter 10. For now, bear in mind that, as we have discussed in previous chapters, these assumptions rarely hold when we are describing the political world.

Table 8.1. Variable types and appropriate bivariate hypothesis tests

		Independent variable type	
		Categorical	Continuous
Dependent	Categorical	*Tabular analysis*	Probit/logit
variable type	Continuous	*Difference of means*	*Correlation coefficient*; bivariate regression model

Notes: Tests in italics are discussed in this chapter.

the first principle for establishing causal relationships. Namely, bivariate hypothesis tests help us to answer the question, "Are X and Y related?" By definition – "bivariate" means "two variables" – these tests cannot help us with the important question, "Is there some confounding variable Z that is related to both X and Y and makes the observed association between X and Y spurious?"

Despite their limitations, the techniques covered in this chapter are important starting points for understanding the underlying logic of statistical hypothesis testing. In the sections that follow we discuss how one chooses which bivariate test to conduct and then provide detailed discussions of three such tests. Throughout this chapter, try to keep in mind the main purpose of this exercise: We are attempting to apply the lessons of the previous chapters with real-world data. We will eventually do this with more appropriate and more sophisticated tools, but the lessons that we learn in this chapter will be crucial to our understanding of these more advanced methods. Put simply, we are trying to get up and walk in the complicated world of hypothesis testing with real-world data. Once we have mastered walking, we will then begin to work on running with more advanced techniques.

8.2 CHOOSING THE RIGHT BIVARIATE HYPOTHESIS TEST

As we discussed in previous chapters, and especially in Chapters 6 and 7, researchers make a number of critical decisions before they test their hypotheses. Once they have collected their data and want to conduct a bivariate hypothesis test, they need to consider the nature of their dependent and independent variables. As we discussed in Chapter 6, we can classify variables in terms of the types of values that cases take on. Table 8.1 shows four different scenarios for testing a bivariate hypothesis; which one is most appropriate depends on the variable type of the independent variable and the dependent variable. For each case, we have listed one or more appropriate type of bivariate hypothesis tests. In cases in which we can describe both the independent and dependent variables as categorical, we use a form of analysis referred to as **tabular analysis** to test our hypothesis. When the dependent variable is continuous and the independent variable is categorical, we use a **difference of means** test. When the independent variable is continuous and the dependent variable is categorical, analysts typically use either a binomial probit or binomial logit model. (These types of statistical models are discussed in Section 11.4.) This particular test is beyond the scope of this book, and thus we will not discuss it. Finally, when both the dependent and independent variables are continuous, we use a **correlation coefficient** in this chapter, and, in Chapter 9, we will discuss the bivariate regression model.

8.3   ALL ROADS LEAD TO p

One common element across a wide range of statistical hypothesis tests is the p-value (the p stands for "probability.") This value, ranging between 0 and 1, is the closest thing that we have to a bottom line in statistics. But it is often misunderstood and misused. In this section we discuss the basic logic of the p-value and relate it back to our discussion in Chapter 7 of using sample data to make inferences about an underlying population.

8.3.1   The Logic of p-Values

If we think back to the four principles for establishing causal relationships that were discussed in Chapter 3, the third hurdle is the question "Is there covariation between X and Y?" To answer this question, we need to apply standards to real-world data for determining whether there appears to be a relationship between our two variables, the independent variable X and the dependent variable Y. The tests listed in the cells in Table 8.1 are commonly accepted tests for each possible combination of data type. In each of these tests, we follow a common logic: We compare the actual relationship between X and Y in sample data with what we would expect to find if X and Y *were not* related in the underlying population. The *more different* the empirically observed relationship is from what we would expect to find if there were *not* a relationship, the more confidence we have that X and Y are related in the population. The logic of this inference from sample to population is the same as what we used in Chapter 7 to make inferences about the population mean from sample data.

The statistic that is most commonly associated with this type of logical exercise is the p-**value**. The p-value, which ranges between 0 and 1, is the probability that we would see the relationship that we are finding because of random chance. Put another way, the p-value tells us the probability that we would see the observed relationship between the two variables in our sample data if there were truly no relationship between them in the unobserved population. Thus, the lower the *p*-value, the greater confidence we have that there *is* a systematic relationship between the two variables for which we estimated the particular *p*-value.

One common characteristic across statistical techniques is that, for a particular measured relationship, the more data on which the measurement is based, the lower our *p*-value will be. This is consistent with one of the lessons of Chapter 7 about sample size: The larger the sample size, the more confident we can be that our sample will more accurately represent the population.[2] (See Subsection 7.3.1 for a reminder.)

8.3.2   The Limitations of *p*-Values

Although *p*-values are powerful indicators of whether or not two variables are related, they are limited. In this subsection we review the limitations of *p*-values. It is important that we also understand what a *p*-value is not: The logic of a *p*-value is not reversible. In other words, $p = .001$ does not mean that there is a .999 chance that something systematic is going on. Also, it is important to realize that, although a *p*-value tells us something about our confidence that there is a relationship between two variables, it does not tell us whether that relationship is causal.

In addition, it might be tempting to assume that, when a *p*-value is very close to zero, this indicates that the relationship between *X* and *Y* is very *strong*. This is not necessarily true (though it might be true). As we previously noted, *p*-values represent our degree of confidence that there is a relationship in the underlying population. So we should naturally expect smaller *p*-values as our sample sizes increase. But a larger sample size does not magically make a relationship stronger; it *does* increase our confidence that the observed relationship in our sample accurately represents the underlying population. We saw a similar type of relationship in Chapter 7 when we calculated standard errors. Because the number of cases is in the denominator of the standard error formula, an increased number of cases leads to a smaller standard error and a more narrow confidence interval for our inferences about the population.

Another limitation of *p*-values is that they do not directly reflect the quality of the measurement procedure for our variables. Thus, if we are more confident in our measurement, we should be more confident in a particular *p*-value. The flip side of this is that, if we are not very confident in our measurement of one or both of our variables, we should be less confident in a particular *p*-value.

---

[2] Also, the smaller the sample size, the more likely it is that we will get a result that is not very representative of the population.

Finally, we should keep in mind that p-values are always based on the assumption that you are drawing a perfectly random sample from the underlying population. Mathematically, this is expressed as

$$p_i = P \; \forall i.$$

This translates into "the probability of an individual case from our population ending up in our sample, p_i, is assumed to equal P for all of the individual cases i." If this assumption were valid, we would have a **truly random sample**. Because this is a standard that is almost never met, we should use this in our assessment of a particular p-value. The further we are from a truly random sample, the less confidence we should have in our p-value.

8.3.3 From p-Values to Statistical Significance

As we outlined in the preceding subsection, lower p-values increase our confidence that there is indeed a relationship between the two variables in question. A common way of referring to such a situation is to state that the relationship between the two variables is **statistically significant**. Although this type of statement has a ring of authoritative finality, it is always a qualified statement. In other words, an assertion of statistical significance depends on a number of other factors. One of these factors is the set of assumptions from the previous section. "Statistical significance" is achieved only to the extent that the assumptions underlying the calculation of the p-value hold. In addition, there are a variety of different standards for what is a statistically significant p-value. Most social scientists use the standard of a p-value of .05. If p is less than .05, they consider a relationship to be statistically significant. Others use a more stringent standard of .01, or a more loose standard[3] of .1.

We cannot emphasize strongly enough that finding that X and Y have a statistically significant relationship does *not* necessarily mean that the relationship between X and Y is strong or especially that the relationship is causal. To evaluate the case for a causal relationship, we need to evaluate how well our theory has performed in terms of all four of the causal hurdles from Chapter 2.

8.3.4 The Null Hypothesis and p-Values

In Chapter 1 we introduced the concept of the null hypothesis. Our definition was "A null hypothesis is also a theory-based statement but it is

---

[3] More recently, there has been a trend toward reporting the estimated p-value and letting readers make their own assessments of statistical significance.

about what we would expect to observe if our theory was incorrect." Thus, following the logic that we previously outlined, if our theory-driven hypothesis is that there is covariation between X and Y, then the corresponding null hypothesis is that there is no covariation between X and Y. In this context, another interpretation of the p-value is that it conveys the level of confidence with which we can reject the null hypothesis.

8.4   THREE BIVARIATE HYPOTHESIS TESTS

We now turn to three specific bivariate hypothesis tests. In each case, we are testing for whether there is a relationship between X and Y. We are doing this with sample data, and then, based on what we find, making inferences about the underlying population.

8.4.1   Example 1: Tabular Analysis

Tabular presentations of data on two variables are still used quite widely. In the more recent political science literature, scholars use them as stepping stones on the way to multivariate analyses. It is worth noting at this point in the process that, in tables and graphs, most of the time the dependent variable is displayed in the rows along the vertical dimension whereas the independent variable is displayed in the columns across horizontal dimension. Any time that you see a table, it is very important to take some time to make sure that you understand what is being conveyed in the table. We can break this into the following three-step process:

1. Figure out what the variables are that define the rows and columns of the table.
2. Figure out what the individual cell values represent. Sometimes they will be the number of cases that take on the particular row and column values; other times the cell values will be proportions (ranging from 0 to 1.0) or percentages (ranging from 0 to 100). If this is the case, it is critical that you figure out whether the researcher calculated the percentages or proportions for the entire table or for each column or row.
3. Figure out what, if any, general patterns you see in the table.

Let's go through these steps with Table 8.2. In this table we are testing the theory that affiliation with trade unions make people more likely to support left-leaning candidates.[4] We can tell from the title and the column

---

[4] Take a moment to assess this theory in terms of the first two of the four hurdles that we discussed in Chapter 3. The causal mechanism is that left-leaning candidates tend to support policies favored by trade unions. Is this credible? What about hurdle 2? Could

Table 8.2. Union households and vote in the 2004 U.S. presidential election

Candidate	From a union household	Not from a union household	Total
Kerry	64.24	45.73	49.19
Bush	35.76	54.27	50.81
Total	100.00	100.00	100.00

Note: Cell entries are column percentages.

and row headings that this table is comparing the votes of people from union households with those not from union households in the 2004 U.S. presidential election. We can use the information in this table to test the hypothesis that voters from union households were more likely to support Democratic Party presidential candidate John Kerry.[5] As the first step in reading this table, we determine that the columns indicate values for the independent variable (whether or not the individual was from a union household) and that the rows indicate values for the dependent variable (presidential vote). The second step is fairly straightforward; the table contains a footnote that tells us that the "cell entries are column percentages." This is the easiest format for pursuing step 3, because the column percentages correspond to the comparison that we want to make. We want to compare the presidential votes of people from union households with the presidential votes of people not from union households. The pattern is fairly clear: People from the union households overwhelmingly supported Kerry (64.24 for Kerry and 35.76 for Bush), whereas people from the nonunion households strongly favored Bush (45.73 for Kerry and 54.27 for Bush). If we think in terms of independent (X) and dependent (Y) variables, the comparison that we have made is between the distribution of the dependent variable ($Y =$ Presidential Vote) across values of the independent variable ($X =$ Type of Household).

In Table 8.2, we follow the simple convention of placing the values of the independent variable in the columns and the values of the dependent variable in the rows. Then, by calculating column percentages for the cell values, this makes comparing across the columns straightforward. It is wise to adhere to these norms, because it is the easiest way to make the

support for left-leaning candidates make one more likely to be affiliated with a trade union?

[5] What do you think about the operationalization of these two variables? How well does it stand up to what we discussed in Chapter 4?

Table 8.3. Gender and vote in the 2004 U.S. presidential election: Hypothetical scenario

Candidate	Male	Female	Row total
Kerry	?	?	49.20
Bush	?	?	50.80
Column total	100.00	100.00	100.00

Note: Cell entries are column percentages.

comparison that we want, and because it is the way many readers will expect to see the information.

In our next example we are going to go step by step through a bivariate test of the hypothesis that gender (X) is related to vote (Y) in U.S. presidential elections. To test this hypothesis about gender and presidential vote, we are going to use data from the 2004 NES. This is an appropriate set of data for testing this hypothesis, because these data are from a randomly selected sample of cases from the underlying population of interest (U.S. adults). Before we look at results obtained by using actual data, think briefly about the measurement of the variables of interest and what we would expect to find if there was no relationship between the two variables.

Table 8.3 shows partial information from a hypothetical example in which we know that 49.2% of our sample respondents report having voted for John Kerry and 50.8% of our sample respondents report having voted for George W. Bush. But, as the question marks inside this table indicate, we do not know how voting breaks down in terms of gender. If there was no relationship between gender and presidential voting in 2004, consider what we would expect to see given what we know from Table 8.3. In other words, what values should replace the question marks in Table 8.3 if there were no relationship between our independent variable (X) and dependent variable (Y)?

If there is not a relationship between gender and presidential vote, then we should expect to see no major differences between males and females in terms of how they vote for John Kerry and George W. Bush. Because we know that 49.2% of our cases voted for Kerry and 50.8% for Bush, what should we expect to see for males and for females? We should expect to see the same proportions of males and females voting for each candidate. In other words, we should expect to see the question marks replaced with the values in Table 8.4.

Table 8.5 shows the total numbers of respondents who fit into each column and row from the 2004 NES. If we do the calculations, we can see that the numbers in the rightmost column of Table 8.5 correspond with the

Table 8.4. Gender and vote in the 2004 U.S. presidential election: Expectations for hypothetical scenario if there were no relationship

Candidate	Male	Female	Row total
Kerry	49.20	49.20	49.20
Bush	50.80	50.80	50.80
Column total	100.00	100.00	100.00

Note: Cell entries are column percentages.

Table 8.5. Gender and vote in the 2004 U.S. presidential election

Candidate	Male	Female	Row total
Kerry	?	?	399
Bush	?	?	412
Column total	374	437	811

Note: Cell entries are number of respondents.

Table 8.6. Gender and vote in the 2004 U.S. presidential election: Calculating the expected cell values if gender and presidential vote are unrelated

Candidate	Male	Female
Kerry	(49.2% of 374)	(49.2% of 437)
	$= 0.492 \times 374 = 184$	$= 0.492 \times 437 = 215$
Bush	(50.8% of 374)	(50.8% of 437)
	$= 0.508 \times 374 = 190$	$= 0.508 \times 437 = 222$

Note: Cell entries are expectation calculations if these two variables are unrelated.

Table 8.7. Gender and vote in the 2004 U.S. presidential election

Candidate	Male	Female	Row total
Kerry	170	229	0.492
Bush	204	208	0.508
Column total	0.4612	0.5388	1.0

Note: Cell entries are number of respondents.

Table 8.8. Gender and vote in the 2004
U.S. presidential election

Candidate	Male	Female
Kerry	$O = 170; E = 184$	$O = 229; E = 215$
Bush	$O = 204; E = 190$	$O = 208; E = 222$

Note: Cell entries are the number observed (O); the number
expected if there were no relationship (E).

percentages from Table 8.3. We can now combine the information from
Table 8.5 with our expectations from Take 8.4 to calculate the number
of respondents that we would expect to see in each cell if gender and
presidential vote were unrelated. We display these calculations in Table
8.6. In Table 8.7, we see the actual numbers of respondents that fell into
each of the four cells.

Finally, in Table 8.8, we compare the observed number of cases in each
cell (O) with the number of cases that we would expect to see if there was
no relationship between our independent and dependent variables (E).

We can see a pattern. Among males, the proportion observed voting
for Kerry is lower than what we would expect if there were no relationship
between the two variables. Also, among men, the proportion voting for
Bush is higher than what we would expect if there were no relationship.
For females this pattern is reversed – the proportion voting for Kerry (Bush)
is higher (lower) than we would expect if there were no relationship between gender and vote for U.S. president. The pattern of these differences
is in line with the theory that women support Democratic Party candidates
more than men do. Although these differences are present, we have not yet
determined that they are of such a magnitude that we should now have increased confidence in our theory. In other words, we want to know whether
or not these differences are statistically significant.

To answer this question, we turn to the **chi-squared** (χ^2) test for tabular
association. Karl Pearson originally developed this test when he was testing
theories about the influence of nature versus nurture at the beginning of the
20th century. His formula for the χ^2 statistic is

$$\chi^2 = \sum \frac{(O - E)^2}{E}.$$

The summation sign in this formula signifies that we sum over each
cell in the table; so a 2×2 table would have four cells to add up. If we
think about an individual cell's contribution to this formula, we can see the
underlying logic of the χ^2 test. If the value observed, O, is exactly equal to

the expected value if there were no relationship between the two variables, E, then we would get a contribution of zero from that cell to the overall formula (because $O - E$ would be zero). Thus, if all observed values were exactly equal to the values that we expect if there were no relationship between the two variables, then $\chi^2 = 0$. The more the O values differ from the E values, the greater the value will be for χ^2. Because the numerator on the right-hand side of the χ^2 formula ($O - E$) is squared, any difference between O and E will contribute positively to the overall χ^2 value.

Here are the calculations for χ^2 mode with the values in Table 8.8:

$$\chi^2 = \sum \frac{(O - E)^2}{E}$$
$$= \frac{(170 - 184)^2}{184} + \frac{(204 - 190)^2}{190} + \frac{(229 - 215)^2}{215} + \frac{(208 - 222)^2}{222}$$
$$= \frac{196}{184} + \frac{196}{190} + \frac{196}{215} + \frac{196}{222}$$
$$= 1.065 + 1.032 + 0.912 + 0.883 = 3.892.$$

So our calculated value of χ^2 is 3.892 based on the observed data. What do we do with this? We need to compare that 3.892 with some predetermined standard, called a **critical value**, of χ^2. If our calculated value is greater than the critical value, then we conclude that there is a relationship between the two variables; and if the calculated value is less than the critical value, we cannot make such a conclusion.

How do we obtain this critical value? First, we need a piece of information known as the **degrees of freedom** (df's) for our test.[6] In this case, the df's calculation is very simple: df $= (r - 1)(c - 1)$, where r is the number of rows in the table, and c is the number of columns in the table. In the example in Table 8.8, there are two rows and two columns, so $(2 - 1)(2 - 1) = 1$.

You can find a table with critical values of χ^2 in Appendix A. If we adopt the standard p-value of .05, we see that the critical value of χ^2 for df $= 1$ is 3.841. Therefore a calculated χ^2 value of 3.892 is just barely over the minimum value needed to achieve a p-value of .05. When we use computer software packages to estimate this p-value, we get $p = .048$.

At this point, we have established that the relationship between our two variables meets a conventionally accepted standard of statistical significance (i.e., $p < .05$). Although this result is supportive of our hypothesis, we have not yet established a causal relationship between gender and presidential voting. To see this, think back to the four hurdles along the route to establishing causal relationships that we discussed in Chapter 3. Thus far,

---

[6] We define degree of freedom in the next section.

we have cleared the third hurdle, by demonstrating that X (gender) and Y (vote) covary. From what we know about politics, we can easily cross hurdle 1, "Is there a credible causal mechanism that links X to Y?" Women might be more likely to vote for Kerry because, among other things, women depend on the social safety net of the welfare state more than men do. If we turn to hurdle 2, "Does Y cause X?," we can pretty easily see that we have met this standard through basic logic. We know with confidence that changing one's vote does not lead to a change in one's gender. We hit the most serious bump in the road to establishing causality for this relationship when we encounter hurdle 4, "Is there some Z associated with X and Y that makes the relationship between X and Y spurious?" Unfortunately, our answer here is that we do not yet know. In fact, with a bivariate analysis, we cannot know whether some other variable Z is relevant because, by definition, there are only two variables in such an analysis.

8.4.2 Example 2: Difference of Means

In our second example, we examine a situation in which we have a continuous dependent variable and a categorical independent variable. In this type of bivariate hypothesis test, we are looking to determine whether the distribution of the dependent variable is different across the values of the independent variable. We follow the basic logic of hypothesis testing: comparing our real-world data with what we would expect to find if there were no relationship between our independent and dependent variables.

Our theory in this section will come from the study of parliamentary governments. When political scientists study phenomena across different forms of government, one of the fundamental distinctions that they draw between different types of democracies is whether the regime is parliamentary or not. A democratic regime is labeled "parliamentary" when the lower house of the legislature is the most powerful branch of government and directly selects the head of the government.[7] One of the interesting

---

[7] An important part of research design is determining which cases are and are not covered by our theory. In this case, our theory, which we will introduce shortly, is going to apply to only parliamentary democracies. As an example, consider whether or not the United States and the United Kingdom fit this description at the beginning of 2007. In the United States in 2007, the head of government was President George W. Bush. Because Bush was selected by a presidential election and not by the lower branch of government, we can already see that the United States at the beginning of 2007 is not covered by our theory. In the UK, we might be tempted at first to say that the head of government at the beginning of 2007 was Queen Elizabeth. But, if we consider that British queens and kings have been mostly ceremonial in UK politics for some time now, we then realize that the head of government was the prime minister, Tony Blair, who was selected from the lower house of the legislature, the House of Commons. If we further consider the relative

features of most parliamentary regimes is that a vote in the lower house of the legislature can remove the government from power. As a result, political scientists have been very interested in the determinants of how long parliamentary governments last when the possibility of such a vote exists.

One factor that is an important difference across parliamentary democracies is whether the party or parties that are in government occupy a majority of the seats in the legislature.[8] By definition, the opposition can vote out of office a minority government, because it does not control a majority of the seats in the legislature. Thus a pretty reasonable theory about government duration is that majority governments will last longer than minority governments.

We can move from this theory to a hypothesis test by using a data set produced by Michael D. McDonald and Silvia M. Mendes titled "Governments, 1950–1995." Their data set covers governments from 21 Western countries. For the sake of comparability, we will limit our sample to those governments that were formed after an election.[9] Our independent variable, "Government Type," takes on one of two values: "majority government" or "minority government." Our dependent variable, "Government Duration," is a continuous variable measuring the number of days that each government lasted in office. Although this variable has a hypothetical range from 1 day to 1461 days, the actual data vary from an Italian government that lasted for 31 days in 1953 to a Dutch government that lasted for 1749 days in the late 1980s and early 1990s.

To get a better idea of the data that we are comparing, we can turn to two graphs that we introduced in Chapter 6 for viewing the distribution of continuous variables. Figure 8.1 presents a box-whisker plot of government duration for minority and majority governments, and Figure 8.2 presents a kernel density plot of government duration for minority and majority governments. From both of these plots, it appears that majority governments last longer than minority governments.

To determine whether the differences from these figures are statistically significant, we turn to a **difference of means test**. In this test we compare what we have seen in the two figures with what we would expect

---

power of the House of Commons compared with the other branches of government at the beginning of 2007, we can see that the United Kingdom met our criteria for being classified as parliamentary.

[8] Researchers usually define a party as being in government if its members occupy one or more cabinet posts, whereas parties not in government are in opposition.

[9] We have also limited the analyses to cases in which the governments had a legal maximum of four years before they must call for new elections. These limitations mean that, strictly speaking, we are only able to make inferences about the population of cases that also fit these criteria.

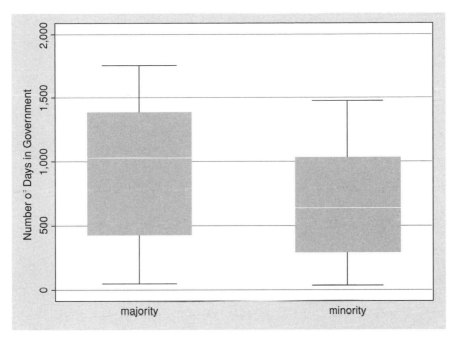

Figure 8.1. Box-whisker plot of Government Duration for majority and minority governments.

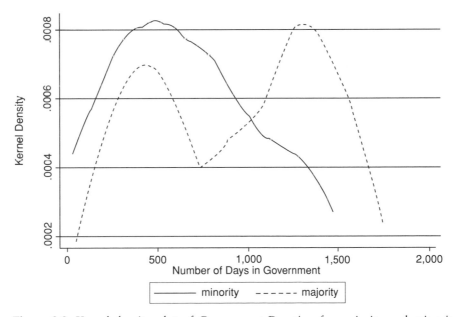

Figure 8.2. Kernel density plot of Government Duration for majority and minority governments.

if there were no relationship between Government Type and Government Duration. If there were no relationship between these two variables, then the world would be such that the duration of governments of both types were drawn from the same underlying distribution. If this were the case, the mean or average value of Government Duration would be the same for minority and majority governments.

To test the hypothesis that these means are drawn from the same underlying distribution, we use another test developed by Karl Pearson for these purposes. The test statistic for this is known as a t-test because it follows the t-distribution. The formula for this particular t-test is

$$t = \frac{\bar{Y}_1 - \bar{Y}_2}{\text{se}(\bar{Y}_1 - \bar{Y}_2)},$$

where $\bar{Y}_1$ is the mean of the dependent variable for the first value of the independent variable and $\bar{Y}_2$ is the mean of the dependent variable for the second value of the independent variable. We can see from this formula that the greater the difference between the mean value of the dependent variable across the two values of the independent variable, the greater the value of t.

In Chapter 7 we introduced the notion of a standard error, which is a measure of uncertainty about a statistical estimate. The basic logic of a standard error is that the larger it is, the more uncertainty (or less confidence) we have in our ability to make precise statements. Similarly, the smaller the standard error, the greater our confidence about our ability to make precise statements. The standard error of the difference between $\bar{Y}_1$ and $\bar{Y}_2$, $\text{se}(\bar{Y}_1 - \bar{Y}_2)$, is calculated from the following formula:

$$\text{se}(\bar{Y}_1 - \bar{Y}_2) = \sqrt{\left(\frac{s_1^2}{n_1}\right) + \left(\frac{s_2^2}{n_2}\right)},$$

where s_1 is the standard deviation of $\bar{Y}_1$, s_2 is the standard deviation of $\bar{Y}_2$, n_1 is the number of cases in the first category of the independent variable, and n_2 is the number of cases in the second category of the independent variable. We can see from this formula that the standard error of the difference between $\bar{Y}_1$ and $\bar{Y}_2$, $\text{se}(\bar{Y}_1 - \bar{Y}_2)$, combines the standard deviations for both Y_1 and Y_2. The larger these standard deviations, the larger the standard error.

To better understand the contribution of the top and bottom parts of the t-calculation for a difference of means, look again at Figure 8.2. The further apart the two means are and the less dispersed the distributions (as

Table 8.9. Government type and government duration			
Government type	Number of observations	Mean duration	Standard deviation
Majority	124	930.5	466.1
Minority	53	674.4	421.4
Combined	177	853.8	467.1

measured by the standard deviations s_1 and s_2), the greater confidence we have that $\bar{Y}_1$ and $\bar{Y}_2$ are different from each other.

Table 8.9 presents the descriptive statistics for government duration by government type. From the values displayed in this table we can calculate the t-test statistic for our hypothesis test. Start with the standard error for the difference:

$$se(\bar{Y}_1 - \bar{Y}_2) = \sqrt{\left(\frac{s_1^2}{n_1}\right) + \left(\frac{s_2^2}{n_2}\right)} = \sqrt{\left(\frac{466.1^2}{124}\right) + \left(\frac{421.4^2}{53}\right)}$$

$$= \sqrt{\left(\frac{217249.21}{124}\right) + \left(\frac{177577.96}{53}\right)}$$

$$= \sqrt{1752 + 3350.5} = \sqrt{5102.5} = 71.43.$$

Now that we have the standard error, we can calculate the t-statistic:

$$t = \frac{\bar{Y}_1 - \bar{Y}_2}{se(\bar{Y}_1 - \bar{Y}_2)} - \frac{930.5 - 674.4}{71.43} = \frac{256.1}{71.43} = 3.59.$$

Now that we have calculated this t-statistic, we need one more piece of information before we can get to our p-value. This is called the **degrees of freedom** (df's). Degrees of freedom reflect the basic idea that we will gain confidence in an observed pattern as the amount of data on which that pattern is based increases. In other words, as our sample size increases, we become more confident about our ability to say things about the underlying population. If we turn to Appendix B, which is a table of critical values for t, we can see that it reflects this logic. This table also follows the same basic logic as the χ^2 table. The way to read such a table is that the columns are defined by targeted p-values, and, to achieve a particular target p-value, you need to obtain a particular value of t. The rows in the t-table indicate the number of degrees of freedom. As the number of degrees of freedom goes up, the t-statistic we need to obtain a particular p-value goes down. We calculate the degrees of freedom for a difference of means t-statistic based on the smaller of the two samples in terms of number of cases minus one. In this case, because we have 53 minority governments and 124 majority governments, our degrees of freedom equal $53 - 1$, or 52. From the p-value, we can look across the row for which df $= 50$ and see the minimum t-value needed to achieve each targeted value of p.[10] In the second column of the t-table, we can see that, to have a p-value of .10 (meaning that there is a 10%, or 1 in 10, chance that we would see this relationship randomly in our sample if there was no relationship between X and Y in the underlying population), we must have a t-statistic greater than or equal to 1.299. Because $3.59 > 1.299$, we can proceed to the next column for $p = .05$ and see that 3.59 is also greater than 1.676. In fact, if we go all the way to the end of the row for df $= 50$, we can see that our t-statistic is greater than 3.261, which is the t-value needed to achieve $p = .001$ (meaning that there is a 0.1%, or 1 in 1000, chance that we would see this relationship randomly in our sample if there were no relationship between X and Y in the underlying population).

8.4.3   Example 3: Correlation Coefficient

In our final example of bivariate hypothesis testing we look at a situation in which both the independent variable and the dependent variable are continuous. We test the hypothesis that there is a positive relationship between economic growth and incumbent-party fortunes in U.S. presidential elections.

In Chapter 6 we discussed the variation (or variance) of a single variable, and in Chapter 1 we introduced the concept of covariation. The statistical measure of covariation is **covariance**. In the three examples that we have looked at so far, we have found there to be covariation between being from a union household and presidential vote, gender and presidential vote, and government type and government duration. All of these examples used at least one limited variable. When we have an independent variable and a dependent variable that are both continuous, we can visually detect covariation pretty easily in graphs. Consider the graph in Figure 8.3, which shows a scatter plot of incumbent vote and economic growth. When we look at this graph, we generally see a pattern that runs from lower-left to upper-right. This indicates that, as expected by our hypothesis, when the economy is doing better (more rightward values on the horizontal axis),

---

[10] Although our degrees of freedom equal 52, we are using the row for df $= 50$. With a computer program, we can calculate an exact p-value.

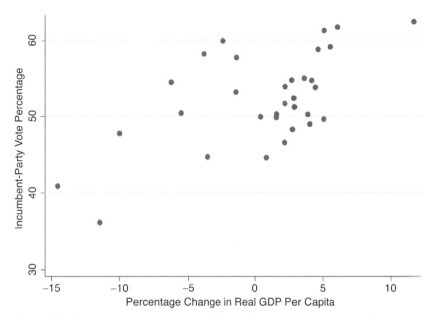

Figure 8.3. Scatter plot of change in GDP and incumbent-party vote share.

we also tend to see higher vote percentages for the incumbent party in U.S. presidential elections (higher values on the vertical axis).

Covariance is a statistical way of summarizing the general pattern of association (or the lack thereof) between two variables. The formula for covariance between two variables X and Y is

$$\text{cov}_{XY} = \frac{\sum_{i=1}^{n}(X_i - \bar{X})(Y_i - \bar{Y})}{n}.$$

To better understand the intuition behind the covariance formula, it is helpful to think of individual cases in terms of their values relative to the mean of X ($\bar{X}$) and the mean of Y ($\bar{Y}$). If an individual case has a value for the independent variable that is greater than the mean of X ($X_i - \bar{X} > 0$) and its value for the dependent variable is greater than the mean of Y ($Y_i - \bar{Y} > 0$), that case's contribution to the numerator in the covariance equation will be positive. If an individual case has a value for the independent variable that is less than the mean of X ($X_i - \bar{X} < 0$) and a value of the dependent variable that is less than the mean of Y ($Y_i - \bar{Y} < 0$), that case's contribution to the numerator in the covariance equation will also be positive, because multiplying two negative numbers yields a positive product. If a case has a combination of one value greater than the mean and one value less than the mean, its contribution to the numerator in the covariance equation will be negative because multiplying a positive number by a negative number yields a negative product. Figure 8.4 illustrates this; we see the same plot of

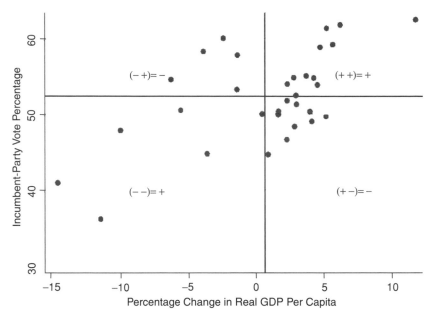

Figure 8.4. Scatter plot of change in GDP and incumbent-party vote share with mean-delimited quadrants.

growth versus incumbent vote, but with the addition of lines showing the mean value of each variable. In each of these mean-delimited quadrants we can see the contribution of the cases to the numerator. If a plot contains cases in mostly the upper-right and lower-left quadrants, the covariance will tend to be positive. On the other hand, if a plot contains cases in mostly the lower-right and upper-left quadrants, the covariance will tend to be negative. If a plot contains a balance of cases in all four quadrants, the covariance calculation will be close to zero because the positive and negative values will cancel out each other. When the covariance between two variables is positive, we describe this situation as a positive relationship between the variables, and when the covariation between two variables is negative, we describe this situation as a negative relationship.

Table 8.10 presents the calculations for each year in the covariance formula for the data that we presented in Figure 8.4. For each year, we have started out by calculating the difference between each X and $\bar{X}$ and the difference between each Y and $\bar{Y}$. If we begin with the year 1880, we can see that the value for growth (X_{1880}) was 3.879 and the value for vote (Y_{1880}) was 50.22. The value for growth is greater than the mean and the value for vote is less than the mean, $X_{1880} - \bar{X} = 3.879 - 0.628 = 3.251$ and $Y_{1880} - \bar{Y} = 50.22 - 52.27022 = -2.050217$. In Figure 8.4, the dot for 1880 is in the lower-right quadrant. When we multiply these two mean deviations together, we get $(X_{1880} - \bar{X})(Y_{1880} - \bar{Y}) = -6.665254$.

Table 8.10. Contributions of individual election years to the covariance calculation

Year	Growth (X_i)	Vote (Y_i)	$X_i - \bar{X}$	$Y_i - \bar{Y}$	$(X_i - \bar{X})(Y_i - \bar{Y})$
1880	3.879	50.22	3.251	−2.050217	−6.665254
1884	1.589	49.846	0.961	−2.424217	−2.329673
1888	−5.553	50.414	−6.181	−1.856216	11.47327
1892	2.763	48.268	2.135	−4.002216	−8.544732
1896	−10.024	47.76	−10.652	−4.51022	48.04286
1900	−1.425	53.171	−2.053	0.9007835	−1.849309
1904	−2.421	60.006	−3.049	7.735783	−23.5864
1908	−6.281	54.483	−6.909	2.212784	−15.28812
1912	4.164	54.708	3.536	2.437782	8.619998
1916	2.229	51.682	1.601	−0.5882187	0.9417382
1920	−11.463	36.119	−12.091	−16.15122	195.2844
1924	−3.872	58.244	−4.5	5.973782	−26.88202
1928	4.623	58.82	3.995	6.549782	26.16638
1932	−14.557	40.841	−15.185	−11.42922	173.5527
1936	11.677	62.458	11.049	10.18778	112.5648
1940	3.611	54.999	2.983	2.728783	8.139958
1944	4.433	53.774	3.805	1.50378	5.721884
1948	2.858	52.37	2.23	0.099781	0.2225117
1952	0.84	44.595	0.212	−7.675217	−1.627146
1956	−1.394	57.764	−2.022	5.493782	−11.10843
1960	0.417	49.913	−0.211	2.35722	0.4973734
1964	5.109	61.344	4.481	9.073784	40.65963
1968	5.07	49.596	4.442	−2.674217	−11.87887
1972	6.125	61.789	5.497	9.518784	52.32475
1976	4.026	48.948	3.398	−3.322216	−11.28889
1980	−3.594	44.697	−4.222	−7.573219	31.97413
1984	5.568	59.17	4.94	6.89978	34.08491
1988	2.261	53.902	1.633	1.631783	2.664701
1992	2.223	46.545	1.595	−5.72522	−9.131725
1996	2.712	54.736	2.084	2.465782	5.13869
2000	1.603	50.265	0.975	−2.005219	−1.955088
2004	2.9	51.2	2.272	−1.070217	−2.431533
	$\bar{X} = 0.628$	$\bar{Y} = 52.27022$			$\sum(X_i - \bar{X})(Y_i - \bar{Y})$ $= 641.6768$

We repeat this same calculation for every case (presidential election year). Each negative calculation like this contributes evidence that the overall relationship between X and Y is negative, whereas each positive calculation contributes evidence that the overall relationship between X and Y is positive. The sum across all 32 years of data in Table 8.10 is 641.6768, indicating that the positive values have outweighed the negative values. When we divide this by 32, we have the sample covariance,

Table 8.11. Covariance table for economic growth and incumbent-party presidential vote, 1880–2004

	Vote	Growth
Vote	36.86	
Growth	20.05	30.68

which equals 20.05. This tells us that we have a positive relationship, but it does not tell us how confident we can be that this relationship is different from what we would see if our independent and dependent variables were not related in our underlying population of interest. To see this, we turn to a third test developed Karl Pearson, Pearson's correlation coefficient. This is also known as **Pearson's** r, the formula for which is

$$r = \frac{\text{cov}_{XY}}{\sqrt{\text{var}_X \text{var}_Y}}.$$

Table 8.11 is a covariance table. In a covariance table, the cells across the main diagonal (from upper-left to lower-right) are cells for which the column and the row reference the same variable. In this case the cell entry is the variance for the referenced variable. All of the cells off of the main diagonal represent the covariance for a pair of variables. In covariance tables, the cells above the main diagonal are often left blank, because the values in these cells are a mirror image of the values in the corresponding cells below the main diagonal. For instance, in Table 8.11 the covariance between growth and vote is the same as the covariance between vote and growth, so the upper-right cell in this table is left blank.

Using the entries in Table 8.11, we can calculate the correlation coefficient:

$$r = \frac{\text{cov}_{XY}}{\sqrt{\text{var}_X \text{var}_Y}},$$

$$r = \frac{20.05}{\sqrt{30.68 \times 36.86}},$$

$$r = \frac{20.05}{\sqrt{1130.8648}},$$

$$r = \frac{20.05}{33.6283},$$

$$r = 0.596.$$

There are a couple of points worth noting about the correlation coefficient. If all of the points in the plot line up perfectly on a straight, positively sloping line, the correlation coefficient will equal 1. If all of the points in the plot line up perfectly on a straight, negatively sloping line, the correlation coefficient will equal −1. Otherwise, the values will lie between positive one and negative one. This standardization of correlation coefficient values is a particularly useful improvement over the covariance calculation. Additionally, we can calculate a t-statistic for a correlation coefficient as

$$t_r = \sqrt{|r| \times \frac{n-2}{1-r^2}},$$

with $n-1$ degrees of freedom, where n is the number of cases. In this case, our degrees of freedom equal $32 - 1 = 31$.

For the current example,

$$t_r = \sqrt{|r| \times \frac{n-2}{1-r^2}},$$

$$t_r = \sqrt{|0.596| \times \frac{32-2}{1-(0.596)^2}},$$

$$t_r = \sqrt{0.596 \times \frac{30}{1-(0.3552)}},$$

$$t_r = \sqrt{0.596 \times \frac{30}{0.6448}},$$

$$t_r = \sqrt{0.596 \times 46.5261},$$

$$t_r = \sqrt{27.7296},$$

$$t_r = 5.2659.$$

With the degrees of freedom equal to 32 ($n - 32$) minus one, or 31, we can now turn to the t-table in Appendix B. Looking across the row for df $= 30$, we can see that our calculated t of 5.2659 is greater even than the critical t at the p-value of .001. Thus we are quite confident that a relationship exists between economic growth and incumbent-party vote share and that our theory has successfully cleared our third causal hurdle.[11]

8.5 WRAPPING UP

We have introduced three methods to conduct bivariate hypothesis tests – tabular analysis, difference of means tests, and correlation coefficients. Which test is most appropriate in any given situation depends on the

---

[11] The first causal hurdle is pretty well cleared if we refer back to the discussion of the theory of economic voting in earlier chapters. The second causal hurdle also can be pretty well cleared logically by the timing of the measurement of each variable. Because economic growth is measured prior to incumbent vote, it is difficult to imagine that Y caused X.

MORAL VALUES – THE TRANSATLANTIC GULF

Q How often do you go to church?

	BRITAIN				US	
	All Voters	Labour voters	Tory voters	Lib Dem voters	Bush voters	Kerry voters
More than weekly	2%	2%	3%	1%	63%	35%
Weekly	10%	10%	13%	7%	58%	41%
Monthly	5%	6%	4%	6%	50%	50%
A few times a year	36%	36%	38%	40%	44%	55%
Never	47%	46%	43%	44%	34%	64%

Q Which of the following is closest to your view of what the law should say about abortion?

	All Voters	Labour voters	Tory voters	Lib Dem voters	Bush voters	Kerry voters
Always legal: absolute right to choose	38%	45%	34%	46%	24%	74%
Mostly legal: some restrictions	36%	35%	40%	32%	37%	62%
Mostly illegal: only in exceptional circumstances	19%	14%	18%	17%	72%	27%
Always illegal	4%	4%	3%	3%	77%	22%

Q Which of the following is closest to your view of what the law should be towards same-sex couples?

	All Voters	Labour voters	Tory voters	Lib Dem voters	Bush voters	Kerry voters
Legal right to marry	28%	33%	18%	31%	22%	77%
Legally civil union but not marriage	37%	37%	39%	47%	51%	48%
No legal recognition of same sex couples	29%	23%	39%	20%	69%	30%

Sources: for British figures, Populus poll for *The Times* (Nov 5–7); for American figures, exit polls conducted by National Election Poll (Nov 2)

Figure 8.5. What is wrong with this table?

measurement metric of your independent and dependent variables. Table 8.1 should serve as a helpful reference for you on this front.

We have yet to introduce the final method for conducting bivariate hypothesis tests covered in this book, namely bivariate regression analysis. That is the topic of our next chapter, and it serves as the initial building block for multiple regression (which we will cover in Chapter 10).

CONCEPTS INTRODUCED IN THIS CHAPTER

chi-squared (χ^2)	difference of means test
correlation coefficient	Pearson's r
covariance	p-value
critical value	statistically significant
degrees of freedom	tabular analysis
difference of means	truly random sample

Table 8.12. Incumbent reelection rates in U.S. congressional elections, 1964–2006		
Year	House	Senate
1964	87	85
1966	88	88
1968	97	71
1970	85	77
1972	94	74
1974	88	85
1976	96	64
1978	94	60
1980	91	55
1982	90	93
1984	95	90
1986	98	75
1988	98	85
1990	96	96
1992	88	83
1994	90	92
1996	94	91
1998	98	90
2000	98	79
2002	96	86
2004	98	96
2006	94	79

EXERCISES

1. Take a look at Figure 8.5. What is the dependent variable? What are the independent variables? What does this table tell us about politics?

2. What makes the table in Figure 8.5 so confusing?

3. Build a crosstab from the information presented in the following hypothetical discussion of polling results: "We did a survey of 800 respondents who were likely Democratic primary voters in the state. Among these respondents, 45% favored Obama whereas 55% favored Clinton. When we split the respondents in half at the median age of 40, we found some stark differences: Among the younger half of the sample respondents, we found that 72.2% favored Obama to be the nominee and among the older sample respondents, we found that 68.2% favored Clinton."

4. For the example in Exercise 3, test the theory that age is related to preference for a Democratic nominee.

5. A lot of people in the United States think that the Watergate scandal in 1972 caused a sea change in terms of U.S. citizens' views toward incumbent politicians. Use the data in Table 8.12 to produce a difference of means test of the null hypothesis that average reelection rates were the same before and after the Watergate scandal.

6. Using the data set "BES2005 Subset," produce a table that shows the combination values for the variables "LabourVote" (Y) and "IraqWarApprovalDich" (X). Read the descriptions of these two variables and write about what this table tells you about politics in the UK in 2005. Compute a χ^2 hypothesis test for these two variables. Write about what this tells you about politics in the UK in 2005.

7. Using the data set "BES2005 Subset," test the hypothesis that values for "BlairFeelings" (Y) are different across different values of "IraqWarApprovalDich" (X). Read the descriptions of these two variables and write about what this table tells you about politics in the UK in 2005.

8. Using the data set "BES2005 Subset," produce a scatter plot of the values for "BlairFeelings" (Y) and "SelfLR" (X). Calculate a correlation coefficient and p-value for the hypothesis that these two variables are related to each other. Read the descriptions of these two variables and write about what this table tells you about politics in the UK in 2005.

9 Bivariate Regression Models

OVERVIEW

Regression models are the workhorses of data analysts in a wide range of fields in the social sciences. We begin this chapter with a discussion of fitting a line to a scatter plot of data, and then we discuss the additional inferences that can be made when we move from a correlation coefficient to a two-variable regression model. We include discussions of measures of goodness-of-fit and on the nature of hypothesis testing and statistical significance in regression models. Throughout this chapter, we present important concepts in text, mathematical formulae, and graphical illustrations. This chapter concludes with a discussion of the assumptions of the regression model and minimal mathematical requirements for estimation.

9.1 TWO-VARIABLE REGRESSION

In Chapter 8 we introduced three different bivariate hypothesis tests. In this chapter we add a fourth, two-variable regression. This is an important first step toward the multiple regression model – which is the topic of Chapter 10 – in which we are able to "control for" another variable (Z) as we measure the relationship between our independent variable of interest (X) and our dependent variable (Y). It is crucial to develop an in-depth understanding of two-variable regression before moving to multiple regression. In the sections that follow, we begin with an overview of the two-variable regression model, in which a line is fit to a scatter plot of data. We then discuss the uncertainty associated with the line and how we use various measures of this uncertainty to make inferences about the underlying population. This chapter concludes with a discussion of the assumptions of the regression model and the minimal mathematical requirements for model estimation.

9.2 FITTING A LINE: POPULATION ⇔ SAMPLE

The basic idea of two-variable regression is that we are fitting the "best" line through a scatter plot of data. This line, which is defined by its slope and y-intercept, serves as a **statistical model** of reality. In this sense, two-variable regression is very different from the three hypothesis-testing techniques that we introduced in Chapter 8; although those techniques allow hypothesis testing, they do not produce a statistical model. You may remember from a geometry course the formula for a line expressed as

$$Y = mX + b,$$

where b is the y-intercept and m is the slope – often explained as the "rise-over-run" component of the line formula. For a one-unit increase (run) in X, m is the corresponding amount of rise in Y (or fall in Y, if m is negative). Together these two elements (m and b) are described as the line's **parameters**.[1] You may remember exercises from junior high or high school math classes in which you were given the values of m and b and then asked to draw the resulting line on graph paper. Once we know these two parameters for a line, we can draw that line across any range of X values.[2]

In a two-variable regression model, we represent the y-intercept parameter by the Greek letter alpha (α) and the slope parameter by the Greek letter beta (β).[3] As foreshadowed by all of our other discussions of variables, Y is the dependent variable and X is the independent variable. Our theory about the underlying population in which we are interested is expressed in the **population regression model**:

$$Y_i = \alpha + \beta X_i + u_i.$$

Note that in this model there is one additional component, u_i, that does not correspond with what we are used to seeing in line formulae from geometry classes. This term is the **stochastic** or "random" component of our dependent variable. We have this term because we do not expect all of our data points to line up perfectly on a straight line. This corresponds directly with our discussion in earlier chapters about the probabilistic (as opposed to deterministic) nature of causal theories about political phenomena. We are,

---

[1] The term "parameter" is a synonym for "boundary" with a more mathematical connotation. In the description of a line, the parameters (m and b in this case) are fixed whereas the variables (X and Y in this case) vary.

[2] If this is not familiar to you, or if you merely want to refresh your memory, you may want to complete Exercise 1 at the end of this chapter before you continue reading.

[3] Different textbooks on regression use slightly different notation for these parameters, so it is important not to assume that all textbooks use the same notation when comparing across them.

after all, trying to explain processes that involve human behavior. Because human beings are complex, there is bound to be a fair amount of random noise in our measures of their behavior. Thus we think about the values of our dependent variable Y_i as having a systematic component, $\alpha + \beta X_i$, and a stochastic component, u_i.

As we have discussed, we rarely work with population data. Instead, we use sample data to make inferences about the underlying population of interest. In two-variable regression, we use information from the **sample regression model** to make inferences about the unseen population regression model. To distinguish between these two, we place hats (^) over terms in the sample regression model that are estimates of terms from the unseen population regression model. Because they have hats, we can describe $\hat{\alpha}$ and $\hat{\beta}$ as being **parameter estimates**. These terms are our best guesses of the unseen population parameters α and β:

$$\text{sample regression model: } Y_i = \hat{\alpha} + \hat{\beta} X_i + \hat{u}_i.$$

Note that, in the sample regression model, α, β, and u_i get hats, but Y_i, and X_i do not. This is because Y_i and X_i are values for cases in the population that ended up in the sample. As such, Y_i and X_i are values that are *measured* rather than *estimated*. We use them to estimate α, β, and the u_i values. The values that define the line are the estimated systematic components of Y. For each X_i value, we use $\hat{\alpha}$ and $\hat{\beta}$ to calculate the predicted value of Y_i, which we call $\hat{Y}_i$, where

$$\hat{Y}_i = \hat{\alpha} + \hat{\beta} X_i.$$

This can also be written in terms of expectations,

$$E(Y|X_i) = \hat{Y}_i = \hat{\alpha} + \hat{\beta} X_i,$$

which means that the expected value of Y given X_i (or $\hat{Y}_i$) is equal to our formula for the two-variable regression line. So we can now talk about each Y_i as having an estimated systematic component, $\hat{Y}_i$, and an estimated stochastic component, $\hat{u}_i$. We can thus write our model as

$$Y_i = \hat{Y}_i + \hat{u}_i,$$

and we can rewrite this in terms of $\hat{u}_i$ to get a better understanding of the estimated stochastic component:

$$\hat{u}_i = Y_i - \hat{Y}_i.$$

From this formula, we can see that the estimated stochastic component ($\hat{u}_i$) is equal to the difference between the actual value of the dependent variable (Y_i) and the predicted value of the dependent variable from our two-variable regression model. Another name for the estimated stochastic component is the **residual**. "Residual" is another word for "leftover," and

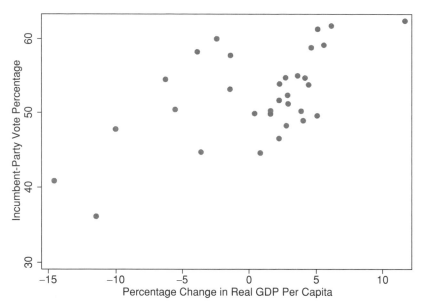

Figure 9.1. Scatter plot of change in GDP and incumbent-party vote share.

this is appropriate, because $\hat{u}_i$ is the leftover part of Y_i after we have drawn the line defined by $\hat{Y}_i = \hat{\alpha} + \hat{\beta} X_i$. Another way to refer to $\hat{u}_i$, which follows from the formula $\hat{u}_i = Y_i - \hat{Y}_i$, is to call it the **sample error term**. Because $\hat{u}_i$ is an estimate of u_i, a corresponding way of referring to u_i is to call it the **population error term**.

9.3 WHICH LINE FITS BEST? ESTIMATING THE REGRESSION LINE

Consider the scatter plot of data in Figure 9.1. Our task is to draw a straight line[4] that describes the relationship between our independent variable X and our dependent variable Y. How do we draw our line? We clearly want to draw a line that comes as close as possible to the cases in our scatter plot of data. Because the data have a general pattern from lower-left to upper-right, we know that our slope will be positive.

In Figure 9.2, we have drawn three lines with positive slopes – labeled A, B, and C – through the scatter plot of growth and vote and written the corresponding parametric formula above each line on the right-hand side of the figure. So, how do we decide which line "best" fits the data that we see in our scatter plot of X_i and Y_i values? Because we are interested in explaining our dependent variable, we want our residual values, $\hat{u}_i$, which are vertical distances between each Y_i and the corresponding $\hat{Y}_i$, to be as

---

[4] By "straight line," we mean a line with a single slope that does not change as we move from left to right in our figure.

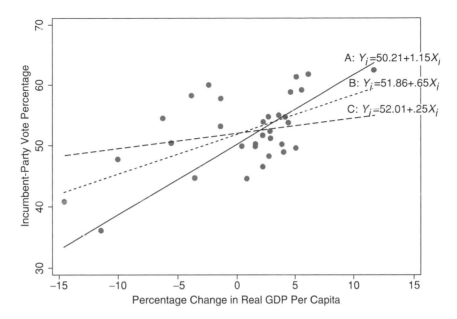

Figure 9.2. Three possible lines.

small as possible. But, because these vertical distances come in both positive and negative values, we cannot just add them up for each line and have a good summary of the "fit" between each line and our data.[5]

So we need a method of assessing the fit of each line in which the positive and negative residuals do not cancel each other out. One possibility is to add together the absolute value of the residuals for each line:

$$\sum_{i=1}^{n} |\hat{u}_i|.$$

Another possibility is to add together the squared value of the residuals for each line:

$$\sum_{i=1}^{n} \hat{u}_i^2.$$

With either choice, we want to choose the line that has the smallest total value. Table 9.1 presents these calculations for the three lines in Figure 9.2.

From both calculations, we can see that line B does a better job of fitting the data than lines A and C. Although the absolute-value calculation is just as valid as the squared residual calculation, statisticians have tended to prefer the latter (both methods identify the same line as being "best"). Thus

---

[5] Initially, we might think that we would want to minimize the sum of our residuals. But the line that minimizes the sum of the residuals is actually a flat line parallel to the x-axis. Such a line does not help us to explain the relationship between X and Y.

Table 9.1. Measures of total residuals for three different lines

Line	Parametric formula	$\sum_{i=1}^{n} \lvert \hat{u}_i \rvert$	$\sum_{i=1}^{n} \hat{u}_i^2$
A	$Y = 50.21 + 1.15X_i$	141.46	1028.11
B	$Y = 51.86 + 0.65X_i$	128.61	736.46
C	$Y = 52.01 + 0.25X_i$	137.69	891.70

we draw a line that minimizes the sum of the *squared* residuals $\sum_{i=1}^{n} \hat{u}_i^2$. This technique for estimating the parameters of a regression model is known as **ordinary least-squares** (OLS) regression. For a two-variable OLS regression, the formulae for the parameter estimates of the line that meet this criterion are[6]

$$\hat{\beta} = \frac{\sum_{i=1}^{n}(X_i - \bar{X})(Y_i - \bar{Y})}{\sum_{i=1}^{n}(X_i - \bar{X})^2},$$

$$\hat{\alpha} = \bar{Y} - \hat{\beta}\bar{X}.$$

If we examine the formula for $\hat{\beta}$, we can see that the numerator is the same as the numerator for calculating the covariance between X and Y. Thus the logic of how each case contributes to this formula, as displayed in Figure 9.2, is the same. The denominator in the formula for $\hat{\beta}$ is the sum of squared deviations of the X_i values from the mean value of X ($\bar{X}$). Thus, for a given covariance between X and Y, the more (less) spread out X is, the less (more) steep the estimated slope of the regression line.

One of the mathematical properties of OLS regression is that the line produced by the parameter estimates goes through the sample mean values of X and Y. This makes the estimation of $\hat{\alpha}$ fairly simple. If we start out at the point defined by the mean value of X and the mean value of Y and then use the estimated slope ($\hat{\beta}$) to draw a line, the value of X where Y equals zero is $\hat{\alpha}$. Figure 9.3 shows the OLS regression line through the scatter plot of data. We can see from this figure that the OLS regression line passes through the point where the line depicting the mean value of X meets the line depicting the mean value of Y.

Using the data presented in Table 8.11 in the preceding formulae, we have calculated $\hat{\alpha} = 51.86$ and $\hat{\beta} = 0.65$, making our sample regression line formula $Y = 51.86 + 0.65X$. If we think about what this tells us about politics, we first need to remember that Y is the incumbent party's share of the major-party vote and X is the real per capita growth in GDP. So, if

---

[6] The formulae for OLS parameter estimates come from setting the sum of squared residuals equal to zero and using differential calculus to solve for the values of $\hat{\beta}$ and $\hat{\alpha}$.

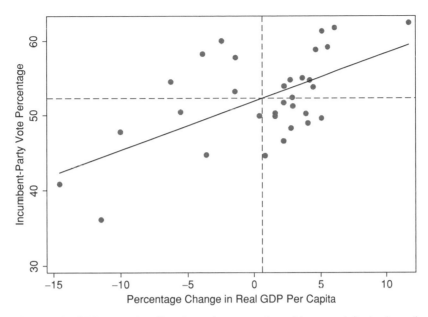

Figure 9.3. OLS regression line through scatter plot with mean-delimited quadrants.

our measure of growth equals zero, we would expect the incumbent party to obtain 51.86% of the vote. If growth is not equal to zero, we multiply the value of growth by 0.65 and add (or subtract, if growth is negative) the result to 51.86 to obtain our best guess of the value of vote. Moving to the right or the left along our sample regression line in Figure 9.3 means that we are increasing or decreasing the value of growth. For each right–left movement, we see a corresponding rise or decline in the value of the expected level of incumbent vote. We can tell from Figure 9.3 that there are points that lie above and below our regression line. We therefore know that our model does not perfectly fit the real world. In the next section we discuss a series of inferences that we can make about the uncertainty associated with our sample regression model.

9.4 MEASURING OUR UNCERTAINTY ABOUT THE OLS REGRESSION LINE

As we have seen in Chapters 7 and 8, inferences about the underlying population of interest from sample data are made with varying degrees of uncertainty. In Chapter 8 we discussed the role of p-values in expressing this uncertainty. With an OLS regression model, we have several different ways in which to measure our uncertainty. We discuss these measures in terms of the overall fit between X and Y first and then discuss the uncertainty about individual parameters. Our uncertainty about individual parameters is used

```
. reg VOTE GROWTH
```

Source	SS	df	MS			
Model	406.285326	1	406.285326			
Residual	736.446506	30	24.5482169			
Total	1142.73183	31	36.8623172			

Number of obs	=	32
F(1, 30)	=	16.55
Prob > F	=	0.0003
R-squared	=	0.3555
Adj R-squared	=	0.3341
Root MSE	=	4.9546

VOTE	Coef.	std. Err.	t	P>|t|	[95% Conf. Interval]	
GROWTH	0.6535869	.1606563	4.07	0.000	.325483	.9816909
_Cons	51.85977	.8816524	58.82	0.000	50.05919	53.66034

Figure 9.4. Stata results for two-variable regression model of VOTE $= \alpha + \beta \times$ GROWTH.

in the testing of our hypotheses. Throughout this discussion, we refer to our example of fitting a regression line to our data on U.S. presidential elections in order to test the theory of economic voting. Numerical results from Stata for this model are displayed in Figure 9.4. These numerical results can be partitioned into three separate areas. The table in the upper-left corner of Figure 9.4 gives us measures of the variation in our model. The set of statistics listed in the upper-right corner of Figure 9.4 gives us a set summary statistics about the entire model. Across the bottom of Figure 9.4 we get a table of statistics on the model's parameter estimates. The name of the dependent variable, "VOTE," is displayed at the top of this table. Underneath we see the name of our independent variable, "GROWTH," and "cons," which is short for "constant" (another name for the y-intercept term), which we also know as $\hat{\alpha}$. Moving to the right in the table at the bottom of Figure 9.4, we see that the next column heading here is "Coef.," which is short for "coefficient," which is another name for parameter estimate. In this column we see the values of $\hat{\beta}$ and $\hat{\alpha}$, which are 0.65 and 51.86 when we round these results to the second decimal place.[7]

[7] The choice of how many decimal places to report should be decided based on the value of the dependent variable. In this case, because our dependent variable is a vote percentage, we have chosen the second decimal place. Political scientists usually do not report election results beyond the first two decimal places.

9.4.1 Goodness-of-Fit: Root Mean-Squared Error

Measures of the overall fit between a regression model and the dependent variable are called goodness-of-fit measures. One of the most intuitive of these measures (despite its name) is **root mean-squared error** (MSE). This statistic is sometimes referred to as the standard error of the regression model. It provides a measure of the average accuracy of the model in the metric of the dependent variable. This statistic ("Root MSE" in Figure 9.4) is calculated as

$$\text{root MSE} = \sqrt{\frac{\sum_{i=1}^{n} \hat{u}_i^2}{n}}.$$

The squaring and then taking the square root of the quantities in this formula are done to adjust for the fact that some of our residuals will be positive (points for which Y_i is above the regression line) and some will be negative (points for which Y_i is below the regression line). Once we realize this, we can see that this statistic is basically the average distance between the data points and the regression line.

From the numeric results depicted in Figure 9.4, we can see that the root MSE for our two-variable model of incumbent-party vote is 4.95. This value is found on the sixth line of the column of results on the right-hand side of Figure 9.4. It indicates that, on average, our model is off by 4.95 points in predicting the percentage of the incumbent party's share of the major-party vote. It is worth emphasizing that the root MSE is always expressed in terms of the metric in which the dependent variable is measured. The only reason why this particular value corresponds to a percentage is because the metric of the dependent variable is vote percentage.

9.4.2 Goodness-of-Fit: R-Squared Statistic

Another popular indicator of the model's goodness-of-fit is the **R-squared statistic** (typically written as R^2). The R^2 statistic ranges between zero and one, indicating the proportion of the variation in the dependent variable that is accounted for by the model. The basic idea of the R^2 statistic is shown in Figure 9.5, which is a Venn diagram depiction of variation in X and Y as well as covariation between X and Y. The idea behind this diagram is that we are depicting variation in each variable with a circle. The larger the circle, the larger the variation. In this figure, the variation in Y consists of two areas, a and b, and variation in X consists of areas b and c. Area a represents variation in Y that is not related to variation in X, and area b represents covariation between X and Y. In a two-variable regression model, area a is the residual or stochastic variation in Y. The R^2

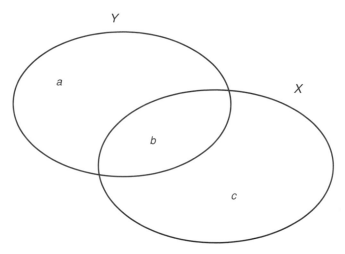

Figure 9.5. Venn diagram of variance and covariance for X and Y.

statistic is equal to area b over the total variation in Y, which is equal to the sum of areas a and b. Thus smaller values of area a and larger values of area b lead to a larger R^2 statistic. The formula for total variation in Y (areas a and b in Figure 9.5), also known as the total sum of squares (TSS), is

$$\text{TSS} = \sum_{i=1}^{n}(Y_i - \bar{Y})^2.$$

The formula for the residual variation in Y, area a that is not accounted for by X, called the residual sum of squares (RSS), is

$$\text{RSS} = \sum_{i=1}^{n}\hat{u}_i^2.$$

Once we have these two quantities, we can calculate the R^2 statistic as

$$R^2 = 1 - \frac{\text{RSS}}{\text{TSS}}.$$

The formula for the other part of TSS that is not the RSS, called the model sum of squares (MSS), is

$$\text{MSS} = \sum_{i=1}^{n}(\hat{Y}_i - \bar{Y})^2.$$

This can also be used to calculate R^2 as

$$R^2 = \frac{\text{MSS}}{\text{TSS}}.$$

From the numeric results depicted in Figure 9.4, we can see that the R^2 statistic for our two-variable model of incumbent-party vote is .355. This number appears on the fourth line of the column of results on the right-hand side of Figure 9.4. It indicates that our model accounts for about 36% of the variation in the dependent variable. We can also see in Figure 9.4 the values for the MSS, RSS, and TSS that are presented under the column labeled "SS" in the table in the upper-left-hand corner of Figure 9.4.

9.4.3   Is That a "Good" Goodness-of-Fit?

A logical question to ask when we see a measure of a model's goodness-of-fit is "What is a good or bad value for the root MSE and/or R^2?" This is not an easy question to answer. In part, the answer depends on what you are trying to do with the model. If you are trying to predict election outcomes, saying that you can predict the outcome with a typical error of 4.95 may not seem very good. After all, most presidential elections are fairly close and, in the scheme of things, 4.95% is a lot of votes. In fact, we can see that, in 12 of the 32 elections that we are looking at, the winning margin was less than 4.95%, making over one-third of our sample of elections too close to call with this model.[8] On the other hand, looking at this another way, we can say that we are able to come this close and, in terms of R^2, explain almost 36% of the variation in incumbent vote from 1880 to 2004 with just one measure of the economy. When we start to think of all of the different campaign strategies, personalities, scandals, wars, and everything else that is not in this simple model, this level of accuracy is rather impressive. In fact, we would suggest that this tells us something pretty remarkable about politics in the United States – the economy is massively important.

9.4.4   Uncertainty about Individual Components of the Sample Regression Model

Before we go through this subsection, we want to warn you that there are a lot of formulae in it. To use a familiar metaphor, as you go through the formulae in this subsection it is important to focus on the contours of the forest and not to get caught up in the details of the many trees that we will see along the way. Instead of memorizing each formula, concentrate on what makes the overall values generated by these equations larger or smaller.

A crucial part of the uncertainty in OLS regression models is the degree of uncertainty about individual estimates of population parameter values

---

[8] We can get this by calculating VOTE (100 – VOTE) for the values in Table 8.11.

from the sample regression model. We can use the same logic that we discussed in Chapter 7 for making inferences from sample values about population values for each of the individual parameters in a sample regression model.

One estimate that factors into the calculations of our uncertainty about each of the population parameters is the estimated variance of the population stochastic component, u_i. This unseen variance, σ^2, is estimated from the residuals ($\hat{u}_i$) after the parameters for the sample regression model have been estimated by the following formula:

$$\hat{\sigma}^2 = \frac{\sum_{i=1}^{n} \hat{u}_i^2}{n-2}.$$

Looking at this formula, we can see two components that play a role in determining the magnitude of this estimate. The first component comes from the individual residual values ($\hat{u}_i$). Remember that these values (calculated as $\hat{u}_i = Y_i - \hat{Y}_i$) are the vertical distance between each observed Y_i value and the regression line. The larger these values are, the further the individual cases are from the regression line. The second component of this formula comes from n, the sample size. By now, you should be familiar with the idea that the larger the sample size, the smaller the variance of the estimate. This is the case with our formula for $\hat{\sigma}^2$.

Once we have estimated $\hat{\sigma}^2$, the variance and standard errors for the slope parameter estimate ($\hat{\beta}$) are then estimated from the following formulae:

$$\text{var}(\hat{\beta}) = \frac{\hat{\sigma}^2}{\sum_{i=1}^{n}(X_i - \bar{X})^2},$$

$$\text{se}(\hat{\beta}) = \sqrt{\text{var}(\hat{\beta})} = \frac{\hat{\sigma}}{\sqrt{\sum_{i=1}^{n}(X_i - \bar{X})^2}}.$$

Both of these formulae can be broken into two components that determine their magnitude. In the numerator, we find $\hat{\sigma}$ values. So the larger these values are, the larger will be the variance and standard error of the slope parameter estimate. This makes sense, because the farther the points representing our data are from the regression line, the less confidence we will have in the value of the slope. If we look at the denominator in this equation, we see the term $\sum_{i=1}^{n}(X_i - \bar{X})^2$, which is a measure of the variation of the X_i values around their mean ($\bar{X}$). The greater this variation, the smaller will be the variance and standard error of the slope parameter estimate. This is an important property; in real-world terms it means that the more variation we have in X, the more precisely we will be able to estimate the relationship between X and Y.

The variance and standard errors for the intercept parameter estimate ($\hat{\alpha}$) are then estimated from the following formulae:

$$\text{var}(\hat{\alpha}) = \frac{\hat{\sigma}^2 \sum_{i=1}^{n} X_i^2}{n \sum_{i=1}^{n} (X_i - \bar{X})^2},$$

$$\text{se}(\hat{\alpha}) = \sqrt{\text{var}(\hat{\alpha})} = \sqrt{\frac{\hat{\sigma}^2 \sum_{i=1}^{n} X_i^2}{n \sum_{i=1}^{n} (X_i - \bar{X})^2}}.$$

The logic for taking apart the components of these formulae is slightly more complicated because we can see that the sum of the X_i values squared appears in the numerator. We can see, however, that the denominator contains the measure of the variation of the X_i values around their mean ($\bar{X}$) multiplied by n, the number of cases. Thus the same basic logic holds for these terms: The larger the $\hat{u}_i$ values are, the larger will be the variance and standard error of the intercept parameter estimate; and the larger the variation of the X_i values around their mean, the smaller will be the variance and standard error of the intercept parameter estimate.

Less obvious – but nevertheless true – from the preceding formulae is the fact that larger sample sizes will also produce smaller standard errors.[9] So, just as we learned about the effects of sample size when calculating the standard error of the mean in Chapter 7, there is an identical effect here. Larger sample sizes will, other things being equal, produce smaller standard errors of our estimated regression coefficients

9.4.5   Confidence Intervals about Parameter Estimates

In Chapter 7 we discussed how we use the normal distribution (supported by the central limit theorem) to estimate confidence intervals for the unseen population mean from sample data. We go through the same logical steps to estimate confidence intervals for the unseen parameters from the population regression model by using the results from the sample regression model. The formulae for estimating confidence intervals are

$$\hat{\beta} \pm [t \times \text{se}(\hat{\beta})],$$

$$\hat{\alpha} \pm [t \times \text{se}(\hat{\alpha})],$$

---

[9] It is true because the numerator of the expression contains $\hat{\sigma}$, which, as seen further previously, has the sample size n in its denominator.

where the value for t is determined from the t-table in Appendix B. So, for instance, if we want to calculate a 95% confidence interval,[10] this means that we are looking down the column for 0.025. Once we have determined the appropriate column, we select our row based on the number of degrees of freedom. The number of degrees of freedom for this t-test is equal to the number of observations (n) minus the number of parameters estimated (k). In the case of the regression model presented in Figure 9.4, $n = 32$ and $k = 2$, so our degrees of freedom equal 30. Looking down the column for 0.025 and across the row for 30, we can see that $t = 2.042$. Thus our 95% confidence intervals are

$$\hat{\beta} \pm [t \times se(\hat{\beta})] = 0.654 \pm (2.042 \times 0.161) = 0.325 \text{ to } 0.982,$$
$$\hat{\alpha} \pm [t \times se(\hat{\alpha})] = 51.86 \pm (2.042 \times 0.88) = 50.06 \text{ to } 53.66.$$

These values are displayed in the lower right-hand corner of the table at the bottom of Figure 9.4.

9.4.6 Hypothesis Testing: Overview

The traditional approach to hypothesis testing with OLS regression is that we specify a null hypothesis and an **alternative hypothesis** and then compare the two. Although we can test hypotheses about either the slope or the intercept parameter, we are usually more concerned with tests about the slope parameter. In particular, we are usually concerned with testing the hypothesis that the population slope parameter is equal to zero. The logic of this hypothesis test corresponds closely with the logic of the bivariate hypothesis tests introduced in Chapter 8. We observe a sample slope parameter, which is an estimate of the population slope. Then, from the value of this parameter estimate, the confidence interval around it, and the size of our sample, we evaluate how likely it is that we observe this sample slope if the true but unobserved population slope is equal to zero. If the answer is "very likely," then we conclude that the population slope is equal to zero.

To understand why we so often focus on a slope value of zero, think about what this corresponds to in the formula for a line. Remember that the slope is the change in Y from a one-unit increase in X. If that change is equal to zero, then there is no covariation between X and Y, and we have failed to clear our third causal hurdle.

[10] To understand this, think back to Chapter 7, where we introduced confidence intervals. A 95% confidence interval would mean that would leave a total of 5% in the tails. Because there are two tails, we are going to use the 0.025 column.

These types of tests are either one or two tailed. Most statistical computer programs report the results from two-tailed hypothesis tests that the parameter in question is not equal to zero. Despite this, many political science theories are more appropriately translated into one-tailed hypothesis tests, which are sometimes referred to as "directional" hypothesis tests. We review both types of hypothesis tests with the example regression from Figure 9.4.

9.4.7 Two-Tailed Hypothesis Tests

The most common form of statistical hypothesis tests about the parameters from an OLS regression model is a two-tailed hypothesis test that the slope parameter is equal to zero. It is expressed as

$$H_0 : \beta = 0,$$

$$H_1 : \beta \neq 0,$$

where H_0 is the null hypothesis and H_1 is the alternative hypothesis. Note that these two rival hypotheses are expressed in terms of the slope parameter from the population regression model. To test which of these two hypotheses is supported, we calculate a *t*-ratio in which β is set equal to the value specified in the null hypothesis (in this case zero because $H_0 : \beta = 0$), which we represent as β^*:

$$t_{n-k} = \frac{\hat{\beta} - \beta^*}{\text{se}(\hat{\beta})}.$$

For the slope parameter in the two-variable regression model presented in Figure 9.4, we can calculate this as

$$t_{30} = \frac{\hat{\beta} - \beta^*}{\text{se}(\hat{\beta})} = \frac{0.654 - 0}{0.161} = 4.07.$$

From what we have seen in previous chapters, we can tell that this *t*-ratio is quite large. Remember that a typical standard for statistical significance in the social sciences is when the *p*-value is less than .05. If we look across the row for degrees of freedom equal to 30 in Appendix B, we can see that, to have a *p*-value of less than .05, we would need a *t*-ratio of 2.042 or larger. We clearly have exceeded this standard.[11] In fact, if we look at the far-right-hand column in Appendix B for 30 degrees of freedom, we can see that this *t*-ratio exceeds the value for *t* needed for *p* to be less than .002. This means that it is extremely unlikely that H_0 is the case, which

---

[11] Because this is a two-tailed hypothesis test, for the standard of $p < .05$ we need to look down the column labeled ".025."

in turn greatly increases our confidence in H_1. If we look at the table at the bottom of Figure 9.4, we can see that the t-ratio and resulting p-value for this hypothesis test are presented in the fourth and fifth columns of the GROWTH row. It is worth noting that although the reported p-value is .000, this does not mean that the probability of the null hypothesis being the case is actually equal to zero. Instead, this means that it is a very small number that gets rounded to zero when we report it to three decimal places.

The exact same logic is used to test hypotheses about the y-intercept parameter. The formula for this t-ratio is

$$t_{n-k} = \frac{\hat{\alpha} - \alpha^*}{se(\hat{\alpha})}.$$

In Figure 9.4 we see the calculation for the following null hypothesis and alternative:

$$H_0 : \alpha = 0,$$
$$H_1 : \alpha \neq 0.$$

The resulting t-ratio is a whopping 58.82! This makes sense when we think about this quantity in real-world terms. Remember that the y-intercept is the expected value of the dependent variable Y when the independent variable X is equal to zero. In our model, this means we want to know the expected value of incumbent-party vote when growth equals zero. Even when the economy is shrinking, there are always going to be some diehard partisans who will vote for the incumbent party. Thus it makes sense that the null hypothesis $H_0 : \alpha = 0$ would be pretty easy to reject.

Perhaps a more interesting null hypothesis is that the incumbents would still obtain 50% of the vote if growth were equal to zero. In this case,

$$H_0 : \alpha = 50,$$
$$H_1 : \alpha \neq 50.$$

The corresponding t-ratio is calculated as

$$t_{30} = \frac{\hat{\alpha} - \alpha^*}{se(\hat{\alpha})} = \frac{51.86 - 50}{0.88} = 2.11.$$

Looking at the row for degrees of freedom equal to 30, we can see that this t-ratio is just larger than 2.042, which is the value for $p < .05$ but not as large as the 2.457 value for $p < .02$. With a more detailed t-table or a computer, we could calculate the exact p-value for this hypothesis test. But, from this table, we can reject the null hypothesis ($H_0: \alpha = 50$) with a fair amount of confidence.

9.4.8   The Relationship between Confidence Intervals and Two-Tailed Hypothesis Tests

In the previous three subsections, we introduced confidence intervals and hypothesis tests as two of the ways for making inferences about the parameters of the population regression model from our sample regression model. These two methods for making inferences are mathematically related to each other. We can tell this because they each rely on the t-table. The relationship between the two is such that, if the 95% confidence interval does not include a particular value, then the null hypothesis that the population parameter equals that value (a two-tailed hypothesis test) will have a p-value smaller than .05. We can see this for each of the three hypothesis tests that we discussed in the section on two-tailed hypothesis tests:

- Because the 95% confidence interval for our slope parameter does not include 0, the p-value for the hypothesis test that $\beta = 0$ is less than .05.
- Because the 95% confidence interval for our intercept parameter does not include 0, the p-value for the hypothesis test that $\alpha = 0$ is less than .05.
- Because the 95% confidence interval for our intercept parameter does not include 50, the p-value for the hypothesis test that $\alpha = 50$ is less than .05.

9.4.9   One-Tailed Hypothesis Tests

As we pointed out in previous sections, the most common form of statistical hypothesis tests about the parameters from an OLS regression model is a two-tailed hypothesis test that the slope parameter is equal to zero. That this is the most common test is somewhat of a fluke. By default, most statistical computer programs report the results of this hypothesis test. In reality, though, most political science hypotheses are that a parameter is either positive or negative and not just that the parameter is different from zero. This is what we call a **directional hypothesis**. Consider, for instance, the theory of economic voting and how we would translate it into a hypothesis about the slope parameter in our current example. Our theory is that the *better* the economy is performing, the *higher* will be the vote percentage for the incumbent-party candidate. In other words, we expect to see a positive relationship between economic growth and the incumbent-party vote percentage, meaning that we expect β to be greater than zero.

When our theory leads to such a directional hypothesis, it is expressed as

$$H_0 : \beta \leq 0,$$
$$H_1 : \beta > 0,$$

where H_0 is the null hypothesis and H_1 is the alternative hypothesis. As was the case with the two-tailed test, these two rival hypotheses are expressed in terms of the slope parameter from the population regression model. To test which of these two hypotheses is supported, we calculate a t-ratio where β is set equal to the value specified in the null hypothesis[12] (in this case zero because $H_0 : \beta \leq 0$), which we represent as β^*:

$$t_{n-k} = \frac{\hat{\beta} - \beta^*}{\text{se}(\hat{\beta})}.$$

For the slope parameter in the two-variable regression model presented in Figure 9.4, we can calculate this as

$$t_{30} = \frac{\hat{\beta} - \beta^*}{\text{se}(\hat{\beta})} = \frac{0.654 - 0}{0.161} = 4.07.$$

Do these calculations look familiar to you? They should, because this t-ratio is calculated exactly the same way that the t-ratio for the two-sided hypothesis about this parameter was calculated. The difference comes in how we use the t-table in Appendix B to arrive at the appropriate p-value for this hypothesis test. Because this is a one-tailed hypothesis test, we use the column labeled ".05" instead of the column labeled ".025" to assess whether we have achieved a t-ratio such that $p < .05$. In other words, we would need a t-ratio of only 1.697 to achieve this level of significance for a one-tailed hypothesis test. For a two-tailed hypothesis test, we needed a t-ratio of 2.047.

We can see from this example and from the t-table that, when we have a directional hypothesis, we can more easily reject a null hypothesis. One of the quirks of political science research is that, even when they have directional hypotheses, researchers often report the results of two-tailed hypothesis tests.

---

[12] We choose 0 when the null hypothesis is $H_0 : \beta \leq 0$ because this is the critical value for the null hypothesis. Under this null hypothesis, zero is the threshold, and evidence that β is equal to any value less than or equal to zero is supportive of this null hypothesis.

9.5 ASSUMPTIONS, MORE ASSUMPTIONS, AND MINIMAL MATHEMATICAL REQUIREMENTS

If assumptions were water, you'd need an umbrella right now. Any time that you estimate a regression model, you are implicitly making a large set of assumptions about the unseen population model. In this section, we break these assumptions into assumptions about the population stochastic component and assumptions about our model specification. In addition, there are some minimal mathematical requirements that must be met before a regression model can be estimated. In this final section we list these assumptions and requirements and briefly discuss them as they apply to our working example of a two-variable regression model of the impact of economic growth on incumbent-party vote. We will provide more elaborate discussions in later chapters.

9.5.1 Assumptions about the Population Stochastic Component

The most important assumptions about the population stochastic component u_i are about its distribution. These can be summarized as

$$u_i \sim N(0, \sigma^2),$$

which means that we assume that u_i is distributed normally ($\sim N$) with the mean equal to zero and the variance[13] equal to σ^2. This compact mathematical statement contains three of the five assumptions that we make about the population stochastic component any time we estimate a regression model. We now go over each one separately.

u_i Is Normally Distributed

The assumption that u_i is normally distributed allows us to use the t-table to make probabilistic inferences about the population regression model from the sample regression model. The main justification for this assumption is the central limit theorem that we discussed in Chapter 7.

$E(u_i) = 0$: No Bias

The assumption that u_i has a mean or expected value equal to zero is also known as the assumption of zero bias. Consider what it would mean if

---

[13] Strictly speaking we do not need to make all of these assumptions to estimate the parameters of an OLS model. But we do need to make all of these assumptions to interpret the results from an OLS model in the standard fashion.

there was a case for which $E(u_i) \neq 0$. In other words, this would be a case for which we would *expect* our regression model to be off. If we have cases like this, we would essentially be ignoring some theoretical insight that we have about the underlying causes of Y. Remember, this term is supposed to be random. If $E(u_i) \neq 0$, then there must be some nonrandom component to this term. It is important to note here that we do not expect *all* of our u_i values to equal zero because we know that some of our cases will fall above and below the regression line. But this assumption means that our best guess or expected value for each individual u_i value is zero.

If we think about the example in this chapter, this assumption means that we do not have any particular cases for which we expect our model, with economic growth as the independent variable, to overpredict or under-predict the value of the incumbent-party vote percentage in any particular election. If, on the other hand, we had some expectation along these lines, we would not be able to make this assumption. Say, for instance, that we expected that during times of war the incumbent party would fare better than we would expect them to fare based on the economy. Under these circumstances, we would not be able to make this assumption. The solution to this problem would be to include another independent variable in our model that measured whether or not the nation was at war at the time of each election. Once we control for all such potential sources of bias, we can feel comfortable making this assumption. The inclusion of additional independent variables is the main subject covered in Chapter 10.

u_i Has Variance σ^2: Homoscedasticity

The assumption that u_i has variance equal to σ^2 seems pretty straightforward. But, because this notation for variance does not contain an i subscript, it means that the variance for every case in the underlying population is assumed to be the same. The word for describing this situation is "homoscedasticity," which means "uniform error variance." If this assumption does not hold, we have a situation in which the variance of u_i is σ_i^2 known as "heteroscedasticity," which means "unequal error variance." When we have heteroscedasticity, our regression model fits some of the cases in the population better than others. This can potentially cause us problems when we are estimating confidence intervals and testing hypotheses.

In our example for this chapter, this assumption would be violated if, for some reason, some elections were harder than others for our model to predict. In this case, our model would be heteroscedastic. It could, for instance, be the case that elections that were held after political debates became televised are harder to predict with our model in which the only independent variable is economic performance. Under these circumstances, the assumption of homoscedasticity would not be reasonable.

No Autocorrelation

We also assume that there is no autocorrelation. Autocorrelation occurs when the stochastic terms for any two or more cases are systematically related to each other. This clearly cuts against the grain of the idea that these terms are stochastic or random. Formally, we express this assumption as

$$\text{cov}_{u_i, u_j} = 0 \; \forall \; i \neq j;$$

in words, this means that the covariance between the population error terms u_i and u_j is equal to zero for all i not equal to j (for any two unique cases).

The most common form of autocorrelation occurs in regression models of time-series data. As we discussed in Chapter 4, time-series data involve measurement of the relevant variables across time for a single spatial unit. In our example for this chapter, we are using measures of economic growth and incumbent-party vote percentage measured every 4 years for the United States. If, for some reason, the error terms for adjacent pairs of elections were correlated, we would have autocorrelation.

X Values Are Measured Without Error

At first, the assumption that X values are measured without error may seem to be out of place in a listing of assumptions about the population stochastic component. But this assumption is made to greatly simplify inferences that we make about our population regression model from our sample regression model. By assuming that X is measured without error, we are assuming that any variability from our regression line is due to the stochastic component u_i and not to measurement problems in X. To put it another way, if X also had a stochastic component, we would need to model X before we could model Y, and that would substantially complicate matters.

With just about any regression model that we estimate with real-world data, we will likely be pretty uncomfortable with this assumption. In the example for this chapter, we are assuming that we have exactly correct measures of the percentage change in real GDP per capita from 1880 to 2004. If we think a little more about this measure, we can think of all kinds of potential errors in measurement. What about illegal economic activities that are hard for the government to measure? Because this is per capita, how confident are we that the denominator in this calculation, population, is measured exactly correctly?

Despite the obvious problems with this assumption, we make it every time that we estimate an OLS model. Unless we move to considerably more complicated statistical techniques, this is an assumption that we have to live with and keep in the back of our minds as we evaluate our overall confidence in what our models tell us.

Recall from Chapter 5, when we discussed measuring our concepts of interest, that we argued that measurement is important because, if we mismeasure our variables, we may make incorrect causal inferences about the real world. This assumption should make the important lessons of that chapter crystal clear.

9.5.2   Assumptions about Our Model Specification

The assumptions about our model specification can be summarized as a single assumption that we have *the* correct model specification. We break this into two separate assumptions to highlight the range of ways in which this assumption might be violated.

No Causal Variables Left Out; No Noncausal Variables Included

This assumption means that if we specify our two-variable regression model of the relationship between X and Y there cannot be some other variable Z that also causes[14] Y. It also means that X must cause Y. In other words, this is just another way of saying that the sample regression model that we have specified *is* the true underlying population regression model.

As we have gone through the example in this chapter, we have already begun to come up with additional variables that we theorize to be causally related to our dependent variable. To comfortably make this assumption, we will need to include all such variables in our model. Adding additional independent variables to our model is the subject of Chapter 10.

Parametric Linearity

The assumption of parametric linearity is a fancy way of saying that our population parameter β for the relationship between X and Y does not

---

[14] One exception to this is the very special case in which there is a Z variable that is causally related to Y but Z is uncorrelated with X and u_i. In this case, we would still be able to get a reasonable estimate of the relationship between X and Y despite leaving Z out of our model. More on this in Chapter 10.

vary. In other words, the relationship between X and Y is the same across all values of X.

In the context of our current example, this means that we are assuming that the impact of a one-unit increase in change in real GDP per capita is the same. So moving from a value of -10 to -9 has the same effect as moving from a value of 1 to 2. In Chapter 11 we discuss some techniques for relaxing this assumption.

9.5.3   Minimal Mathematical Requirements

For a two-variable regression model, we have two minimal requirements that must be met by our sample data before we can estimate our parameters. We will add to these requirements when we expand to multiple regression models.

X Must Vary

Think about what the scatter plot of our sample data would look like if X did not vary. Basically, we would have a stack of Y values at the same point on the x-axis. The only reasonable line that we could draw through this set of points would be a straight line parallel to the y axis. Remember that our goal is to explain our dependent variable Y. Under these circumstances we would have failed miserably because any Y value would be just as good as any other given our single value of X. Thus we need some variation in X in order to estimate an OLS regression model.

n > k

To estimate a regression model, the number of cases (n) must exceed the number of parameters to be estimated (k). Thus, as a minimum, when we estimate a two-variable regression model with two parameters (α and β) we must have *at least* three cases.

9.5.4   How Can We Make All of These Assumptions?

The mathematical requirements to estimate a regression model aren't too severe, but a sensible question to ask at this point is, "How we can reasonably make all of the assumptions just listed every time that we run a regression model?" To answer this question, we refer back to the discussion in Chapter 1 of the analogy between models and maps. We *know* that all of our assumptions cannot possibly be met. We also know that we are trying to simplify complex realities. The only way that we can do this is to make a large set of unrealistic assumptions about the world. It is crucial, though, that we never lose sight of the fact that we are making these assumptions. In the next chapter we relax one of these most unrealistic assumptions made in the two-variable regression model by controlling for a second variable, Z.

CONCEPTS INTRODUCED IN THIS CHAPTER

alternative hypothesis	root mean-squared error
directional hypothesis	R-squared statistic
ordinary least-squares	sample error term
parameters	sample regression model
parameter estimates	statistical model
population error term	stochastic
population regression model	t-ratio
residual	

EXERCISES

1. Draw an X–Y axis through the middle of a 10×10 grid. The point where the X and Y lines intersect is known as the "origin" and is defined as the point at which both X and Y are equal to zero. Draw each of the following lines across the values of X from -5 to 5 and write the corresponding regression equation:

    (a) y-intercept $= 2$, slope $= 2$;
    (b) y-intercept $= -2$, slope $= 2$;
    (c) y-intercept $= 0$, slope $= -1$;
    (d) y-intercept $= 2$, slope $= -2$.

2. Estimate and interpret the results from a two-variable regression model by using your own data. Try to check the calculations made by the computer by using the formulae that we have presented in this chapter.

3. Think through the assumptions that you made when you carried out Exercise 2. Which do you feel least and most comfortable making? Explain your answers.

4. In Exercise 8 for Chapter 8, you calculated a correlation coefficient for the relationship between two continuous variables. Now, estimate a two-variable regression model for these same two variables. Produce a table of the results and write about what this table tells you about politics in the UK in 2005.

10 Multiple Regression Models I: The Basics

OVERVIEW

Despite what we have learned in the preceding chapters on hypothesis testing and statistical significance, we have not yet crossed all four of our hurdles for establishing causal relationships. Recall that all of the techniques we have learned in Chapters 8 and 9 are simply bivariate, X-and-Y-type analyses. But, to fully assess whether X causes Y, we need to control for other possible causes of Y, which we have not yet done. In this chapter, we show how multiple regression – which is an extension of the two-variable model we covered in Chapter 9 – does exactly that. We explicitly connect the formulae that we include to the key issues of research design that tie the entire book together. We also discuss some of the problems in multiple regression models when key causes of the dependent variable are omitted, which ties this chapter to the fundamental principles presented in Chapters 3 and 4.

10.1 MODELING MULTIVARIATE REALITY

From the very outset of this book, we have emphasized that almost all interesting phenomena in social reality have more than one cause. And yet most of our theories are simply bivariate in nature.

We have shown you (in Chapter 4) that there are distinct methods for dealing with the nature of reality in our designs for social research. If we are fortunate enough to be able to conduct an experiment, then the process of randomly assigning our participants to treatment groups will automatically "control for" those other possible causes that are not a part of our theory.

But in observational research – which represents the vast majority of political science research – there is no automatic control for the other possible causes of our dependent variable; we have to control for them statistically. The main way that social scientists accomplish this is through multiple regression. The math in this model is an extension of the math involved in the two-variable regression model you just learned in Chapter 9.

10.2   THE POPULATION REGRESSION FUNCTION

We can generalize the population regression model that we learned in Chapter 9,

$$\text{bivariate population regression model: } Y_i = \alpha + \beta X_i + u_i,$$

to include more than one systematic cause of Y, which we have been calling Z throughout this book:

$$\text{multiple population regression model: } Y_i = \alpha + \beta_1 X_i + \beta_2 Z_i + u_i.$$

The interpretation of the slope coefficients in the three-variable model is similar to interpreting bivariate coefficients, with one very important difference. In both, the coefficient in front of the variable X (β in the two-variable model, β_1 in the multiple regression model) represents the "rise-over-run" effect of X on Y. In the multiple regression case, though, β_1 actually represents the effect of X on Y while holding constant the effects of Z. If this distinction sounds important, it is. We show how these differences arise in the next section.

10.3   FROM TWO-VARIABLE TO MULTIPLE REGRESSION

Recall from Chapter 9 that the formula for a two-variable regression line (in a sample) is

$$Y_i = \hat{\alpha} + \hat{\beta} X_i + \hat{u}_i.$$

And recall that, to understand the nature of the effect that X has on Y, the estimated coefficient $\hat{\beta}$ tells us, on average, how many units of change in Y we should expect given a one-unit increase in X. The formula for $\hat{\beta}$ in the two-variable model, as we learned in Chapter 9, is

$$\hat{\beta} = \frac{\sum_{i=1}^{n}(X_i - \bar{X})(Y_i - \bar{Y})}{\sum_{i=1}^{n}(X_i - \bar{X})^2}.$$

Given that our goal is to control for the effects of some third variable, Z, how exactly is that accomplished in regression equations? If a scatter plot in two dimensions (X and Y) leaves the formula for a *line*, then adding a third dimension leaves the formula for a *plane*. And the formula for that plane is

$$Y_i = \hat{\alpha} + \hat{\beta}_1 X_i + \hat{\beta}_2 Z_i.$$

That might seem deceptively simple. A formula representing a plane simply adds the additional $\hat{\beta}_2 Z_i$ term to the formula for a line.[1]

Pay attention to how the notation has changed. In the two-variable formula for a line, there were no numeric subscripts below the β coefficient – because, well, there was only one of them. But now we have two independent variables, X and Z, that help to explain the variation in Y, and therefore we have two different coefficients β, and so we subscript them β_1 and β_2 to be clear that the values of these two effects are different from one another.[2]

The key message from this chapter is that, in the preceding formula, the coefficient β_1 represents more than the effect of X on Y; in the multiple regression formula, it represents *the effect of X on Y while controlling for the effect of Z*. Simultaneously, the coefficient β_2 represents *the effect of Z on Y while controlling for the effect of X*. And in observational research, this is the key to crossing our fourth causal hurdle that we introduced all the way back in Chapter 3.

How is it the case that the coefficient for β_1 actually controls for Z? After all, β_1 is not connected to Z in the formula; it is, quite obviously, connected to X. The first thing to realize here is that the preceding multiple regression formula for β_1 is different from the two-variable formula for β from Chapter 9. (We'll get to the formula shortly.) The key consequence of this is that the value of β derived from the two-variable formula, representing the effect of X on Y, will almost always be different – perhaps only trivially different, or perhaps wildly different – from the value of β_1 derived from the multiple regression formula, representing the effect of X on Y while controlling for the effects of Z.

But how does β_1 control for the effects of Z? Let's assume that X and Z are correlated. They need not be related in a *causal* sense, and they need

---

[1] All of the subsequent math about adding one more independent variable, Z, generalizes quite easily to adding still more independent variables. We use the three-variable case for ease of illustration.

[2] In many other textbooks on regression analysis, just as we distinguish between β_1 and β_2, the authors choose to label their independent variables X_1, X_2, and so forth. We have consistently used the notation of X, Y, and Z to emphasize the concept of controlling for other variables while examining the relationship between an independent and a dependent variable of theoretical interest. Therefore we will stick with this notation throughout this chapter.

not be related *strongly*. They simply have to be related to one another – that is, for this example, their covariance is not exactly equal to zero. Now, assuming that they are related somehow, we can write their relationship just like that of a two-variable regression model:

$$X_i = \hat{\alpha}' + \hat{\beta}' Z_i + \hat{e}_i.$$

Note some notational differences here. Instead of the parameters $\hat{\alpha}$ and $\hat{\beta}$, we are calling the estimated parameters $\hat{\alpha}'$ and $\hat{\beta}'$ just so you are aware that their values will be different from the $\hat{\alpha}$ and $\hat{\beta}$ estimates in previous equations. And note also that the residuals, which we labeled u_i in previous equations, are now labeled e_i here.

If we use Z to predict X, then the predicted value of X (or $\hat{X}$) based on Z is simply

$$\hat{X}_i = \hat{\alpha}' + \hat{\beta}' Z_i,$$

which is just the preceding equation, but without the error term, because it is expected (on average) to be zero. Now, we can just substitute the left-hand side of the preceding equation into the previous equation and get

$$X_i = \hat{X}_i + \hat{e}_i$$

or, equivalently,

$$\hat{e}_i = X_i - \hat{X}_i.$$

These $\hat{e}_i$, then, are the exact equivalents of the residuals from the two-variable regression of Y on X that you learned from Chapter 9. So their interpretation is identical, too. That being the case, the $\hat{e}_i$ are the portion of the variation in X that Z cannot explain. (The portion of X that Z *can* explain is the predicted portion – the $\hat{X}_i$.)

So what have we done here? We have just documented the relationship between Z and X and partitioned the variation in X into two parts – the portion that Z *can* explain (the $\hat{X}_i$) and the portion that Z *cannot* explain (the $\hat{e}_i$). Hold this thought.

We can do the exact same thing for the relationship between Z and Y that we just did for the relationship between Z and X. The process will look quite similar, with a bit of different notation to distinguish the processes. So we can model Y as a function of Z in the following way:

$$Y_i = \hat{\alpha}^* + \hat{\beta}^* Z_i + \hat{v}_i.$$

Here, the estimated slope is $\hat{\beta}^*$ and the error term is represented by $\hat{v}_i$.

Just as we did with Z and X, if we use Z to predict Y, then the predicted value of Y (or $\hat{Y}$) (which we will label $\hat{Y}^*$) based on Z is simply

$$\hat{Y}_i^* = \hat{\alpha}^* + \hat{\beta}^* Z_i,$$

which, as before, is identical to the preceding equation, but without the error term, because the residuals are expected (on average) to be zero. And again, as before, we can substitute the left-hand side of the preceding equation into the previous equation, and get

$$Y_i = \hat{Y}_i^* + \hat{v}_i$$

or, equivalently,

$$\hat{v}_i = Y_i - \hat{Y}_i^*.$$

These $\hat{v}_i$, then, are interpreted in an identical way to that of the preceding $\hat{e}_i$. They represent the portion of the variation in Y that Z cannot explain. (The portion of Y that Z *can* explain is the predicted portion – the $\hat{Y}_i^*$.)

Now what has this accomplished? We have just documented the relationship between Z and Y and partitioned the variation in Y into two parts – the portion that Z *can* explain and the portion that Z *cannot* explain.

So we have now *let* Z try to explain X and found the residuals (the $\hat{e}_i$ values); similarly, we have also now *let* Z try to explain Y, and found those residuals as well (the $\hat{v}_i$ values). Now back to our three-variable regression model that we have seen before, with Y as the dependent variable, and X and Z as the independent variables:

$$Y_i = \hat{\alpha} + \hat{\beta}_1 X_i + \hat{\beta}_2 Z_i + \hat{u}_i.$$

The formula for $\hat{\beta}_1$, representing the effect of X on Y while controlling for Z, is

$$\hat{\beta}_1 = \frac{\sum_{i=1}^n \hat{e}_i \hat{v}_i}{\sum_{i=1}^n \hat{e}_i^2}.$$

Now, we know what $\hat{e}_i$ and $\hat{v}_i$ are from the previous equations. So, substituting, we get

$$\hat{\beta}_1 = \frac{\sum_{i=1}^n (X_i - \hat{X}_i)(Y_i - \hat{Y}_i^*)}{\sum_{i=1}^n (X_i - \hat{X}_i)^2}.$$

Pay careful attention to this formula. The "hatted" components in these expressions are from the two-variable regressions involving Z that we previously learned about. The key components of the formula for the effect of X on Y, while controlling for Z, are the $\hat{e}_i$ and $\hat{v}_i$, which, as we just learned, are the portions of X and Y (respectively) that Z cannot account for. And that is how, in the multiple regression model, the parameter β_1, which represents the effects of X on Y, *controls for* the effects of Z. How? Because the only components of X and Y that it uses are components that Z cannot account for – that is, the $\hat{e}_i$ and $\hat{v}_i$.

Comparing this formula for β_1 with the two-variable formula for β is very revealing. Instead of using the factors $(X_i - \bar{X})$ and $(Y_i - \bar{Y})$ in the numerator, which were the components of the *two-variable* regression of Y on X from Chapter 9, in the multiple regression formula that controls for Z the factors in the numerator are $(X_i - \hat{X}_i)$ and $(Y_i - \hat{Y}_i^*)$, where, again, the hatted portions represent X as predicted by Z and Y as predicted by Z.

Note something else in the comparison of the two-variable formula for β and the multiple regression formula for β_1. The result of $\hat{\beta}$ in the two-variable regression of Y and X and $\hat{\beta}_1$ in the three-variable regression of Y on X while controlling for Z will be different almost all the time. In fact, it is quite rare – though mathematically possible in theory – that those two values will be identical.[3]

And the formula for β_2, likewise, represents the effects of Z on Y while controlling for the effects of X. These processes, in fact, happen simultaneously.

It's been a good number of chapters – six of them, to be precise – between the first moment when we discussed the importance of controlling for Z and the point, just above, when we showed you precisely how to do it. The fourth causal hurdle has never been too far from front-and-center since Chapter 3, and now you know the process of crossing it.

Don't get too optimistic too quickly, though. As we noted, the three-variable setup we just mentioned can easily be generalized to more than three variables. But the formula for β_1 controls only for the effects of the Z variable that are included in the regression equation. It does not control for other variables that are not measured and not included in the model. And what happens when we fail to include a relevant cause of Y in our regression model? Bad things. And those bad things are the focus of the next section.

10.4   WHAT HAPPENS WHEN WE FAIL TO CONTROL FOR *Z*?

Controlling for the effects of other possible causes of our dependent variable Y, we have maintained, is critical to making the correct causal inferences. Some of you might be wondering something like the following: "How does omitting Z from a regression model affect my inference of whether X causes Y? Z isn't X, and Z isn't Y, so why should omitting Z matter?"

---

[3] In the next section, you will see that there are two situations in which the two-variable and multiple regression parameter estimates of β will be the same.

Consider the following three-variable regression model involving our now-familiar trio of X, Y, and Z:

$$Y_i = \alpha + \beta_1 X_i + \beta_2 Z_i + u_i.$$

And assume, for the moment, that this is the *correct* model of reality. That is, the only systematic causes of Y are X and Z; and, to some degree, Y is also influenced by some random error component, u.

Now let's assume that, instead of estimating this correct model, we fail to estimate the effects of Z. That is, we estimate

$$Y_i = \alpha + \beta_1^* X_i + u_i^*.$$

As we previously hinted, the value of β_1 in the correct, three-variable equation and the value of β_1^* will not be identical under most circumstances. (We'll see the exceptions in a moment.) And that, right there, should be enough to raise red flags of warning. For, if we know that the three-variable model is the *correct* model – and what that means, of course, is that the estimated value of β_1 that we obtain from the data will be equal to the true population value – and if we know that β_1 will not be equal to β_1^*, then there is a problem with the estimated value of β_1^*. That problem is a statistical problem called **bias**, which means that the expected value of the parameter estimate that we obtain from a sample will not be equal to the true population parameter. The specific type of bias that results from the failure to include a variable that belongs in our regression model is called **omitted-variables bias**.

Let's get specific about the nature of omitted-variables bias. If, instead of estimating the true three-variable model, we estimate the incorrect two-variable model, the formula for the slope β_1^* will be

$$\hat{\beta}_1^* = \frac{\sum_{i=1}^{n}(X_i - \bar{X})(Y_i - \bar{Y})}{\sum_{i=1}^{n}(X_i - \bar{X})^2}.$$

Notice that this is simply the bivariate formula for the effect of X on Y. (Of course, the model we just estimated is a bivariate model, in spite of the fact that we know that Z, as well as X, affects Y.) But because we know that Z *should* be in the model, and we know from Chapter 9 that regression lines travel through the mean values of each variable, we can figure out that the following is true:

$$(Y_i - \bar{Y}) = \beta_1(X_i - \bar{X}) + \beta_2(Z_i - \bar{Z}) + (u_i - \bar{u}).$$

We can do this because we know that the plane will travel through each mean.

Now notice that the left-hand side of the preceding equation – the $(Y_i - \bar{Y})$ – is identical to one portion of the numerator of the slope for $\hat{\beta}_1^*$.

Therefore we can substitute the right-hand side of the preceding equation – yes, that entire mess – into the numerator of the formula for $\hat{\beta}_1^*$.

The resulting math isn't anything that is beyond your skills in algebra, but it is cumbersome, so we won't derive it here. After a few lines of multiplying and reducing, though, the formula for $\hat{\beta}_1^*$ will reduce to

$$E(\hat{\beta}_1^*) = \beta_1 + \beta_2 \frac{\sum_{i=1}^n (X_i - \bar{X})(Z_i - \bar{Z})}{\sum_{i=1}^n (X_i - \bar{X})^2}.$$

This might seem like a mouthful – a fact that's rather hard to deny – but there is a very important message in it. What the equation says is that the estimated effect of X on Y, $\hat{\beta}_1^*$, in which we do not include the effects of Z on Y (but should have), will be equal to the true β_1 – that is, the effect with Z taken into account – plus a bundle of other stuff. That other stuff, strictly speaking, is bias. And because this bias came about as a result of omitting a variable (Z) that should have been in the model, this type of bias is known as omitted-variables bias.

Obviously, we'd like the expected value of our $\hat{\beta}_1^*$ (estimated without Z) to equal the true β_1 (as if we had estimated the equation with Z). And if the things on the right-hand side of the "+" sign in the preceding equation equal zero, it will. When will that happen? In two circumstances, neither of which is particularly likely. First, $\hat{\beta}_1^* = \beta_1$ if $\beta_2 = 0$. Second, $\hat{\beta}_1^* = \beta_1$ if the large quotient at the end of the equation is equal to zero. What is that quotient? It should look familiar; in fact, it is the bivariate slope parameter of a regression of Z on X.

In the first of these two special circumstances, the bias term will equal zero if and only if the effect of Z on Y – that is, the parameter β_2 – is zero. Okay, so it's safe to omit an independent variable from a regression equation if it has no effect on the dependent variable. (If that seems obvious to you, good.) The second circumstance is a bit more interesting: It's safe to omit an independent variable Z from an equation if it is entirely unrelated to the other independent variable X. Of course, if we omit Z in such circumstances, we'll still be deprived of understanding how Z affects Y; but at least, so long as Z and X are absolutely unrelated, omitting Z will not adversely affect[4] our estimate of the effect of X on Y.

We emphasize that this second condition is unlikely to occur in practice. Therefore, if Z affects Y, and Z and X are related, then if we omit Z from our model, our bias term will not equal zero. In the end, omitting Z will cause us to misestimate the effect of X on Y.

That might seem unfair, but it's true. If we estimate a regression model that omits an independent variable (Z) that belongs in the model, then

---

[4] Omitting Z from our regression model also drives down the R^2 statistic.

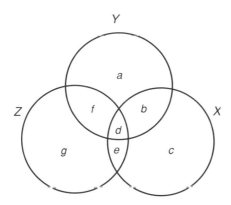

Figure 10.1. Venn diagram in which *X*, *Y*, and *Z* are correlated.

the effects of that *Z* will somehow work their way into the parameter estimates for the independent variable that we do estimate (*X*) and pollute our estimate of the effect of *X* on *Y*.

The preceding equation also suggests when the magnitude of the bias is likely to be large and when it is likely to be small. If either or both of the components of the bias term [β_2 and $\frac{\sum_{i=1}^{n}(X_i-\bar{X})(Z_i-\bar{Z})}{\sum_{i=1}^{n}(X_i-\bar{X})^2}$] are *close to* zero, then the bias is likely to be small (because the bias term is the product of both components); but if both are likely to be large, then the bias is likely to be quite large.

Moreover, the equation also suggests the likely *direction* of the bias. All we have said thus far is that the coefficient $\hat{\beta}_1^*$ will be biased – that is, it will not equal its true value. But will it be too large or too small? If we have good guesses about the values of β_2 and the correlation between *X* and *Z*, then we can suspect the direction of the bias. For example, suppose that β_1, β_2, and the correlation between *X* and *Z* are all positive. That means that our estimated coefficient $\hat{\beta}_1^*$ will be larger than it is supposed to be, because a positive number plus the product of two positive numbers will be a still-larger positive number. And so on.[5]

To better understand the importance of controlling for other possible causes of the dependent variable and the importance of the relationship (or the lack of one) between *X* and *Z*, consider the following graphical illustrations. In Figure 10.1, we represent the total variation of *Y*, *X*, and *Z* each with a circle. The covariation between any of these two variables – or among all three – is represented by the places where the circles overlap. Thus, in the figure, the total variation in *Y* is represented as the sum of the area $a + b + d + f$. The covariation between *Y* and *X* is represented by the area $b + d$.

Note in the figure, though, that the variable *Z* is related to both *Y* and *X* (because the circle for *Z* overlaps with both *Y* and *X*). In particular, the relationship between *Y* and *Z* is accounted for by the area $f + d$, and the relationship between *Z* and *X* is accounted for by the area $d + e$. As we have already seen, *d* is also a portion of the relationship between *Y* and *X*. If, hypothetically, we erased the circle for *Z* from the figure, we would

---

[5] With more than two independent variables, it becomes more complex to figure out the direction of the bias.

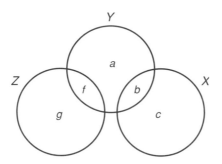

Figure 10.2. Venn diagram in which X and Z are correlated with Y, but not with each other.

(incorrectly) attribute all of the area $b + d$ to X, when in fact the d portion of the variation in Y is shared by *both* X and Z. This is why, when Z is related to both X and Y, if we fail to control for Z, we will end up with a biased estimate of X's effect on Y.

Consider the alternative scenario, in which both X and Z affect Y, but X and Z are completely unrelated to one another. That scenario is portrayed graphically in Figure 10.2. There, the circles for both X and Z overlap with the circle for Y, but they do not overlap at all with one another. In that case – which, we have noted, is unlikely in applied research – we can safely omit consideration of Z when considering the effects of X on Y. In that figure, the relationship between X and Y – the area b – is unaffected by the presence (or absence) of Z in the model.[6]

10.4.1 An Additional Minimal Mathematical Requirement in Multiple Regression

We outlined a set of assumptions and minimal mathematical requirements for the two-variable regression model in Chapter 9. In multiple regression, all of these assumptions are made and all of the same minimal mathematical requirements remain in place. In addition to those, however, we need to add one more minimal mathematical requirement to be able to estimate our multiple regression models: It must be the case that *there is no exact linear relationship* between any two or more of our independent variables (which we have called X and Z). This is also called the assumption of no **perfect multicollinearity** (as in X and Z cannot be *perfectly* collinear).

What does it mean to say that X and Z cannot exist in an exact linear relationship? Refer back to Figure 10.1. If X and Z had an *exact* linear relationship, instead of having some degree of overlap – that is, some imperfect degree of correlation – the circles would be exactly on top of one another. In such cases, it is literally impossible to estimate the regression model, as separating out the effects of X on Y from the effects of Z on Y is impossible.

---

[6] For identical reasons, we could safely estimate the effect of Z on Y – the area f – without considering the effect of X.

Table 10.1. Three regression models of U.S. presidential elections

Variable	A	B	C
Growth	0.65*	–	0.57*
	(0.16)	–	(0.16)
Good News	–	0.96*	0.72*
	–	(0.34)	(0.30)
Constant	51.86*	47.20*	48.12*
	(0.88)	(2.07)	(1.75)
R^2	.36	.20	.46
n	32	32	32

Notes: Standard errors are in parentheses.
* $= p < .05$

This is not to say that we must assume that X and Z are entirely uncorrelated with one another (as in Figure 10.2). In fact, in almost all applications, X and Z will have some degree of correlation between them. Things become complicated only as that correlation approaches 1.0; and when it hits 1.0, the regression model will fail to be estimable with both X and Z as independent variables. In Chapter 11 we will discuss these issues further.

10.5 INTERPRETING MULTIPLE REGRESSION

For an illustration of how to interpret multiple regression coefficients, let's return to our example from Chapter 9, in which we showed you the results of a regression of U.S. presidential election results on the previous year's growth rate in the U.S. economy (see Figure 9.4). The model we estimated, you will recall was Vote $= \alpha + (\beta \times Growth)$, and the estimated coefficients there were $\hat{\alpha} = 51.86$ and $\hat{\beta} = 0.65$. Those results are in column A of Table 10.1.

In column A, you see the parameter estimates for the annual growth rate in the U.S. economy (in the row labeled "Growth"), and the standard error of that estimated slope, 0.16. In the row labeled "Constant," you see the estimated y-intercept for that regression, 51.86, and its associated standard error, 0.88. Both parameter estimates are statistically significant.

Recall that the interpretation of the slope coefficient in a two-variable regression indicates that, for every one-unit increase in the independent variable, we expect to see β units of change in the dependent variable. In the current context, $\hat{\beta} = 0.65$ means that for every extra one percentage point in growth rate in the U.S. economy, we expect to see, on average, an extra 0.65% in vote percentage for the incumbent party in presidential elections.[7]

But recall our admonition, throughout this book, about being too quick to interpret any bivariate analysis as evidence of a causal relationship. We have not shown, in column A of Table 10.1, that higher growth rates in the economy *cause* incumbent-party vote totals to be higher. To be sure, the evidence in column A is consistent with a causal connection, but it does not *prove* it. Why not? Because we have not controlled for other possible causes of election outcomes. Surely there are other causes, in addition to how the economy has (or has not) grown in the last year, of how well the incumbent party will fare in a presidential election. Indeed, we can even imagine other *economic* causes that might bolster our statistical explanation of presidential elections.[8]

Consider the fact that the growth variable accounts for economic growth over the past year. But perhaps the public rewards or punishes the incumbent party for *sustained* economic growth over the long run. In particular, it does not necessarily make sense for the public to reelect a party that has presided over three years of subpar growth in the economy but a fourth year with solid growth. And yet, with our single measure of growth, we are assuming – rather unrealistically – that the public would pay attention to the growth rate only in the past year. Surely the public does pay attention to recent growth, but the public might also pay heed to growth over the long run.

In column B of Table 10.1, we estimate another two-variable regression model, this time using the number of consecutive quarters of strong economic growth leading up to the presidential election – the variable is labeled "Good News" – as our independent variable.[9] (Incumbent-Party Vote Share remains our dependent variable.) In the row labeled "Good News," we see that the parameter estimate is 0.96, which means that, on average, for every additional consecutive quarter of good economic news, we expect to see a 0.96% increase in incumbent-party vote share. The coefficient is statistically significant.

---

[7] Be sure not to invert the independent and dependent variables in describing results. It is *not* correct to interpret column A to say "for every 0.65-point change in growth rate in the U.S. economy, we should expect to see, on average, an extra 1% in vote percentage for the incumbent party in presidential elections." Be sure that you can see the difference in those descriptions.

[8] And, of course, we can imagine variables relating to success or failure in foreign policy, for example, as other, noneconomic causes of election outcomes.

[9] Fair's operationalization of this variable is "the number of quarters in the first 15 quarters of the administration in which the growth rate of real per capita GDP is greater than 3.2 percent."

Our separate two-variable regressions each show a relationship between the independent variable in the particular model and incumbent-party vote shares. But none of the parameter estimates in columns A or B controls for the other independent variable. We rectify that situation in column C, in which we estimate the effects of both the Growth and Good News variables on vote shares simultaneously.

Compare column C with columns A and B. In the row labeled "Good News," we see that the estimated parameter of $\hat{\beta} = 0.72$ indicates that, for every extra quarter of a year with strong growth rates, the incumbent party should expect to see an additional 0.72% of the national vote share, *while controlling for the effects of Growth*. Note the additional clause in the interpretation as well as the emphasis that we place on it. Multiple regression coefficients always represent the effects of a one-point increase in that particular independent variable on the dependent variable, *while controlling for the effects of all other independent variables in the model*. The higher the number of quarters of continuous strong growth in the economy, the higher the incumbent-party vote share should be in the next election, controlling for the previous year's growth rate.

But, critical to this chapter's focus on multiple regression, notice in column C how including the "Good News" variable changes the estimated effect of the "Growth" variable from an estimated 0.65 in column A to 0.57 in column C. The effect in column C is different because it *controls for the effects of Good News*. That is, when the effects of long-running economic expansions are controlled for, the effects of short-term growth falls a bit. The effect is still quite strong and is still statistically significant, but it is more modest once the effects of long-term growth are taken into account.[10] Note also that the R^2 statistic rises from .36 in column A to .46 in column C, which means that adding the "Good News" variable increased the proportion of the variance of our dependent variable that we have explained[11] by 10%.

---

[10] And we can likewise compare the bivariate effects of Good News on Vote shares in column B with the multivariate results in column C, noting that the effect of Good News, in the multivariate context, appears to have fallen by approximately one-fourth.

[11] It is important to be cautious when reporting contributions to R^2 statistics by individual independent variables, and this table provides a good example of why this is the case. If we were estimate Model A first and C second, we might be tempted to conclude that Growth explains 36% of Vote and Good News explains 10%. But if we estimated Model B and then C, we might be tempted to conclude that Growth explains 26% of Vote and Good News explains 20%. Actually, both of these sets of conclusions are faulty. The R^2 is always a measure of the overall fit of the model to the dependent variable. So, all that we can say about the R^2 for Model C is that Growth, Good News, and the constant term together explain 45% of the variation in Vote. So, although we can talk about how the addition or subtraction of a particular variable to a model increases or decreases the

In this particular example, the whole emphasis on controlling for other causes might seem like much ado about nothing. After all, comparing the two columns in Table 10.1 did not change our interpretation of whether short-term growth rates affect incumbent-party fortunes at the polls. But we didn't know this until we tested for the effects of long-term growth. And in Chapter 12, we will see examples in which controlling for new causes of the dependent variable substantially changes our interpretations about causal relationships. We should be clear about one other thing regarding Table 10.1: Despite controlling for another variable, we still have a ways to go before we can say that we've controlled for all other possible causes of the dependent variable. As a result, we should be cautious about interpreting those results as proof of causality. However, as we continue to add independent variables to our regression model, we inch closer and closer to saying that we've controlled for every other possible cause that comes to mind. Recall that, all the way back in Chapter 1, we noted that one of the "rules of the road" of the scientific enterprise is to always be willing to consider new evidence. New evidence – in the form of controlling for other independent variables – can change our inferences about whether any particular independent variable is causally related to the dependent variable.

10.6 WHICH EFFECT IS "BIGGEST"?

In the preceding analysis, we might be tempted to look at the coefficients in column C of Table 10.1 for Growth (0.57) and for Good News (0.72) and conclude that the effect for Good News is roughly one-third larger than the effect for Growth. As tempting as such a conclusion might be, it must be avoided for one critical reason: The two independent variables are measured in different metrics, which makes that comparison misleading. Short-run growth rates are measured in a different metric – ranging from negative numbers for times during which the economy shrunk, all the way through stronger periods during which growth exceeded 5% per year – than are the number of quarters of consecutive strong growth – which ranges from 0 in the data set through 10. That makes comparing the coefficients misleading.

Because the coefficients in Table 10.1 each exist in the native metric of each variable, they are referred to as **unstandardized coefficients**.

model's R^2, we should not be tempted to attribute particular values of R^2 to specific independent variables. If we return to Figure 10.1, we can get some intuition on why this is the case. The R^2 statistic for the model represented in this figure is $\frac{f+d+b}{a+f+d+b}$. It is the presence of area d that confounds our ability to make definitive statements about the contribution of individual variables to R^2.

Although they are normally not comparable, there is a rather simple method to remove the metric of each variable to make them comparable with one another. As you might imagine, such coefficients, because they are on a standardized metric, are referred to as **standardized coefficients**. We compute them, quite simply, by taking the unstandardized coefficients and taking out the metrics – in the forms of the standard deviations – of both the independent and dependent variables:

$$\hat{\beta}_{\text{Std}} = \hat{\beta}\frac{s_X}{s_Y},$$

where $\hat{\beta}_{\text{Std}}$ is the standardized regression coefficient, β is the unstandardized coefficient (as in Table 10.1), and s_X and s_Y are the standard deviations of X and Y, respectively. The interpretation of the standardized coefficients changes, not surprisingly. Whereas the unstandardized coefficients represent the expected change in Y given a one-unit increase in X, the standardized coefficients represent the expected *standard deviation* change in Y given a *one-standard-deviation* increase in X. Now, because all parameter estimates are in the same units – that is, the standard deviations – they become comparable.

Implementing this formula for the unstandardized coefficients in column C of Table 10.1 produces the following results. First, for Growth,

$$\hat{\beta}_{\text{Std}} = 0.57\left(\frac{5.54}{6.07}\right) = 0.52.$$

Next, for Good News,

$$\hat{\beta}_{\text{Std}} = 0.72\left(\frac{2.85}{6.07}\right) = 0.34.$$

These coefficients would be interpreted as follows: For a one-standard-deviation increase in Growth, on average, we expect a 0.52-standard-deviation increase in the incumbent-party vote share, controlling for the effects of Good News. And for a one-standard-deviation increase in Good News, we expect to see, on average, a 0.34-standard-deviation increase in the incumbent-party vote shares, controlling for the effects of Growth. Note how, when looking at the unstandardized coefficients, we might have mistakenly thought that the effect of Good News was larger than the effect of Growth. But the standardized coefficients (correctly) tell the opposite story: The estimated effect of Growth is about 150% of the size of the effect of Good News.[12]

---

[12] Some objections have been raised about the use of standardized coefficients (King 1986). From a technical perspective, because standard deviations can differ across samples, this makes the results of standardized coefficients particularly sample specific. Additionally, and from a broader perspective, one-unit or one-standard-deviation shifts in different independent variables have different substantive meanings regardless of the metrics in

10.7 STATISTICAL AND SUBSTANTIVE SIGNIFICANCE

Related to the admonition about which effect is "biggest," consider the following, seemingly simpler, question: Are the effects found in column C of Table 10.1 "big?" A tempting answer to that question is "Well of course they're big. Both coefficients are statistically significant. Therefore, they're big."

That logic, although perhaps appealing, is faulty. Recall the discussion from Chapter 7 (specifically, Subsection 7.3.2) on the effects of sample size on the magnitude of the standard error of the mean. And we noted the same effects of sample size on the magnitude of the standard error of our regression coefficients (specifically, Section 9.4). What this means is that, even if the strength of the relationship (as measured by our coefficient estimates) remains constant, by merely increasing our sample size we can affect the statistical significance of those coefficients. Why? Because statistical significance is determined by a t-test (see Subsection 9.4.7) in which the standard error is in the denominator of that quotient. What you can remember is that larger sample sizes will shrink standard errors and therefore make finding statistically significant relationships more likely.[13] It is also apparent from Appendix B that, when the number of degrees of freedom is greater, it is easier to achieve statistical significance.

We hope that you can see that arbitrarily increasing the size of a sample, and therefore finding statistically significant relationships, does not in any way make an effect "bigger" or even "big." Recall, such changes to the standard errors have no bearing on the rise-over-run nature of the slope coefficients themselves.

How, then, should you judge whether an effect of one variable on another is "big?" One way is to use the method just described – using standardized coefficients. By placing the variances of X and Y on the same metric, it is possible to come to a judgment about how big an effect is. This is particularly helpful when the independent variables variables X and Z, or the dependent variable Y, or both, are measured in metrics that are unfamiliar or artificial.

When the metrics of the variables in a regression analysis are intuitive and well known, however, rendering a judgment about whether an effect is large or small becomes something of a matter of interpretation. For example, in Chapter 12, we will see an example relating the effects of

---

which the variables are measured. We might therefore logically conclude that there isn't much use in trying to figure out which effect is biggest.

[13] To be certain, it's not always possible to increase sample sizes, and, even when possible, it is nearly always costly to do so. The research situations in which increasing sample size is most likely, albeit still expensive, is in mass-based survey research.

changes in the unemployment rate (X) on a president's approval rating (Y). It is very simple to interpret that a slope coefficient of, say, -1.51, means that, for every additional point of unemployment, we expect approval to go down by 1.51 points, controlling for other factors in the model. Is that effect large, small, or moderate? There is something of a judgment call to be made here, but at least in this case, the metrics of both X and Y are quite familiar; no one needs to explain what unemployment rates mean or what approval polls mean. Independent of the statistical significance of that estimate – which, you should note, we have not mentioned here – discussions of this sort represent attempts to judge the **substantive significance** of a coefficient estimate. Substantive significance is more difficult to judge than statistical significance because there are no numeric formulae for making such judgements. Instead, substantive significance is a judgment call about whether or not statistically significant relationships are "large" or "small" in terms of their real-world impact.

From time to time we will see a "large" parameter estimate that is not statistically significant. Although it is tempting to describe such a result as substantively significant, it is not. We can understand this by thinking about what it means for a particular result to be statistically significant. As we discussed in Chapter 9, in most cases we are testing the null hypothesis that the population parameter is equal to zero. In such cases, even when we have a large parameter estimate, if it is statistically insignificant this means that it is not statistically distinguishable from zero. Therefore a parameter estimate can be substantively significant only when it is also statistically significant.

10.8 IMPLICATIONS

What are the implications of this chapter? The key take-home point of this chapter – that failing to control for all relevant independent variables will often lead to mistaken causal inferences for the variables that do make it into our models – applies in several contexts. If you are reading a research article in one of your other classes, and it shows a regression analysis between two variables, but fails to control for the effects of some other possible cause of the dependent variable, then you have some reason to be skeptical about the reported findings. In particular, if you can think of another independent variable that is likely to be related to *both* the independent variable and the dependent variable, then the relationship that the article does show that fails to control for that variable is likely to be plagued with bias. And if that's the case, then there is substantial reason to doubt the findings. The findings *might* be right, but you can't know that from the evidence presented in the article; in particular, you'd need to control for the omitted variable to know for sure.

But this critical issue isn't just encountered in research articles. When you read a news article from your favorite media web site that reports a relationship between some presumed cause and some presumed effect – news articles don't usually talk about "independent variables" or "dependent variables" – but fails to account for some other cause that you can imagine might be related to both the independent and dependent variables, then you have reason to doubt the conclusions.

It might be tempting to react to omitted-variables bias by saying, "Omitted-variables bias is such a potentially serious problem that I don't want to use regression analysis." That would be a mistake. In fact, the logic of omitted-variables bias applies to any type of research, no matter what type of statistical technique used – in fact, no matter whether the research is qualitative or quantitative.

Sometimes, as we have seen, controlling for other causes of the dependent variable changes the discovered effects only at the margins. That happens on occasion in applied research. At other times, however, failure to control for a relevant cause of the dependent variable can have serious consequences for our causal inferences about the real world. In Chapter 12, you will see several such examples. But first, in Chapter 11, we present you with some crucial extensions of the multiple regression model that you are likely to encounter when consuming or conducting research.

CONCEPTS INTRODUCED IN THIS CHAPTER

bias	standardized coefficients
omitted-variables bias	substantive significance
perfect multicollinearity	unstandardized coefficients

EXERCISES

1. Identify an article from a prominent web site that reports a causal relationship between two variables. Can you think of another variable that is related to both the independent variable and the dependent variable?

2. In Exercise 1, estimate the direction of the bias resulting from omitting the third variable.

3. Fill in the values in the third column of Table 10.2.

4. In your own research you have found evidence from a bivariate regression model that supports your theory that your independent variable X_i is positively related to your dependent variable Y_i (the slope parameter for X_i was statistically significant and positive when you estimated a bivariate regression

Table 10.2. Bias in $\hat{\beta}_1$ when the true population model is $Y_i = \alpha + \beta_1 X_i + \beta_2 Z_i + u_i$ but we leave out Z

β_2	$\frac{\sum_{i=1}^{n}(X_i-\bar{X})(Z_i-\bar{Z})}{\sum_{i=1}^{n}(X_i-\bar{X})^2}$	Resulting bias in $\hat{\beta}_1$
0	+	?
0	−	?
+	0	?
−	0	?
+	+	?
−	−	?
+	−	?
−	+	?

model). You go to a research presentation in which other researchers present a theory that their independent variable Z_i is negatively related to their dependent variable Y_i. They report the results from a bivariate regression model in which the slope parameter for Z_i was statistically significant and negative. Your Y_i and their Y_i are the same variable. What would be your reaction to these findings under each of the following circumstances?

(a) You are confident that the correlation between Z_i and X_i is equal to zero.
(b) You think that the correlation between Z_i and X_i is positive.
(c) You think that the correlation between Z_i and X_i is negative.

11 Multiple Regression Models II: Crucial Extensions

OVERVIEW

In this chapter we provide introductory *discussions of* and *advice for* commonly encountered research scenarios involving multiple regression models. Issues covered include dummy independent variables, interactive specifications, dummy dependent variables, influential cases, multicollinearity, and models of time-series data.

11.1 EXTENSIONS OF OLS

In the previous two chapters we discussed in detail various aspects of the estimation and interpretation of OLS regression models. In this chapter we go through a series of research scenarios commonly encountered by political science researchers as they attempt to test their hypotheses within the OLS framework. The purpose of this chapter is twofold – first, to help you to identify when you have hit these issues and, second, to help you to figure out what to do to continue on your way.

We begin with a discussion of "dummy" independent variables and how to properly use them to make inferences. We then discuss how to test interactive hypotheses with dummy variables. Our third topic with dummy variables involves the interpretation of models in which our dependent variable is a dummy variable. We next turn our attention to two frequently encountered problems in OLS – outliers and multicollinearity. With both of these topics, at least half of the battle is identifying that you have the problem. Finally, we conclude with a discussion of a series of problems specific to the analysis of time-series data.

11.2 BEING SMART WITH DUMMY INDEPENDENT VARIABLES IN OLS

In Chapter 6 we discussed how an important part of knowing your data involves knowing the metric in which each of your variables is measured. Throughout the examples that we have examined thus far, almost all of the variables, both the independent and dependent variables, have been continuous. This is not by accident. We chose examples with continuous variables because they are, in many cases, easier to interpret than models in which the variables are noncontinuous. In this section, though, we consider a series of scenarios involving independent variables that are *not* continuous. We begin with a relatively simple case in which we have a categorical independent variable that takes on one of two possible values for all cases. Categorical variables like this are commonly referred to as **dummy variables**. Although any two values will do, the most common form of dummy variable is one that takes on values of one or zero. We then consider more complicated examples in which we have an independent variable that is categorical with more than two categories.

11.2.1 Using Dummy Variables to Test Hypotheses about a Categorical Independent Variable with Only Two Values

During the 1996 U.S. presidential election between incumbent Democrat Bill Clinton and Republican challenger Robert Dole, Clinton's wife Hillary was a prominent and polarizing figure. Throughout the next couple of examples, we will use her "thermometer ratings" by individual respondents to the NES survey as our dependent variable. A thermometer rating is a survey respondent's answer to a question about how they *feel* (as opposed to how they *think*) toward particular individuals or groups on a scale that typically runs from 0 to 100. Scores of 50 indicate that the individual feels neither warm nor cold about the individual or group in question. Scores from 50 to 100 represent increasingly warm (or favorable) feelings feelings, and scores from 50 to 0 represent increasingly cold (or unfavorable) feelings.

During the 1996 campaign, Ms. Clinton was identified as a being a left-wing feminist. Given this, we theorize that there may have been a causal relationship between respondents' family incomes and their thermometer rating of Ms. Clinton – with wealthier individuals, holding all else constant, liking her less – as well as a relationship between respondents' gender and their thermometer rating of Ms. Clinton – with women, holding all else constant, liking her more. For the sake of this example, we are going to assume that both our dependent variable and our income independent

.reg hillary_thermo income male female

Source	SS	df	MS
Model	80916.663	2	40458.3315
Residual	1266234.71	1539	822.764595
Total	1347151.37	1541	874.205954

Number of obs =	1542
F(2, 1539) =	49.17
Prob > F =	0.0000
R–Squared =	0.0601
Adj R–Squared =	0.0588
Root MSE =	28.684

hillary_th~o	Coef.	Std. Err.	t	P>|t|	[95% Conf. Interval]	
income	−.8407732	.117856	− 7.13	0.000	−1.071948	−.6095978
male	(dropped)					
female	8.081448	1.495216	5.40	0.000	5.148572	11.01432
_cons	61.1804	2.220402	27.55	0.000	56.82507	65.53573

Figure 11.1. Stata output when we include both gender dummy variables in our model.

variable are continuous.[1] Each respondent's gender was coded as equaling either 1 for "male" or 2 for "female." Although we could leave this gender variable as it is and run our analyses, we chose to use this variable to create two new dummy variables, "male" equaling 1 for "yes" and 0 for "no," and "female" equaling 1 for "yes" and 0 for "no."

Our first inclination is to estimate an OLS model in which the specification is the following:

$$\text{Hillary Thermometer}_i = \alpha + \beta_1 \text{Income}_i + \beta_2 \text{Male}_i + \beta_3 \text{Female}_i + u_i.$$

But if we try to estimate this model, our statistical computer program will revolt and give us an error message.[2] Figure 11.1 shows a screen shot of what this output looks like in Stata. We can see that Stata has reported the results from the following model instead of what we asked for:

$$\text{Hillary Thermometer}_i = \alpha + \beta_1 \text{Income}_i + \beta_3 \text{Female}_i + u_i.$$

Instead of the estimates for β_2 on the second row of parameter estimates, we get a note that this variable was "dropped." This is the case because we have failed to meet the additional minimal mathematical criteria that we introduced when we moved from two-variable OLS to multiple OLS in Chapter 10 – "no perfect multicollinearity." The reason that we have failed to meet this is that, for two of the independent variables in our model, Male_i and Female_i, it is the case that

$$\text{Male}_i + \text{Female}_i = 1 \; \forall \; i.$$

---

[1] In this survey, respondents' family income was measured on a scale ranging from 1 to 24 according to which category of income ranges they chose as best describing their family's income during 1995.

[2] Most programs will throw one of the two variables out of the model and report the results from the resulting model along with an error message.

Table 11.1. Two models of the effects of gender and income on Hillary Clinton Thermometer scores		
Independent variable	Model 1	Model 2
Male	–	−8.08***
		(1.50)
Female	8.08***	–
	(1.50)	
Income	−0.84***	−0.84***
	(0.12)	(0.12)
Intercept	61.18***	69.26***
	(2.22)	(1.92)
n	1542	1542
R^2	.06	.06

Notes: The dependent variable in both models is the respondent's thermometer score for Hillary Clinton. Standard errors in parentheses. Two-sided t-tests: ***indicates $p < .01$; **indicates $p < .05$; *indicates $p < .10$.

In other words, our variables "Male" and "Female" are perfectly correlated: If we know a respondent's value on the "Male" variable, then we know their value on the "Female" variable with perfect certainty.

When this happens with dummy variables, we call this situation the **dummy-variable trap**. To avoid the dummy-variable trap, we have to omit one of our dummy variables. But we want to be able to compare the effects of being male with the effects of being female to test our hypothesis. How can we do this if we have to omit of one our two variables that measures gender? Before we answer this question, let's look at the results in Table 11.1 from the two different models in which we omit one of these two variables. We can learn a lot by looking at what is and what is not the same across these two models. In both models, the parameter estimate and standard error for income is identical. The R^2 statistic is also identical. The parameter estimate and the standard error for the intercept are different across the two models. The parameter estimate for male is −8.08, whereas that for female is 8.08, although the standard error for each of these parameter estimates is 0.12. If you're starting to think that all of these similarities cannot have happened by coincidence, you are correct. In fact, these two models are, mathematically speaking, the same model. All of the $\hat{y}$ values and residuals for the individual cases are *exactly* the same. With income held constant, the estimated difference between being male and being female is 8.08. The sign on this parameter estimate switches from positive to negative when we go from Model 1 to Model 2 because we are phrasing the question differently across the two models:

- For Model 1: "What is the estimated difference for a female compared with a male?"
- For Model 2: "What is the estimated difference for a male compared with a female?"

So why are the intercepts different? Think back to our discussions in Chapters 9 and 10 about the interpretation of the intercept – it is the estimated value of the dependent variable when the independent variables are all equal to zero. In Model 1 this means the estimated value of the dependent variable for a low-income man. In Model 2 this means the estimated value of the dependent variable for a low-income woman. And the difference between these two values – you guessed it – is $61.18 - 69.26 = -8.08$!

What does the regression line from Model 1 or Model 2 look like? The answer is that it depends on the gender of the individual for which we are plotting the line, but that it does not depend on which of these two models we use. For men, where $Female_i = 0$ and $Male_i = 1$, the predicted values are calculated as follows:

$$\text{Model 1 for Men: } \hat{Y}_i = 61.18 + (8.08 \times Female_i) - (0.84 \times Income_i),$$

$$\hat{Y}_i = 61.18 + (8.08 \times 0) - (0.84 \times Income_i),$$

$$\hat{Y}_i = 61.18 - (0.84 \times Income_i);$$

$$\text{Model 2 for Men: } \hat{Y}_i = 69.26 - (8.08 \times Male_i) - (0.84 \times Income_i),$$

$$\hat{Y}_i = 69.26 - (8.08 \times 1) - (0.84 \times Income_i),$$

$$\hat{Y}_i = 61.18 - (0.84 \times Income_i).$$

So we can see that, for men, regardless of whether we use the results from Model 1 or Model 2, the formula for predicted values is the same. For women, where $Female_i = 1$ and $Male_i = 0$, the predicted values are calculated as follows:

$$\text{Model 1 for Women: } \hat{Y}_i = 61.18 + (8.08 \times Female_i) - (0.84 \times Income_i),$$

$$\hat{Y}_i = 61.18 + (8.08 \times 1) - (0.84 \times Income_i),$$

$$\hat{Y}_i = 69.26 - (0.84 \times Income_i);$$

$$\text{Model 2 for Women: } \hat{Y}_i = 69.26 - (8.08 \times Male_i) - (0.84 \times Income_i),$$

$$\hat{Y}_i = 69.26 - (8.08 \times 0) - (0.84 \times Income_i),$$

$$\hat{Y}_i = 69.26 - (0.84 \times Income_i).$$

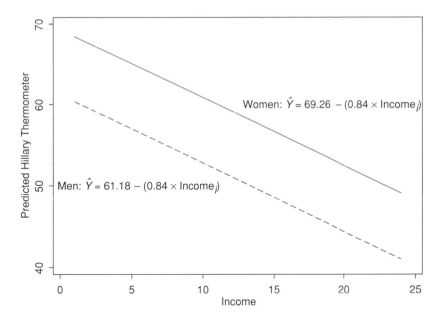

Figure 11.2. Regression lines from the interactive model.

Again, the formula from Model 1 is the same as the formula from Model 2 for women. To illustrate these two sets of predictions, we have plotted them in Figure 11.2. Given that the two predictive formulae have the same slope, it is not surprising to see that the two lines in this figure are parallel to each other with the intercept difference determining the space between the two lines.

11.2.2 Using Dummy Variables to Test Hypotheses about a Categorical Independent Variable with More Than Two Values

As you might imagine, when we have a categorical variable with more than two categories and we want to include it in an OLS model, things get more complicated. We'll keep with our running example of modeling Hillary Clinton Thermometer scores as a function of individuals' characteristics and opinions. In this section we work with respondents' religious affiliation as an independent variable. The frequency of different responses to this item in the 1996 NES is displayed in Table 11.2.

Could we use the Religious Identification variable as it is in our regression models? That would be a bad idea. Remember, this is a categorical variable, in which the values of the variable are not ordered from lowest to highest. Indeed, there is no such thing as "lowest" or "highest" on this variable. So running a regression model with the data as is would be meaningless. But beware: *Your statistics package does not know that this*

Table 11.2. Religious Identification in the 1996 NES			
Value	Category	Frequency	Percent
0	Protestant	683	39.85
1	Catholic	346	20.19
2	Jewish	22	1.28
3	Other	153	8.93
4	None	510	29.75

is a categorical variable. It will be more than happy to run the regression and report parameter estimates to you, even though these estimates will be nonsensical.

In the previous subsection, in which we had a categorical variable (Gender) with only two possible values, we saw that, when we switched which value was represented by "1" and "0," the estimated parameter switched signs. This was the case because we were asking a different question. With a categorical independent variable that has more than two values, we have more than two possible questions that we can ask. Because using the variable as is is not an option, the best strategy for modeling the effects of such an independent variable is to include a dummy variable for all values of that independent variable *except one.*[3] The value of the independent variable for which we do not include a dummy variable is known as the **reference category**. This is the case because the parameter estimates for all of the dummy variables representing the other values of the independent variable are estimated in reference to that value of the independent variable. So let's say that we choose to estimate the following model:

$$\text{Hillary Thermometer}_i = \alpha + \beta_1 \text{Income}_i + \beta_2 \text{Protestant}_i + \beta_3 \text{Catholic}_i$$
$$+ \beta_4 \text{Jewish}_i + \beta_5 \text{Other}_i + u_i.$$

For this model we would be using "None" as our reference category for religious identification. This would mean that $\hat{\beta}_2$ would be the estimated effect of being protestant *relative to* being nonreligious, and we could use this value along with its standard error to test the hypothesis that this effect was statistically significant, controlling for the effects of income. The remaining parameter estimates ($\hat{\beta}_3$, $\hat{\beta}_4$, and $\hat{\beta}_5$) would all also be interpreted

---

[3] If our theory was that only one category, such as Catholics, was different from all of the others, then we would collapse the remaining categories of the variable in question together and we would have a two-category independent variable. We should do this only if we have a theoretical justification for doing so.

Table 11.3. The same model of religion and income on Hillary Clinton Thermometer scores with different reference categories

Independent variable	Model 1	Model 2	Model 3	Model 4	Model 5
Income	−0.97***	−0.97***	−0.97***	−0.97***	−0.97***
	(0.12)	(0.12)	(0.12)	(0.12)	(0.12)
Protestant	−4.24*	−6.66*	−24.82***	−6.30**	
	(1.77)	(2.68)	(6.70)	(2.02)	
Catholic	2.07	−0.35	−18.51**		6.30**
	(2.12)	(2.93)	(6.80)		(2.02)
Jewish	20.58**	18.16**		18.51**	24.82***
	(6.73)	(7.02)		(6.80)	(6.70)
Other	2.42		−18.16**	0.35	6.66*
	(2.75)		(7.02)	(2.93)	(2.68)
None		−2.42	−20.58**	−2.07	4.24*
		(2.75)	(6.73)	(2.12)	(1.77)
Intercept	68.40***	70.83***	88.98***	70.47***	64.17***
	(2.19)	(2.88)	(6.83)	(2.53)	(2.10)
n	1542	1542	1542	1542	1542
R^2	.06	.06	.06	.06	.06

Notes: The dependent variable in both models is the respondent's thermometer score for Hillary Clinton. Standard errors in parentheses.

Two-sided t-tests: ***indicates $p < .01$; **indicates $p < .05$; *indicates $p < .10$.

as the estimated effect of being in the each of the remaining categories relative to "None." The value that we choose to use as our reference category does not matter, as long as we interpret our results appropriately. But we can use the choice of the reference category to focus on the relationships in which we are particularly interested. For each possible pair of categories of the independent variable, we can conduct a separate hypothesis test. The easiest way to get all of the p-values in which we are interested is to estimate the model multiple times with different reference categories. Table 11.3 displays a model of Hillary Clinton Thermometer scores with the five different choices of reference categories. It is worth emphasizing that this is *not* a table with five different models, but that this *is* a table with the same model displayed five different ways. From this table we can see that, when we control for the effects of income, some of the categories of religious affiliation are statistically different from each other in their evaluations of Hillary Clinton whereas others are not. This raises an interesting question: Can we say the effect of religious affiliation, controlling for income, is statistically significant? The answer is that it depends on which categories of religious affiliation we want to compare.

11.3 TESTING INTERACTIVE HYPOTHESES WITH DUMMY VARIABLES

All of the OLS models that we have examined so far have been **additive models**. To calculate the $\hat{Y}$ value for a particular case from an additive model, we simply multiply each independent variable value for that case by the appropriate parameter estimate and *add* these values together. In this section we explore some **interactive models**. Interactive models contain at least one independent variable that we create by multiplying together two or more independent variables. When we specify interactive models, we are testing theories about how the effects of one independent variable on our dependent variable may be contingent on the value of another independent variable. We will continue with our running example of modeling respondents' thermometer scores for Hillary Clinton. We begin with an additive model with the following specification:

$$\text{Hillary Thermometer}_i = \alpha + \beta_1 \text{Women's Movement Thermometer}_i$$
$$+ \beta_2 \text{Female}_i + u_i.$$

In this model we are testing the theory that respondents' feelings toward Hillary Clinton are a function of their feelings toward the women's movement and their own gender. This specification seems pretty reasonable, but we also want to test an additional theory that the effect of feelings toward the women's movement have a stronger effect on feelings toward Hillary Clinton among women than they do among men. Notice the difference in phrasing there. In essence, we want to test the hypothesis that the slope of the line representing the relationship between Women's Movement Thermometer and Hillary Clinton Thermometer is *steeper* for women than it is for men. To test this hypothesis, we need to create a new variable that is the product of the two independent variables in our model and include this new variable in our model:

$$\text{Hillary Thermometer}_i = \alpha + \beta_1 \text{Women's Movement Thermometer}_i$$
$$+ \beta_2 \text{Female}_i + \beta_3 (\text{Women's Movement Thermometer}_i \times \text{Female}_i) + u_i.$$

By specifying our model as such, we have created two different models for women and men. So we can rewrite our model as

$$\text{for Men (Female = 0)} : \text{Hillary Thermometer}_i = \alpha$$
$$+ \beta_1 \text{Women's Movement Thermometer}_i + u_i;$$
$$\text{for Women (Female = 1)} : \text{Hillary Thermometer}_i = \alpha$$
$$+ \beta_1 \text{Women's Movement Thermometer}_i$$
$$+ (\beta_2 + \beta_3)(\text{Women's Movement Thermometer}_i) + u_i.$$

Table 11.4. The effects of gender and feelings toward the women's movement on Hillary Clinton Thermometer scores

Independent variable	Additive model	Interactive model
Women's Movement Thermometer	0.68***	0.75***
	(0.03)	(0.05)
Female	7.13***	15.21***
	(1.37)	(4.19)
Women's Movement Thermometer × Female	–	−0.13**
		(0.06)
Intercept	5.98**	1.56
	(2.13)	(3.04)
n	1466	1466
R^2	.27	.27

Notes: The dependent variable in both models is the respondent's thermometer score for Hillary Clinton. Standard errors in parentheses. Two-sided t-tests: ***indicates $p < .01$; **indicates $p < .05$; *indicates $p < .10$.

And we can rewrite the formula for women as

$$\text{for Women (Female} = 1) : \text{Hillary Thermometer}_i = (\alpha + \beta_2)$$
$$+ (\beta_1 + \beta_3)(\text{Women's Movement Thermometer}_i) + u_i.$$

What this all boils down to is that we are allowing our regression line to be different for men and women. For men, the intercept is α and the slope is β_1. For women, the intercept is $\alpha + \beta_2$ and the slope is $\beta_1 + \beta_3$. However, if $\beta_2 = 0$ and $\beta_3 = 0$, then the regression lines for men and women will be the same. Table 11.4 shows the results for our additive and interactive models of the effects of gender and feelings toward the women's movement on Hillary Clinton Thermometer scores. We can see from the interactive model that we can reject the null hypothesis that $\beta_2 = 0$ and the null hypothesis that $\beta_3 = 0$, so our regression lines for men and women are different. We can also see that the intercept for the line for women $(\alpha + \beta_2)$ is higher than the intercept for men (α). But, perhaps contrary to our expectations, the estimated effect of the Women's Movement Thermometer for men is greater than the effect of the Women's Movement Thermometer for women.

The best way to see the combined effect of all of the results from the interactive model in Table 11.4 is to look at them graphically in a figure such as Figure 11.3. From this figure we can see the regression lines for men and for women across the range of the independent variable. It is clear from this figure that, although women are generally more favorably inclined toward Hillary Clinton, this gender gap narrows when we compare those individuals who feel more positively toward the feminist movement.

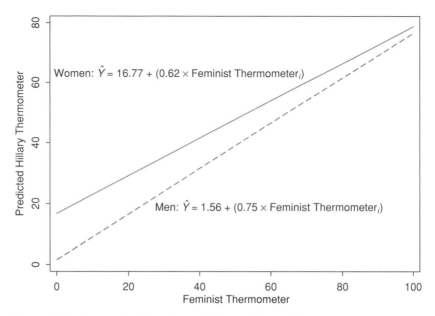

Figure 11.3. Regression lines from the interactive model.

11.4 DUMMY DEPENDENT VARIABLES

Thus far, our discussion of dummy variables has been limited to situations in which the variable in question is one of the independent variables in our model. The obstacles in those models are relatively straightforward. Things get a bit more complicated, however, when our dependent variable is a dummy variable.

Certainly, many of the dependent variables of theoretical interest to political scientists are not continuous. Very often, this means that we need to move to a statistical model other than OLS if we want to get reasonable estimates for our hypothesis testing. One exception to this is the **linear probability model** (LPM). The LPM is an OLS model in which the dependent variable is a dummy variable. It is called a "probability" model because we can interpret the $\hat{Y}$ values as "predicted probabilities." But, as we will see, it is not without problems. Because of these problems, most political scientists do not use the LPM. We provide a brief discussion of the popular alternatives to the LPM and then conclude this section with a discussion of goodness-of-fit measures when the dependent variable is a dummy variable.

11.4.1 The Linear Probability Model

As an example of a dummy dependent variable, we use the choice that most U.S. voters in the 2004 presidential election made between voting for the incumbent George W. Bush and his Democratic challenger John

Table 11.5. The effects of partisanship and performance evaluations on votes for Bush in 2004

Independent variable	Parameter estimate
Party Identification	0.09***
	(0.01)
Evaluation: War on Terror	0.08***
	(0.01)
Evaluation: Health of the Economy	0.08***
	(0.01)
Intercept	0.60***
	(0.01)
n	780
R^2	.73

Notes: The dependent variable is equal to one if the respondent voted for Bush and equal to zero if they voted for Kerry. Standard errors in parentheses. Two-sided t-tests: ***indicates $p < .01$; **indicates $p < .05$; *indicates $p < .10$.

Kerry.[4] Our dependent variable, which we will call "Bush," is equal to one for respondents who reported voting for Bush and equal to zero for respondents who reported voting for Kerry. For our model we theorize that the decision to vote for Bush or Kerry is a function of an individual's partisan identification (ranging from -3 for strong Democrats, to 0 for independents, to $+3$ for strong Republican identifiers) and their evaluation of the job that Bush did in handling the war on terror and the health of economy (both of these evaluations range from $+2$ for "approve strongly" to -2 for "disapprove strongly"). The formula for this model is:

$$Bush_i = \alpha + \beta_1 \text{Party ID}_i + \beta_2 \text{War Evaluation}_i$$

$$+ \beta_3 \text{Economic Evaluation}_i + u_i.$$

Table 11.5 presents the OLS results from this model. We can see from the table that all of the parameter estimates are statistically significant in the expected (positive) direction. Not surprisingly, we see that people

[4] There was only a handful of respondents to the NES who refused to reveal their vote to the interviewers or voted for a different candidate. But there were a large number of respondents who reported that they did not vote. By excluding all of these categories, we are defining the population about which we want to make inferences as those who voted for Kerry or Bush. Including respondents who voted for other candidates, refused to report their vote, or those who did not vote would amount to changing from a dichotomous categorical dependent variable to a multichotomous categorical dependent variable. The types of models used for this type of dependent variable are substantially more complicated.

who identified with the Republican Party and who had more approving evaluations of the president's handling of the war and the economy were more likely to vote for him. This model performs pretty well overall, with an R^2 statistic equal to .73.

To examine how the interpretation of this model is different from that of a regular OLS model, let's calculate some individual $\hat{Y}$ values. We know from Table 11.5 that the formula for $\hat{Y}$ is

$$\hat{Y}_i = 0.6 + 0.09 \times \text{Party ID}_i + 0.08 \times \text{War Evaluation}_i$$
$$+ 0.08 \times \text{Economic Evaluation}_i.$$

For a respondent who reported being a pure independent (Party ID = 0) with a somewhat approving evaluation of Bush's handling of the war on terror (War Evaluation = 1) and a somewhat disapproving evaluation of Bush's handling of the health of the economy (Economic Evaluation = -1), we would calculate $\hat{Y}_i$ as follows:

$$\hat{Y}_i = 0.6 + (0.09 \times 0) + (0.08 \times 1) + (0.08 \times -1) = 0.6.$$

One logical way to interpret this predicted value is to think of it as a **predicted probability** that the dummy dependent variable is equal to one. Using the example for which we just calculated $\hat{Y}_i$, we would predict that such an individual would have a 0.6 probability (or 60% chance) of voting for Bush in 2004. As you can imagine, if we change the values of our three independent variables around, the predicted probability of the individual voting for Bush changes correspondingly. This means that the LPM is a special case of OLS for which we can think of the predicted values of the dependent variable as predicted probabilities. From here on, we represent predicted probabilities for a particular case as "$\hat{P}_i$" or "$\hat{P}(Y_i = 1)$" and we can summarize this special property of the LPM as $\hat{P}_i = \hat{P}(Y_i = 1) = \hat{Y}_i$.

One of the problems with the LPM comes when we arrive at extreme values of the predicted probabilities. Consider, for instance, a respondent who reported being a strong Republican (Party ID = 3) with a strongly approving evaluation of Bush's handling of the war on terror (War Evaluation = 2) and a somewhat strongly approving evaluation of Bush's handling of the health of the economy (Economic Evaluation = 2). For this individual, we would calculate $\hat{P}_i$ as follows:

$$\hat{P}_i = \hat{Y}_i = 0.6 + (0.09 \times 3) + (0.08 \times 2) + (0.08 \times 2) = 1.19.$$

This means that we would predict that such an individual would have a 119% chance of voting for Bush in 2004. Such a predicted probability is, of course, nonsensical because probabilities cannot be smaller than zero or greater than one. So, one of the problems with the LPM is that it can produce such values. In the greater scheme of things, though, this problem is not so severe, as we can make sensible interpretations of predicted values higher than one or lower than zero – these are cases for which we are very confident that probability is close to one (for $\hat{P}_i > 1$) or close to zero (for $\hat{P}_i < 0$).

To the extent that the LPM has potentially more serious problems, they come in two forms – heteroscedasticity and functional form. We discussed heteroscedasticity in Chapter 9 when we noted that any time that we estimate an OLS model we assume that there is homoscedasticity (or equal error variance). We can see that this assumption is particularly problematic with the LPM because the values of the dependent variable are all equal to zero or one, but the $\hat{Y}$ or predicted values range anywhere between zero and one (or even beyond these values). This means that the errors (or residual values) will tend to be largest for cases for which the predicted value is close to .5. Any nonuniform pattern of model error variance such as this is called heteroscedasticity, which means that the estimated standard errors may be too high or too low. We care about this because standard errors that are too high or too low will have bad effects on our hypothesis testing and thus ultimately on our conclusions about causal relationships.

The problem of functional form is related to the assumption of parametric linearity that we also discussed in Chapter 9. In the context of the LPM, this assumption amounts to saying that the impact of a one-unit change in an independent variable X is equal to the corresponding parameter estimate $\hat{\beta}$ regardless of the value of X or any other independent variable. This assumption may be particularly problematic for LPMs because the effect of a change in an independent variable may be greater for cases that would otherwise be at 0.5 than for those cases for which the predicted probability would otherwise be close to zero or one. Obviously the extent of both of these problems will vary across different models.

For these reasons, the typical political science solution to having a dummy dependent variable is to avoid using the LPM. Most applications that you will come across in political science research will use a **binomial logit** (BNL) or **binomial probit** (BNP) model instead of the LPM for models in which the dependent variable is a dummy variable. BNL and BNP models are similar to regression models in many ways, but they involve an additional step in interpreting them. In the next subsection we provide a brief overview of these types of models.

11.4.2   Binomial Logit and Binomial Probit

In cases in which their dependent variable is dichotomous, most political scientists use a BNL or a BNP model instead of a LPM. In this subsection we provide a brief introduction to these two models, using the same example that we used for our LPM in the previous subsection. To understand these models, let's first rewrite our LPM from our preceding example in terms of a probability statement:

$$P_i = P(Y_i = 1) = \alpha + \beta_1 \times \text{Party ID}_i + \beta_2 \times \text{War Evaluation}_i + \beta_3$$
$$\times \text{Economic Evaluation}_i + u_i.$$

This is just a way of expressing the probability part of the LPM in a formula in which "$P(Y_i = 1)$" translates to "the probability that Y_i is equal to one," which in the case of our running example is the probability that the individual cast a vote for Bush. We then further collapse this to

$$P_i = P(Y_i = 1) = \alpha + \beta_1 X_{1i} + \beta_2 X_{2i} + \beta_3 X_{3i} + u_i,$$

and yet further to

$$P_i = P(Y_i = 1) = X_i \beta + u_i,$$

where we define $X_i \beta$ as the systematic component of Y such that $X_i \beta = \alpha + \beta_1 X_{1i} + \beta_2 X_{2i} + \beta_3 X_{3i}$.[5] The term u_i continues to represent the stochastic or random component of Y. So if we think about our predicted probability for a given case, we can write this as

$$\hat{Y}_i = \hat{P}_i = \hat{P}(Y_i = 1) = X_i \hat{\beta} = \hat{\alpha} + \hat{\beta}_1 X_{1i} + \hat{\beta}_2 X_{2i} + \hat{\beta}_3 X_{3i}.$$

A BNL model with the same variables would be written as

$$P_i = P(Y_i = 1) = \Lambda(\alpha + \beta_1 X_{1i} + \beta_2 X_{2i} + \beta_3 X_{3i} + u_i) = \Lambda(X_i \beta + u_i).$$

The predicted probabilities from this model would be written as

$$\hat{P}_i = \hat{P}(Y_i = 1) = \Lambda(\hat{\alpha} + \hat{\beta}_1 X_{1i} + \hat{\beta}_2 X_{2i} + \hat{\beta}_3 X_{3i} = \Lambda(X_i \hat{\beta}).$$

A BNP with the same variables would be written as

$$P_i = P(Y_i = 1) = \Phi(\alpha + \beta_1 X_{1i} + \beta_2 X_{2i} + \beta_3 X_{3i} + u_i) = \Phi(X_i \beta + u_i).$$

The predicted probabilities from this model would be written as

$$\hat{P}_i = \hat{P}(Y_i = 1) = \Phi(\hat{\alpha} + \hat{\beta}_1 X_{1i} + \hat{\beta}_2 X_{2i} + \hat{\beta}_3 X_{3i} = \Phi(X_i \hat{\beta}).$$

The difference between the BNL model and the LPM is the Λ, and the difference between the BNP model and the LPM is the Φ. Λ and Φ are known as **link functions**. A link function *links* the linear component of a

---

[5] This shorthand comes from matrix algebra. Although matrix algebra is a very useful tool in statistics, it is not needed to master the material in this text.

Table 11.6. The effects of partisanship and performance evaluations on votes for Bush in 2004: Three different types of models

Variable	LPM	BNL	BNP
Party Identification	0.09***	0.82***	0.45***
	(0.01)	(0.09)	(0.04)
Evaluation: War on Terror	0.08***	0.60***	0.32***
	(0.01)	(0.09)	(0.05)
Evaluation: Health of the Economy	0.08***	0.59***	0.32***
	(0.01)	(0.10)	(0.06)
Intercept	0.60***	1.11***	0.58***
	(0.01)	(0.20)	(0.10)

Notes: The dependent variable is equal to one if the respondent voted for Bush and equal to zero if they voted for Kerry. Standard errors in parentheses. Two-sided significance tests: ***indicates $p < .01$; **indicates $p < .05$; *indicates $p < .10$.

logit or probit model, $X_i\hat{\beta}$, to the quantity in which we are interested, the predicted probability that the dummy dependent variable equals one $\hat{P}(Y_i = 1)$ or $\hat{P}_i$. A major result of using these link functions is that the relationship between our independent and dependent variables is no longer assumed to be linear. In the case of a logit model, the link function, abbreviated as Λ, uses the cumulative logistic distribution function (and thus the name "logit") to link the linear component to the probability that $Y_i = 1$. In the case of the probit function, the link function abbreviated as Φ uses the cumulative normal distribution function to link the linear component to the predicted probability that $Y_i = 1$. Appendices C (for the BNL) and D (for the BNP) provide tables for converting $X_i\hat{\beta}$ values into predicted probabilities.

The best way to understand how the LPM, BNL, and BNP work similarly to and differently from each other is to look at them all with the same model and data. An example of this is presented in Table 11.6. From this table it is apparent that across the three models the parameter estimate for each independent variable has the same sign and significance level. But it is also apparent that the magnitude of these parameter estimates is different across the three models. This is mainly due to the difference of link functions. To better illustrate the differences between the three models presented in Table 11.6, we plotted the predicted probabilities from them in Figure 11.4. These predicted probabilities are for an individual who strongly approved of the Bush administration's handling of the war on terror but who strongly disapproved of the Bush administration's handling

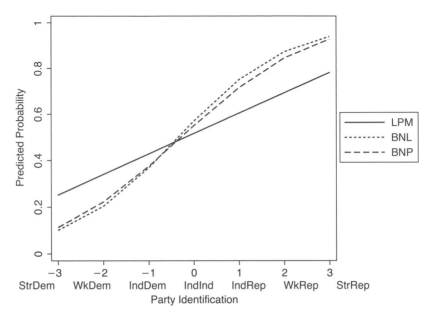

Figure 11.4. Three different models of Bush vote.

of the economy.[6] The horizontal axis in this figure is this individual's party identification ranging from strong Democratic Party identifiers on the left end to strong Republican Party identifiers on the right end. The vertical axis is the predicted probability of voting for Bush. We can see from this figure that the three models make very similar predictions. The main differences come as we move away from a predicted probability of 0.5.

The LPM line has, by definition, a constant slope across the entire range of X. The BNL and BNP lines of predicted probabilities change their slope such that they slope more and more gently as we move farther from predicted probabilities of 0.5. The differences between the BNL and BNP lines are trivial. This means that the effect of a movement in Party Identification on the predicted probability is constant for the LPM. But for the BNL and BNP, the effect of a movement in Party Identification *depends* on the value of the other variables in the model. It is important to realize that the differences between the LPM and the other two types of models are by construction instead of some novel finding. In other words, our choice of model determines the shape of our predicted probability line.

---

[6] These were the modal answers to the two evaluative questions that were included in the model presented in Table 11.6. It is fairly common practice to illustrate the estimated impact of a variable of interest from this type of model by holding all other variables constant at their mean or modal values and then varying that one variable to see how the predicted probabilities change.

Table 11.7. Classification table from LPM of the effects of partisanship and performance evaluations on votes for Bush in 2004

Actual Vote	Model-based expectations	
	Bush	Kerry
Bush	361	36
Kerry	28	355

Notes: Cell entries are the number of cases. Predictions are based on a cutoff of $\hat{Y} > 0.5$

11.4.3 Goodness-of-Fit with Dummy Dependent Variables

Although we can calculate an R^2 statistic when we estimate a linear probability model, R^2 doesn't quite capture what we are doing when want to assess the fit of such a model. What we are trying to assess is the ability of our model to separate our cases into those in which $Y = 1$ and those in which $Y = 0$. So it is helpful to think about this in terms of a 2×2 table of model-based expectations and actual values. To figure out the model's expected values, we need to choose a cutoff point at which we interpret the model as predicting that $Y = 1$. An obvious value to use for this cutoff point is $\hat{Y} > 0.5$. Table 11.7 shows the results of this in what we call a **classification table**. Classification tables compare model-based expectations with actual values of the dependent variable.

In this table, we can see the differences between the LPM's predictions and the actual votes reported by survey respondents to the 2004 NES. One fairly straightforward measure of the fit of this model is to look at the percentage of cases that were correctly classified through use the model. So if we add up the cases correctly classified and divide by the total number of cases we get

$$\text{correctly classified } LPM_{0.5} = \frac{361 + 355}{780} = \frac{716}{780} = 0.918$$

So our LPM managed to correctly classify 0.918 or 91.8% of the respondents and to erroneously classify the remaining 0.082 or 8.2%.

Although this seems like a pretty high classification rate, we don't really know what we should be comparing it with. One option is to compare our model's classification rate with the classification rate for a naive model (NM) that predicts that all cases will be in the modal category. In this case, the NM would predict that all respondents voted for Bush. So, if we calculate the correctly classified for the NM,

$$\text{correctly classified NM} = \frac{361 + 36}{780} = \frac{397}{780} = 0.509$$

This means that the NM correctly classified 0.509 or 50.9% of the respondents and erroneously classified the remaining 0.491 or 49.1%.

Turning now to the business of comparing the performance of our model with that of the NM, we can calculate the **proportionate reduction of error** when we move from the NM to our LPM with party identification and two performance evaluations as independent variables. The percentage erroneously classified in the naive model was 49.1 and the percentage erroneously classified in our LPM was 8.2. So we have reduced the error proportion by $49.1 - 8.2 = 40.9$. If we now divide this by the total error percentage of the naive model, we get $\frac{40.9}{49.1} = 0.833$. This means that we have a proportionate reduction of error equal to 0.833. Another way of saying this is that when we moved from the NM to our LPM we reduced the classification errors by 83.3%.

11.5   OUTLIERS AND INFLUENTIAL CASES IN OLS

In Section 6.4 we advocated using descriptive statistics to identify outlier values for each continuous variable. In the context of a single variable, an outlier is an extreme value relative to the other values for that variable. But in the context of an OLS model, when we say that a single case is an outlier, we could mean several different things.

We should always strive to know our data well. This means looking at individual variables and identifying univariate outliers. But just because a case is an outlier in the univariate sense does not necessarily imply that it will be an outlier in all senses of this concept in the multivariate world. Nonetheless, we should look for outliers in the single-variable sense before we run our models and make sure that when we identify such cases that they are actual values and not values created by some type of data management mistake.

In the regression setting, individual cases can be outliers in several different ways:

1. They can have unusual independent variable values. This is known as a case having large **leverage**. This can be the result of a single case having an unusual value for a single variable. A single case can also have large leverage because it has an unusual *combination* of values across two or more variables. There are a variety of different measures of leverage, but they all make calculations across the values of independent variables in order to identify individual cases that are particularly different.
2. They can have large residual values (usually we look at squared residuals to identify outliers of this variety).

3. They can have both large leverage and large residual values.

The relationship among these different concepts of outliers for a single case in OLS is often summarized as separate contributions to "influence" in the following formula:

$$\text{influence}_i = \text{leverage}_i \times \text{residual}_i.$$

As this formula indicates, the influence of a particular case is determined by the combination of its leverage and residual values. There are a variety of different ways to measure these different factors. We explore a couple of them in the following subsections with a controversial real-world example.

11.5.1 Identifying Influential Cases

One of the most famous cases of outliers/influential cases in political data comes from the 2000 U.S. presidential election in Florida. In an attempt to measure the extent to which ballot irregularities may have influenced election results, a variety of models were estimated in which the raw vote numbers for candidates across different counties were the dependent variables of interest. These models were fairly unusual because the parameter estimates and other quantities that are most often the focus of our model interpretations were of little interest. Instead, these were models for which the most interesting quantities were the diagnostics of outliers. As an example of such a model, we will work with the following:

$$\text{Buchanan}_i = \alpha + \beta \text{Gore}_i + u_i.$$

In this model the cases are individual counties in Florida, the dependent variable (Buchanan$_i$) is the number of votes in each Florida county for the independent candidate Patrick Buchanan, and the independent variable is the number of votes in each Florida county for the Democratic Party's nominee Al Gore (Gore$_i$). Such models are unusual in the sense that there is no claim of an underlying causal relationship between the independent and dependent variables. Instead, the theory behind this type of model is that there should be a strong systematic relationship between the number of votes cast for Gore and those cast for Buchanan across the Florida counties.[7] There was a suspicion that the ballot structure used in some counties – especially the infamous "butterfly ballot" – was such that it confused some voters who intended to vote for Gore into voting for Buchanan. If this

---

[7] Most of the models of this sort make adjustments to the variables (for example, logging the values of both the independent and dependent variables) to account for possibilities of nonlinear relationships. In the present example we avoided doing this for the sake of simplicity.

Table 11.8. Votes for Gore and Buchanan in Florida counties in the 2000 U.S. presidential election

Independent variable	Parameter estimate
Votes for Gore	0.004***
	(0.0005)
Intercept	80.63*
	(46.4)
n	67
R^2	.48

Notes: The dependent variable is the number of votes for Patrick Buchanan. Standard errors in parentheses. Two-sided t-tests: ***indicates $p < .01$; **indicates $p < .05$; *indicates $p < .10$.

was the case, we should see these counties appearing as outliers after we estimate our model.

We can see from Table 11.8 that there was indeed a statistically significant positive relationship between Gore and Buchanan votes, and that this simple model accounts for 48% of the variation in Buchanan votes across the Florida counties. But, as we said before, the more interesting inferences from this particular OLS model are in the outlier/influence of particular cases. Figure 11.5 presents a Stata lvr2plot (short for

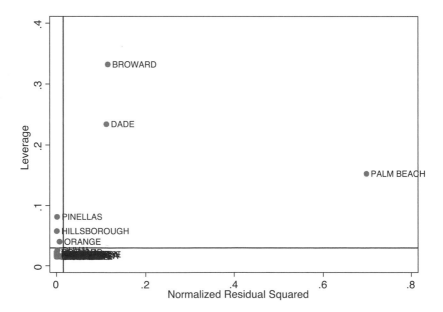

Figure 11.5. Stata lvr2plot for the model presented in Table 11.8.

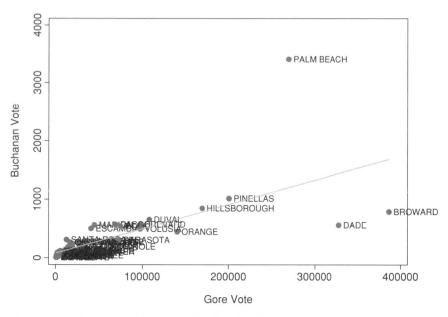

Figure 11.6. OLS line with scatter plot for Florida 2000.

"leverage-versus-residual-squared plot") that displays Stata's measure of leverage on the vertical dimension and a normalized measure of the squared residuals on the horizontal dimension. The logic of this figure is that, as we move to the right of the vertical line through this figure, we are seeing cases with unusually large residual values, and that, as we move above the horizontal line through this figure, we are seeing cases with unusually large leverage values. Cases with both unusually large residual and leverage values are highly influential. From this figure it is apparent that Pinellas, Hillsborough, and Orange counties had large leverage values but not particularly large squared residual values, whereas Dade, Broward, and Palm Beach counties were highly influential with both large leverage values and large squared residual values.

We can get a better idea of the correspondence between Figure 11.5 and Table 11.8 from Figure 11.6, in which we plot the OLS regression line through a scatter plot of the data. From this figure it is clear that Palm Beach was well above the regression line whereas Broward and Dade counties were well below the regression line. By any measure, these three cases were substantial outliers and thus quite influential in our model.

A more specific method for detecting the influence of an individual case involves estimating our model with and without particular cases to see how much this changes specific parameter estimates. The resulting calculation is known as the **DFBETA score** (Belsley, Kuh, and Welsch 1980). DFBETA scores are calculated as the difference in the parameter

Table 11.9. The five largest (absolute-value) DFBETA scores for β from the model presented in Table 11.8

County	DFBETA
Palm Beach	6.993
Broward	−2.514
Dade	−1.772
Orange	−0.109
Pinellas	0.085

estimate without each case divided by the standard error of the original parameter estimate. Table 11.9 displays the five largest absolute values of DFBETA for the slope parameter (β) from the model presented in Table 11.8. Not surprisingly, we see that omitting Palm Beach, Broward, or Dade has the largest impact on our estimate of the slope parameter. By any measure, these cases exerted considerable influence on our model.

11.5.2 Dealing With Influential Cases

Now that we have discussed the identification of particularly influential/outlier cases on our models, we turn to the subject of what to do once we have identified such cases. The first thing to do when we identify a case with substantial influence is to double-check the values of all variables for such a case. We want to be certain that we have not "created" an influential case through some error in our data management procedures. Once we have corrected for any errors of data management and determined that we still have some particularly influential case(s), it is important that we report our findings about such cases along with our other findings. There are a variety of strategies for doing so. Table 11.10 shows five different models that reflect various approaches to reporting results with highly influential cases. In Model 1 we have the original results as reported in Table 11.8. In Model 2 we have added a dummy variable that identifies and isolates the effect of Palm Beach County. This approach is sometimes referred to as **dummying out** influential cases. We can see why this is called dummying out from the results in Model 3, which is the original model with the observation for Palm Beach County dropped from the analysis. The parameter estimates and standard errors for the intercept and slope parameters are identical from Models 2 and 3. The only differences are the model R^2 statistic, the number of cases, and the additional parameter estimate reported in Model 2 for the Palm Beach County dummy variable.[8] In Model 4 and Model 5,

[8] This parameter estimate was viewed by some as an estimate of how many votes the ballot irregularities cost Al Gore in Palm Beach County. But if we look at Model 4, where we include dummy variables for Broward and Dade Counties, we can see the basis for an argument that in these two counties there is evidence of bias in the opposite direction.

Table 11.10. Votes for Gore and Buchanan in Florida counties in the 2000 U.S. presidential election

Independent variable	Model 1	Model 2	Model 3	Model 4	Model 5
Gore	0.004***	0.003***	0.003***	0.005***	0.005***
	(0.0005)	(0.0002)	(0.0002)	(0.0003)	(0.0003)
Palm Beach dummy		2606.3***		2095.5***	
		(150.4)		(110.6)	
Broward dummy				−1066.0***	
				(131.6)	
Dade dummy				−1025.6***	
				(120.6)	
Intercept	80.6*	110.8***	110.8***	59.0***	59.0***
	(46.4)	(19.7)	(19.7)	(13.8)	(13.8)
n	67	67	66	67	64
R^2	.48	.91	.63	.96	.82

Notes: The dependent variable is the number of votes for Patrick Buchanan.

Standard errors in parentheses.

Two-sided t-tests: ***indicates $p < .01$; **indicates $p < .05$; *indicates $p < .10$.

we see the results from dummying out the three most influential cases and then from dropping them out of the analysis.

Across all five of the models shown in Table 11.10, the slope parameter estimate remains positive and statistically significant. In most models, this would be the quantity in which we are most interested (testing hypotheses about the relationship between X and Y). Thus the relative robustness of this parameter across model specifications would be comforting. Regardless of the effects of highly influential cases, it is important first to know that they exist and, second, to report accurately what their influence is and what we have done about them.

11.6 MULTICOLLINEARITY

When we specify and estimate a multiple OLS model, what is the interpretation of each individual parameter estimate? It is our best guess of the causal impact of a one-unit increase in the relevant independent variable on the dependent variable, controlling for all of the other variables in the model. Another way of saying this is that we are looking at the impact of a one-unit increase in one independent variable on the dependent

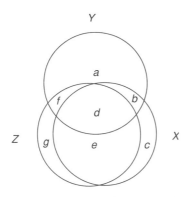

Figure 11.7. Venn diagram with multicollinearity.

variable when we "hold all other variables constant." We know from Chapter 10 that a minimal mathematical property for estimating a multiple OLS model is that there is no perfect multicollinearity. Perfect multicollinearity, you will recall, occurs when one independent variable is an exact linear function of one or more other independent variables in a model.

In practice, perfect multicollinearity is usually the result of a small number of cases relative to the number of parameters we are estimating, limited independent variable values, or model misspecification. As we have noted, if there exists perfect multicollinearity, OLS parameters cannot be estimated. A much more common and vexing issue is less-than-perfect multicollinearity. As a result, when people refer to multicollinearity, they almost always mean "less-than-perfect multicollinearity." From here on, when we refer to "multicollinearity," we will mean "high, but less-than-perfect, multicollinearity." This means that two or more of the independent variables in the model are extremely highly correlated with one another.

11.6.1 How Does Multicollinearity Happen?

Multicollinearity is induced by a small number of degrees of freedom and/or high correlation between independent variables. Figure 11.7 provides a Venn diagram illustration that is useful for thinking about the effects of multicollinearity in the context of an OLS regression model. As you can see from this figure, X and Z are fairly highly correlated. Our regression model is

$$Y_i = \alpha + \beta_1 X_i + \beta_2 Z_i + u_i.$$

Looking at the figure, we can see that the R^2 from our regression model will be fairly high ($R^2 = \frac{f+d+b}{a+f+d+b}$). But we can see from this figure that the areas for the estimation of our two slope parameters – area f for β_1 and area b for β_2 – are pretty small. Because of this, our standard errors for our slope parameters will tend to be fairly large, which makes discovering statistically significant relationships more difficult, and we will have difficulty making precise inferences about the impacts of both X and Z on Y. It is possible that because of this problem we would conclude neither X nor Z has much of an impact on Y. But clearly this is not the case. As we can see from the diagram, both X and Z *are* related to Y. The problem is that much of the covariation between X and Y and X and Z is also covariation between X and Z. In other words, it is the size of area d that is causing us problems. We have precious little area in which to examine the effect of X on Y while holding Z constant, and likewise, there is little leverage to understand the effect of Z on Y while controlling for X.

It is worth emphasizing at this point that multicollinearity is not a statistical problem (examples of statistical problems include autocorrelation, bias, and heteroscedasticity). Rather, multicollinearity is a data problem. It is possible to have multicollinearity even when all of the assumptions of OLS from Chapter 9 are valid and all of the the minimal mathematical requirements for OLS from Chapters 9 and 10 have been met. So, you might ask, what's the big deal about multicollinearity? To underscore the notion of multicollinearity as a data problem instead of a statistical problem, Christopher Achen (1982) has suggested that the word "multicollinearity" should be used interchangeably with "micronumerosity." Imagine what would happen if we could double or triple the size of the diagram in Figure 11.7 without changing the relative sizes of any of the areas. As we expanded all of the areas, areas f and b would eventually become large enough for us to estimate accurate standard errors.

11.6.2   Detecting Multicollinearity

It is very important to know when you have multicollinearity. In particular, it is important to distinguish situations in which estimates are statistically insignificant because the relationships just aren't there from situations in which estimates are statistically insignificant because of multicollinearity. The diagram in Figure 11.7 shows us one way in which we might be able to detect multicollinearity: If we have a high R^2 statistic, but none (or very few) of our parameter estimates is statistically significant, we should be suspicious of multicollinerity. We should also be suspicious of multicollinearity if we see that, when we add and remove independent variables from our model, the parameter estimates for other independent variables (and especially their standard errors) change substantially. If we estimated the model represented in Figure 11.7 with just one of the two independent variables, we would get a statistically significant relationship. But, as we know from the discussions in Chapter 10, this would be problematic. Presumably we have a theory about the relationship between each of these independent variables (X and Z) and our dependent variable (Y). So, although the estimates from a model with just X or just Z as the independent variable would help us to detect multicollinearity, they would suffer from bias. And, as we argued in Chapter 10, omitted-variables bias is a severe problem.

A more formal way to diagnose multicollinearity is to calculate the **variance inflation factor** (VIF) for each of our independent variables. This calculation is based on an **auxiliary regression model** in which one independent variable, which we will call X_j, is the dependent variable and all of the other independent variables are independent variables.[9] The R^2 statistic from this auxiliary model, R_j^2, is then used to calculate the VIF for variable j as follows:

$$\text{VIF}_j = \frac{1}{(1 - R_j^2)}.$$

Many statistical programs report the VIF and its inverse ($\frac{1}{VIF}$) by default. The inverse of the VIF is sometimes referred to as the tolerance index measure. The higher the VIF_j value, or the lower the tolerance index, the higher will be the estimated variance of X_j in our theoretically specified model. Another useful statistic to examine is the square root of the VIF. Why? Because the VIF is measured in terms of variance, but most of our hypothesis-testing inferences are made with standard errors. Thus the square root of the VIF provides a useful indicator of the impact the multicollinearity is going to have on hypothesis-testing inferences.

11.6.3   Multicollinearity: A Simulated Example

Thus far we have made a few scattered references to simulation. In this subsection we make use of simulation to better understand multicollinearity. Almost every statistical computer program has a set of tools for simulating data. When we use these tools, we have an advantage that we do not ever have with real-world data: We can *know* the underlying "population" characteristics (because we create them). When we know the population parameters for a regression model and draw sample data from this population, we gain insights into the ways in which statistical models work.

---

[9] Students facing OLS diagnostic procedures are often surprised that the first thing that we do after we estimate our theoretically specified model of interest is to estimate a large set of atheoretical auxiliary models to test the properties of our main model. We will see that, although these auxiliary models lead to the same types of output that we get from our main model, we are often interested in only one particular part of the results from the auxiliary model. With our "main" model of interest, we have learned that we should include every variable that our theories tell us should be included and exclude all other variables. In auxiliary models, we do not follow this rule. Instead, we are running these models to test whether certain properties have or have not been met in our original model.

So, to simulate multicollinearity, we are going to create a population with the following characteristics:

1. Two variables X_{1i} and X_{2i} such that the correlation $r_{X_{1i}, X_{2i}} = 0.9$.
2. A variable u_i randomly drawn from a normal distribution, centered around 0 with variance equal to 1 $[u_i \sim N(0, 1)]$.
3. A variable Y_i such that $Y_i = 0.5 + 1 X_{1i} + 1 X_{2i} + u_i$.

We can see from the description of our simulated population that we have met all of the OLS assumptions, but that we have a high correlation between our two independent variables. Now we will conduct a series of random draws (samples) from this population and look at the results from the following regression models:

$$\text{Model 1: } Y_i = \alpha + \beta_1 X_{1i} + \beta_2 X_{2i} + u_i,$$

$$\text{Model 2: } Y_i = \alpha + \beta_1 X_{1i} + u_i,$$

$$\text{Model 3: } Y_i = \alpha + \beta_2 X_{2i} + u_i.$$

In each of these random draws, we increase the size of our sample starting with 5, then 10, and finally 25 cases. Results from models estimated with each sample of data are displayed in Table 11.11. In the first column of results ($n = 5$), we can see that both slope parameters are positive, as would be expected, but that the parameter estimate for X_1 is statistically insignificant and the parameter estimate for X_2 is on the borderline of statistical significance. The VIF statistics for both variables are equal to 5.26, indicating that the variance for each parameter estimate is substantially inflated by multicollinearity. The model's intercept is statistically significant and positive, but pretty far from what we know to be the true population value for this parameter. In Models 2 and 3 we get statistically significant positive parameter estimates for each variable, but both of these estimated slopes are almost twice as high as what we know to be the true population parameters. The 95% confidence interval for $\hat{\beta}_2$ does not include the true population parameter. This is a clear case of omitted-variables bias. When we draw a sample of 10 cases, we get closer to the true population parameters with $\hat{\beta}_1$ and $\hat{\alpha}$ in Model 1. The VIF statistics remain the same because we have not changed the underlying relationship between X_1 and X_2. This increase in sample size does not help us with the omitted-variables bias in Models 2 and 3. In fact, we can now reject the true population slope parameter for both models with substantial confidence. In our third sample with a sample of 25 cases, Model 1 is now very close to our true population model, in the sense of both the parameter values and that all of

Table 11.11. Random draws of increasing size from a population with substantial multicollinearity

Estimate	Sample: $n = 5$	Sample: $n = 10$	Sample: $n = 25$
Model 1:			
$\hat{\beta}_1$	0.546	0.882	1.012**
	(0.375)	(0.557)	(0.394)
$\hat{\beta}_2$	1.422*	1.450**	1.324***
	(0.375)	(0.557)	(0.394)
$\hat{\alpha}$	1.160**	0.912***	0.579***
	(0.146)	(0.230)	(0.168)
R^2	.99	.93	.89
VIF_1	5.26	5.26	5.26
VIF_2	5.26	5.26	5.26
Model 2:			
$\hat{\beta}_1$	1.827**	2.187***	2.204***
	(0.382)	(0.319)	(0.207))
$\hat{\alpha}$	1.160**	0.912**	0.579***
	(0.342)	(0.302)	(0.202)
R^2	.88	.85	.83
Model 3:			
$\hat{\beta}_2$	1.914***	2.244***	2.235***
	(0.192)	(0.264)	(0.192)
$\hat{\alpha}$	1.160***	0.912***	0.579***
	(0.171)	(0.251)	(0.188)
R^2	.97	.90	.86

Notes: The dependent variable is $Y_i = .5 + 1X_{1i} + 1X_{2i} + u_i$. Standard errors in parentheses. Two-sided t-tests: ***indicates $p < .01$; **indicates $p < .05$; *indicates $p < .10$.

these parameter estimates are statistically significant. In Models 2 and 3, the omitted-variables bias is even more pronounced.

The findings in this simulation exercise mirror more general findings in the theoretical literature on OLS models. *Adding more data will alleviate multicollinearity, but not omitted-variables bias.* We now turn to an example of multicollinearity with real-world data.

11.6.4   Multicollinearity: A Real-World Example

In this subsection, we estimate a model of the thermometer scores for U.S. voters for George W. Bush in 2004. Our model specification

Table 11.12. Pairwise correlations between independent variables					
	Bush Therm.	Income	Ideology	Education	Party ID
Bush Therm.	1.00				
Income	0.09***	1.00			
Ideology	0.56***	0.13***	1.00		
Education	−0.07***	0.44***	−0.06*	1.00	
Party ID	0.69***	0.15***	0.60***	0.06*	1.00

Notes: Cell entries are correlation coefficients. Two-sided t-tests: ***indicates $p < .01$; **indicates $p < .05$; *indicates $p < .10$.

is the following:

$$\text{Bush Thermometer}_i = \alpha + \beta_1 \text{Income}_i + \beta_2 \text{Ideology}_i + \beta_3 \text{Education}_i$$
$$+ \beta_4 \text{Party ID}_i + u_i.$$

Although we have distinct theories about the causal impact of each independent variable on peoples' feelings toward Bush, Table 11.12 indicates that some of these independent variables are substantially correlated with each other.

In Table 11.13, we present estimates of our model using three different samples from the NES 2004 data. In Model 1, estimated with data from 20 randomly chosen respondents, we see that none of our independent variables are statistically significant despite the rather high R^2 statistic. The VIF statistics for Ideology and Party ID indicate that multicollinearity might be a problem. In Model 2, estimated with data from 74 randomly chosen respondents, Party ID is highly significant in the expected (positive) direction whereas Ideology is near the threshold of statistical significance. None of the VIF statistics for this model are stunningly high, though they are greater than 1.5 for Ideology, Education, and Party ID.[10] Finally, in Model 3, estimated with all 820 respondents for whom data on all of the variables were available, we see that Ideology, Party ID, and Education are all significant predictors of peoples' feelings toward Bush. The sample size is more than sufficient to overcome the VIF statistics for Party ID and Ideology. Of our independent variables, only Income remains statistically insignificant. Is this due to multicollinearity? After all, when we look at Table 11.12, we see that income has a highly significant positive correlation with Bush Thermometer scores. For the answer to this question, we need to go back to the lessons that we learned in Chapter 10: Once we control

---

[10] When we work with real-world data, there tend to be many more changes as we move from sample to sample.

Table 11.13. Model results from random draws of increasing size from the 2004 NES

Independent variable	Model 1	Model 2	Model 3
Income	0.77	0.72	0.11
	(0.90)	(0.51)	(0.15)
	{1.63}	{1.16}	{1.24}
Ideology	7.02	4.57*	4.26***
	(5.53)	(2.22)	(0.67)
	{3.50}	{1.78}	{1.58}
Education	−6.29	−2.50	−1.88***
	(3.32)	(1.83)	(0.55)
	{1.42}	{1.23}	{1.22}
Party ID	6.83	8.44***	10.00***
	(3.98)	(1.58)	(0.46)
	{3.05}	{1.70}	{1.56}
Intercept	21.92	12.03	13.73***
	(23.45)	(13.03)	(3.56)
n	20	74	821
R^2	.71	.56	.57

Notes: The dependent variable is the the respondent's thermometer score for George W. Bush. Standard errors in parentheses; VIF statistics in braces.
Two-sided t-tests: *** indicates $p < .01$; ** indicates $p < .05$;
* indicates $p < .10$.

for the effects of Ideology, Party ID, and Education, the effect of income on peoples' feelings toward George W. Bush goes away.

11.6.5 Multicollinearity: What Should I Do?

In the introduction to this section on multicollinearity, we described it as a "common and vexing issue." The reason why multicollinearity is "vexing" is that there is no magical statistical cure for it. What is the best thing to do when you have multicollinearity? Easy (in theory): *Collect more data.* But data are expensive to collect. If we had more data, we would use them and we wouldn't have hit this problem in the first place. So, if you do not have an easy way increase your sample size, then multicollinearity ends up being something that you just have to live with. It is important to know that you have multicollinearity and to present your multicollinearity by reporting the results of VIF statistics or what happens to your model when you add and drop the "guilty" variables.

11.7   BEING CAREFUL WITH TIME SERIES

In recent years there has been a massive proliferation of valuable time-series data in political science. Although this growth has led to exciting new research opportunities, it has also been the source of a fair amount of controversy. Swirling at the center of this controversy is the danger of spurious regressions that are due to trends in time-series data. As we will see, a failure to recognize this problem can lead to mistakes about inferring causality. In the remainder of this section we first introduce time-series notation, discuss the problems of spurious regressions, and then discuss the trade-offs involved with two possible solutions: the lagged dependent variable and the differenced dependent variable.

11.7.1   Time-Series Notation

In Chapter 4 we introduced the concept of a time-series observational study. Although we have seen some time-series data (such as the Ray Fair data set used in Chapters 8–10), we have not been using the mathematical notation specific to time- series data. Instead, we have been using a generic notation in which the subscript i represents an individual case. In time-series notation, individual cases are represented with the subscript t, and the numeric value of t represents the temporal order in which the cases occurred, and this ordering is very likely to matter.[11] Consider the following OLS population model written in the notation that we have worked with thus far:

$$Y_i = \alpha + \beta_1 X_{1i} + \beta_2 X_{2i} + u_i.$$

If the data of interest were time-series data, we would rewrite this model as

$$Y_t = \alpha + \beta_1 X_{1t} + \beta_2 X_{2t} + u_t.$$

In most political science applications, time-series data occur at regular intervals. Common intervals for political science data are weeks, months, quarters, and years. In fact, these time intervals are important enough that they are usually front-and-center in the description of a data set. For instance, the data presented in Figure 2.1 would be described as a "monthly time series of presidential popularity."

Using this notation, we talk about the observations in the order in which they came. As such, it is often useful to talk about values of variables relative to their **lagged values** or **lead values**. Both lagged and lead values are expressions of values relative to a current time, which we call time t. A

---

[11] In cross-sectional data sets, it is almost always the case that the ordering of the cases is irrelevant to the analyses being conducted.

lagged value of a variable is the value of the variable from a previous time period. For instance, a lagged value from one period previous to the current time is referenced as being from time $t-1$. A lead value of a variable is the value of the variable from a future time period. For instance, a lead value from one period into the future from the current time is referenced as being from time $t+1$. Note that we would not want to specify a model with a leading value for an independent variable because this would amount to a theory that the future value of the independent variable exerted a causal influence on the past.

11.7.2 Memory and Lags in Time-Series Analysis

You might be wondering what, aside from changing a subscript from an i to a t, is so different about time-series modeling. We would like to bring special attention to one particular feature of time-series analysis that sets it apart from modeling cross-sectional data.

Consider the following simple model of presidential popularity, and assume that the data are in monthly form:

$$\text{Popularity}_t = \alpha + \beta_1 \text{Economy}_t + \beta_2 \text{Peace}_t + u_t,$$

where Economy and Peace refer to some measures of the health of the national economy and international peace, respectively. Now look at what the model assumes, quite explicitly. A president's popularity in any given month t is a function of that month's economy and that month's level of international peace (plus some random error term), *and nothing else, at any points in time*. What about last month's economic shocks, or the war that ended three months ago? They are nowhere to be found in this equation, which means quite literally that they can have no effect on a president's popularity ratings in this month. Every month – according to this model – the public starts from scratch evaluating the president, as if to say, on the first of the month: "Okay, let's just forget about last month. Instead, let's check this month's economic data, and also this month's international conflicts, and render a verdict on whether the president is doing a good job or not." There is no memory from month to month whatsoever. Every independent variable has an immediate impact, and that impact lasts exactly one month, after which the effect immediately dies out entirely.

This is preposterous, of course. The public does not erase its collective memory every month. Shifts in independent variables from many months in the past can have lingering effects into current evaluations of the president. In most cases, we imagine that the effects of shifts in independent variables eventually die out over a period of time, as new events become more salient in the minds of the public, and, indeed, some collective "forgetting" occurs. But surely this does not happen in a single month.

And let's be clear what the problems are with a model like the preceding simple model of approval. If we are convinced that at least some past values of the economy still have effects today, and if at least some past values of international peace still have effects today, but we instead estimate only the contemporary effects (from period t), then we have committed omitted-variables bias – which, as we have emphasized over the last two chapters, is one of the most serious mistakes a social scientist can make. Failing to account for how past values of our independent variables might affect current values of our dependent variable is a serious issue in time-series observational studies, and nothing quite like this issue exists in the cross-sectional world. In time-series analysis, even if we know that Y is caused by X and Z, we still have to worry about how many past lags of X and Z might affect Y.

The clever reader might have a ready response to such a situation: Specify additional lags of our independent variables in our regression models:

$$\text{Popularity}_t = \alpha + \beta_1\text{Economy}_t + \beta_2\text{Economy}_{t-1} + \beta_3\text{Economy}_{t-2}$$
$$+\beta_4\text{Economy}_{t-3} + \beta_5\text{Peace}_t + \beta_6\text{Peace}_{t-1} + \beta_7\text{Peace}_{t-2}$$
$$+\beta_8\text{Peace}_{t-3} + u_t.$$

This is, indeed, one possible solution to the question of how to incorporate the lingering effects of the past on the present. But the model is getting a bit unwieldy, with lots of parameters to estimate. More important, though, it leaves several questions unanswered:

1. How many lags of the independent variables should we include in our model? We have included lags from period t though $t - 3$ in the preceding specification, but how do we know that this is the correct choice? From the outset of the book, we have emphasized that you should have *theoretical* reasons for including variables in your statistical models. But what theory tells with any specificity that we should include 3, 4, or 6 periods' worth of lags of our independent variables in our models?

2. If we do include several lags of all of our independent variables in our models, we will almost surely induce multicollinearity into them. That is, X_t, X_{t-1}, and X_{t-2} are likely to be highly correlated with one another. (Such is the nature of time series.) Those models, then, would have all of the problems associated with high multicollinearity

just identified – in particular, large standard errors and the adverse consequences on hypothesis testing.

Before showing two alternatives to saturating our models with lots of lags of variables, we need to confront a different problem in time-series analysis.

11.7.3 Trends and the Spurious Regression Problem

When discussing presidential popularity data, it's easy to see how a time series might have a "memory" – by which we mean that the current values of a series seem to be highly dependent of its past values.[12] Some series have memories of their pasts that are sufficiently long to induce statistical problems. In particular, we mention one, called the **spurious regression problem**.[13]

By way of example, consider the following facts: In post–World War II America, golf became an increasingly popular sport. As its popularity grew, perhaps predictably the number of golf courses in America grew to accommodate the demand for places to play. That growth continued steadily into the early 21st century. We can think of the number of golf courses in America as a time series, of course, presumably one on an annual metric. Over the same period of time, divorce rates in America grew and grew. Whereas divorce was formerly an uncommon practice, today it is commonplace in American society. We can think of family structure as a time series, too – in this case, the percentage of households in which a married couple is present.[14]

And both of these time series – likely for different reasons – have long memories. In the case of golf courses, the number of courses in year t obviously depends heavily on the number of courses in the previous year. In the case of divorce rates, the dependence on the past presumably stems from the lingering, multiperiod influence of the social forces that lead to divorce in the first place. Both the number of golf facilities in America and the percentage of families in which a married couple is present are shown

---

[12] In any time series representing some form of public opinion, the word "memory" is a particularly apt term, though its use applies to all other time series as well.

[13] The problem of spurious regressions was something that economists like John Maynard Keynes worried about long before it had been mathematically demonstrated by Granger and Newbold (1974) in the 1970s. Their main source of concern was the existence of general trends in a variable over time. To be clear, the word "trend" obviously has several popular meanings. In time-series analysis, though, we generally use the word trend to refer to a long-lasting movement in the history of a variable, not a temporary drift in one direction or another.

[14] For the purposes of this illustration, we are obscuring the difference between divorce and unmarried cohabitation.

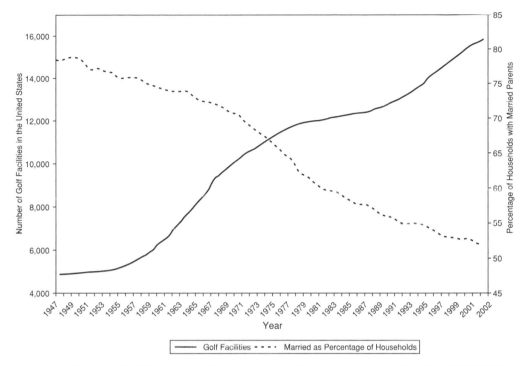

Figure 11.8. The growth of golf and the decline of the American family, 1947–2002.

in Figure 11.8.[15] And it's clear that, consistent with our description, both variables have trends. In the case of golf facilities, that trend is upward; for marriage, the trend is down.

What's the problem here? Any time one time series with a long memory is placed in a regression model with another series that also has a long memory, it can lead to falsely finding evidence of a causal connection between the two variables. This is known as the "spurious regression problem." If we take the demise of marriage as our dependent variable and use golf facilities as our independent variable, we would surely see that these two variables are related, statistically. In substantive terms, we might be tempted to jump to the conclusion that the growth of golf in America has led to the breakdown of the nuclear family. We show the results of that regression in Table 11.14. The dependent variable there is the percentage of households with a married couple, and the independent variable is the number of golf courses (in thousands). The results are exactly as feared. For every thousand golf facilities built in the United States, there are 2.53% fewer families with a married couple present. The R^2 statistic is quite high, suggesting that roughly 93% of the variance in divorce rates is explained by the growth of the golf industry.

---

[15] The National Golf Foundation kindly gave us the data on golf facilities. Data on family structure are from the Current Population Reports.

Table 11.14. Golf and the decline of the family, 1947–2002

Variable	Coefficient (Std. Err.)
Golf Facilities	−2.53*
	(0.09)
Constant	91.36*
	(1.00)
n	56
R^2	.93

Note: *indicates $p < .05$.

We're quite sure that some of you – presumably nongolfers – are nodding your heads and thinking, "But maybe golf *does* cause divorce rates to rise! Does the phrase 'golf widow' ring a bell?" But here's the problem with trending variables, and why it's such a potentially nasty problem in the social sciences. We could substitute *any* variable with a trend in it and come to the same "conclusion." To prove the point, let's take another example. Instead of examining the growth of golf, let's look at a different kind of growth – economic growth. In post-war America, GDP has grown steadily, with few interruptions in its upward trajectory. Figure 11.9 shows GDP, in annual terms, along with the now-familiar time series of the decline in marriage. Obviously, GDP is a long-memoried series, with a sharp upward trend, in which current values of the series depend extremely heavily on past values.

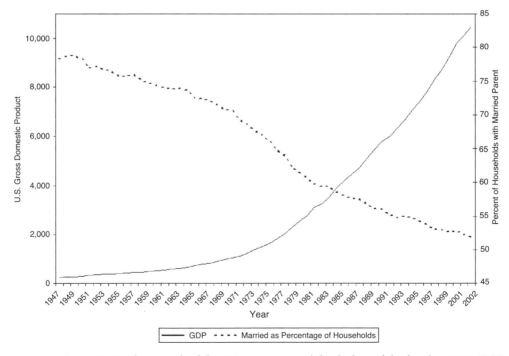

Figure 11.9. The growth of the U.S. economy and the decline of the family, 1947–2002.

Table 11.15. GDP and the decline of the family, 1947–2002	
Variable	Coefficient (Std. Err.)
GDP (in trillions)	−2.71*
	(0.16)
Constant	74.00*
	(0.69)
n	56
R^2	.84

Note: *indicates $p < .05$.

The spurious regression problem has some bite here, as well. Using Divorce as our dependent variable and GDP as our independent variable, the regression results in Table 11.15 show a strong, negative, and statistically significant relationship between the two. This is not occurring because higher rates of economic output have led to the destruction of the American family. It is occurring because both variables have trends in them, and a regression involving two variables with trends – even if they are not truly associated – will produce spurious evidence of a relationship.

The two issues just mentioned – how to deal with lagged effects in a time series and whether or not the spurious regression problem is relevant – are tractable ones. Moreover, new solutions to these issues arise as the study of time-series analysis becomes more sophisticated. We subsequently present two potential solutions to both problems.

11.7.4 The Differenced Dependent Variable

One way to avoid the problems of spurious regressions is to use a **differenced dependent variable**. We calculate a differenced (or, equivalently, "first differenced") variable by subtracting the first lag of the variable (Y_{t-1}) from the current value Y_t. The resulting time series is typically represented as $\Delta Y_t = Y_t - Y_{t-1}$.

In fact, when time series have long memories, taking first differences of both independent and dependent variables can be done. In effect, instead of Y_t representing the *levels* of a variable, ΔY_t represents the period-to-period *changes* in the level of the variable. For many (but not all) variables with such long memories, taking first differences will eliminate the visual pattern of a variable that just seems to keep going up.

Figure 11.10 presents the first differences of the number of golf courses in the United States, as well as the first differences of the U.S. annual divorce rates. You will notice, of course, that the time series in these figures look drastically different from their counterparts in levels from Figure 11.8. In fact, the visual "evidence" of an association between the two variables that appeared in Figure 11.8 has now vanished. The misleading culprit? Trends in both time series.

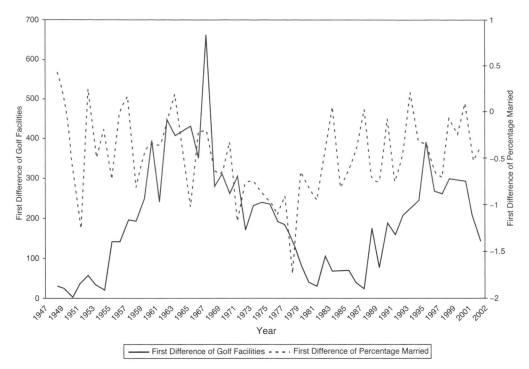

Figure 11.10. First differences of the number of golf courses and percentage of married families, 1947–2002.

Because, in these cases, taking first differences of the series removes the long memories from the series, these transformed time series will not be subject to the spurious regression problem. But we caution against thoughtless differencing of time series. In particular, taking first differences of time series can eliminate some (true) evidence of an association between time series in certain circumstances.

We recommend that, wherever possible, you use theoretical reasons to either difference a time series or to analyze it in levels. In effect, you should ask yourself if your theory about a causal connection between X and Y makes more sense in levels or in first differences. For example, if you are analyzing budgetary data from a government agency, does your theory specify particular things about the sheer amount of agency spending (in which case, you would analyze the data in levels), or does it specify particular things about what causes budgets to shift from year to year (in which case, you would analyze the data in first differences)?

It is also worth noting that taking first differences of your time series does not directly address the issue of the number of lags of independent variables to include in your models. For that, we turn to the lagged-dependent-variable specification.

11.7.5   The Lagged Dependent Variable

Consider for a moment a simple two-variable system with our familiar variables Y and X, except where, to allow for the possibility that previous lags of X might affect current levels of Y, we include a large number of lags of X in our model:

$$Y_t = \alpha + \beta_0 X_t + \beta_1 X_{t-1} + \cdots + \beta_k X_{t-k} + u_t.$$

This model is known as a **distributed lag model**. Notice the slight shift in notation here, in which we are subscripting our β coefficients by the number of periods that that variable is lagged from the current value; hence, the β for X_t is β_0 (because $t - 0 = t$). Under such a setup, the **cumulative impact** β of X on Y is

$$\beta = \beta_0 + \beta_1 + \beta_2 + \cdots + \beta_k = \sum_{i=0}^{k} \beta_i.$$

It is worth emphasizing that we are interested in that cumulative impact of X on Y, not merely the **instantaneous effect** of X_t on Y_t represented by the coefficient β_0.

But how can we capture the effects of X on Y without estimating such a cumbersome model like the preceding one? We have noted that a model like this would surely suffer from multicollinearity.

If we are willing to assume that the effect of X on Y is greatest initially and decays geometrically each period (eventually, after enough periods, becoming effectively 0), then a few steps of algebra would yield the following model that is mathematically identical to the preceding one,[16] That model looks like

$$Y_t = \lambda Y_{t-1} + \alpha + \beta_0 X_t + v_t.$$

This is known as the **Koyck transformation**, and is commonly referred to as the **lagged-dependent-variable** model, for reasons we hope are obvious. Compare the Koyck transformation with the preceding equivalent distributed lag model. Both have the same dependent variable, Y_t. Both have a variable representing the immediate impact of X_t on Y_t. But whereas the distributed lag model also has a slew of coefficients for variables representing all of the lags of 1 through k of X on Y_t, the lagged-dependent-variable model instead contains a single variable and coefficient, λY_{t-1}. Because, as we said, the two setups are equivalent, then this means that the lagged

---

[16] We realize that the model does not *look* mathematically identical, but it is. For ease of presentation, we skip the algebra necessary to demonstrate the equivalence.

dependent variable does *not* represent how Y_{t-1} somehow causes Y_t, but instead Y_{t-1} is a stand-in for the cumulative effects of all past lags of X (that is, lags 1 through k) on Y_t. We achieve all of that through estimating a single coefficient instead of a very large number of them.

The coefficient λ, then, represents the ways in which past values of X affect current values of Y, which nicely solves the problem outlined at the start of this section. Normally, the values of λ will range between 0 and 1.[17] You can readily see that if $\lambda = 0$ then there is literally no effect of past values of X on Y_t. Such values are uncommon in practice. As λ gets larger, that indicates that the effects of past lags of X on Y_t persist longer and longer into the future.

In these models, the cumulative effect of X on Y is conveniently described as

$$\beta = \frac{\beta_0}{1 - \lambda}.$$

Examining the formula, we easily see that, when $\lambda = 0$, the denominator is equal to 1 and the cumulative impact is exactly equal to the instantaneous impact. There is no lagged effect at all. When $\lambda = 1$, however, we run into problems; the denominator equals 0, so the quotient is undefined. But as λ approaches 1, you can see that the cumulative effect grows. Thus, as the values of the coefficient on the lagged dependent variable move from 0 toward 1, the cumulative impact of changes in X on Y grows.

This brief foray into time-series analysis obviously just scratches the surface. When reading research that uses time-series techniques, or especially when embarking on your own time-series analysis, it is important to be aware of both the issues of how the effects of shifts in independent variables can persist over several time periods, and also of the potential pitfalls of long-memoried trends.

11.8   WRAPPING UP

Even in its simplest varieties, OLS regression – and especially multiple OLS regression – can be complicated enough. What we've encountered in this chapter shows that there are additional (but not insurmountable!) obstacles to overcome when we consider that some of our theories involve noncontinuous variables and that there are some unique obstacles involving time-series data.

---

[17] In fact, values close to 1, and especially those greater than 1, indicate that there are problems with the model, most likely related to trends in the data.

Some of these techniques might seem intimidating at first, but we encourage you to press onward. One way to do this is to see how these techniques work in actual examples of political science research. In our final chapter, we examine three pieces of research that attempt to answer compelling theoretical questions.

CONCEPTS INTRODUCED IN THIS CHAPTER

additive models	interactive models
auxiliary regression model	Koyck transformation
	lagged dependent variable
binomial logit	lagged values
binomial probit	lead values
classification table	leverage
cumulative impact	linear probability model
DFBETA score	link functions
differenced (or "first differenced") dependent variable	micronumerosity
	multicollinearity
distributed lag model	predicted probability
dummying out	proportionate reduction of error
dummy variables	reference category
dummy-variable trap	spurious regression problem
instantaneous effect	variance inflation factor

12 Multiple Regression Models III: Applications

OVERVIEW

In this chapter, we show how political scientists across a variety of sub-fields have used multiple regression to test theories about causal processes involving politics. In particular, we show how clever research design and accompanying statistical analyses uncover interesting patterns of causal dynamics in the domain of American presidential popularity, in economic voting in European democracies, and in patterns of international conflict and cooperation. One of the core principles of this chapter – and of the book – is that solid research design is a prerequisite for insightful data analysis.

12.1 WHY CONTROLLING FOR Z MATTERS

Thus far, the discussion of the effects of multiple regression has been mostly abstract, referring to X, Y, and Z instead of to real social phenomena that most political scientists – and most political science students – care about. Some of this abstraction is necessary, of course, but we want you to see examples from actual research on how multiple regression is used, and how including new variables can change our theoretical conclusions. That is the goal of this chapter. What you will see, in these varying examples, is how introducing new controls for variables can change our inferences about the causal structure of the political world, which is what we have emphasized throughout this book.

To highlight the changes that result to parameter estimates when we change our model by adding a new variable, we show only a small portion of the results from the different models that we feature in this chapter. It is worth pointing out that these results come from models that contained (and thus controlled for) other variables.

Figure 12.1. A simple causal model of the relationship between the economy and presidential popularity.

12.2 EXAMPLE 1: THE ECONOMY AND PRESIDENTIAL POPULARITY

All of you, we suspect, are familiar with presidential popularity (or presidential approval) polls. **Presidential popularity**, in fact, is one of the great resources that presidents have at their disposal; they use approval as leverage in bargaining situations. It is not easy, after all, to say "no" to a popular president. In contrast, unpopular presidents are often not influential presidents. Hence all presidents care about their approval ratings.

But why do approval ratings fluctuate, both in the short term and the long term? What systematic forces cause presidents to be popular or unpopular over time? Since the early 1970s, the reigning conventional wisdom held that *economic reality* – usually measured by inflation and unemployment rates – drove approval ratings up and down. When the economy was doing well – that is, when inflation and unemployment were both low – the president enjoyed high approval ratings; and when the economy was performing poorly, the opposite was true.[1] That conventional wisdom is represented graphically in Figure 12.1. Considerable amounts of research over many years supported that wisdom.

In the early 1990s, however, a group of three political scientists questioned the traditional understanding of approval dynamics, suggesting that it was not actual *economic reality* that influenced approval ratings, but the public's perceptions of the economy – which we usually call **consumer confidence** (see MacKuen, Erikson, and Stimson 1992). Their logic was that it doesn't matter for a president's approval ratings if inflation and unemployment are low if people don't *perceive* the economy to be doing well. Their revised causal model is presented in Figure 12.2.

What these researchers needed to do, then, was to test the conventional wisdom to see how it held up to a control for a new variable. By use of quarterly survey data from 1954:2 through 1988:2, this is what they did. Table 12.1 re-creates a portion of MacKuen, Erikson, and Stimson's Table 2. In column A, we see a confirmation of the conventional wisdom. (Can you think why the authors might include a column in their tables like this?) You should think of this column of results as testing the causal model in

---

[1] It has always been the case that scholars have recognized other systematic causes of presidential approval ratings, including scandals, international crises, and battle fatalities. We focus, in this example, exclusively on the economy for simplicity of presentation.

Table 12.1. Excerpts from the table of MacKuen, Erikson, and Stimson on the relationship between the economy and presidential popularity

Variable	A	B
Approval$_{t-1}$	0.87*	0.82*
	(0.04)	(0.04)
Inflation	−0.39*	−0.17
	(0.13)	(0.13)
Change in Unemployment	−1.51*	0.62
	(0.74)	(0.91)
Consumer Confidence	−	0.21*
	−	(.05)
R^2	.93	.94
n	126	117

Note: Standard errors are in parentheses; * = $p < 0.05$.
Other variables were estimated as a part of the regression model but were excluded from this table for ease of presentation.

Figure 12.1. The coefficient for the inflation rate, −0.39, indicates that, for every 1-point increase in the inflation rate, presidential approval will immediately fall by 0.39 points, on average, controlling for the effects of unemployment (and other variables in their model, which we do not show). According to the table, the ratio of the coefficient to the standard error places this effect easily past the threshold of statistical significance.

Similarly, column A presents the results for the effects of changes in the unemployment rate on presidential approval. The slope of −1.51 indicates that, for every 1-point increase in the unemployment rate, presidential approval falls by 1.51 points, on average, controlling for the effects of inflation (and other variables that we do not show). This parameter estimate is also statistically significant.

Notice also the presence of a lagged dependent variable in the model, labeled Approval$_{t-1}$. Recalling our discussion of time-series issues in Chapter 11, we find that the coefficient of 0.87, which is statistically significant, indicates that 87% of the effects of a shift in one of the independent variables persists into the following period. Thus the effects of shifts in X do not die out instantly; rather, a large portion of those effects persist

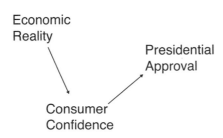

Figure 12.2. A revised model of presidential popularity.

into the future.[2] What this means is that, for example, the coefficient for Inflation of -0.39 represents only the *immediate* effects of inflation, not the *cumulative* effects of Inflation. The cumulative effect for Inflation, as we learned in Chapter 11, is equal to the immediate impact divided by one minus the coefficient for the lagged dependent variable, or,

$$\beta = \frac{\beta_0}{1 - \lambda} = \frac{-0.39}{1 - 0.87} = -3.0.$$

The immediate impact of -0.39, then, considerably understates the total impact of a shift in the Inflation rate, which, because of the strong dynamics in the model – the value of the lagged dependent variable, 0.87, is a lot closer to 1 than it is to 0 – is considerably more impressive in substantive terms. A 1-point shift in the Inflation rate eventually costs a president 3 points of approval.

In short, the first column of data in Table 12.1 provides some confirmation for the conventional wisdom. But the results in column A do not control for the effects of Consumer Confidence. The results from when MacKuen, Erikson, and Stimson did control for Consumer Confidence are provided in column B of Table 12.1. Notice first that Consumer Confidence has a coefficient of 0.21. That is, for every 1-point increase in Consumer Confidence, we expect to see an immediate increase in presidential approval of 0.21 points, *controlling for the effects of Inflation and Unemployment.* This effect is statistically significant.[3]

Notice also, however, what happens to the coefficients for Inflation and Unemployment. Comparing the estimated effects in column A with those in column B reveals some substantial differences. When there was no control for Consumer Confidence in column A, it appeared that Inflation and Unemployment had modestly strong and statistically significant effects. But in column B, the coefficients change because of the control for Consumer Confidence. The effect of unemployment shrinks from -0.39 to -0.17, which reflects the control for Consumer Confidence. The effect is not close to being statistically significant. We can no longer reject the null hypothesis that there is no relationship between Inflation and presidential Approval.

The same thing happens to the effect for the Change in the Unemployment rate. In column B, when Consumer Confidence is controlled for, the effect for the Change in Unemployment changes from -1.51 to 0.62,

---

[2] Indeed, in the second period, 0.87^2 of the effect of a shift in X at time t remains, and 0.87^3 remains in the third period, and so forth.

[3] Again, notice that the cumulative effect of a 1-point shift in Consumer Confidence will be larger, because of the strong dynamics in the model represented by the lagged value of the dependent variable.

a substantial reduction in magnitude, but also a change in the *direction* of the relationship. No matter, because the coefficient is no longer statistically significant, which means we cannot reject the null hypothesis that it is truly zero.

The second column of Table 12.1, then, is consistent with Figure 12.2, which shows no direct connection between Economic Reality and presidential Approval. There is, however, a direct connection between Consumer Confidence and Approval ratings. In this case, introducing a new variable (Consumer Confidence) produced very different findings about a concept (Economic Reality) that scholars had thought for decades exerted a direct causal influence on Approval.

12.3   EXAMPLE 2: POLITICS, ECONOMICS, AND PUBLIC SUPPORT FOR DEMOCRACY

After the Cold War ended in 1989, the formerly communist states in Eastern Europe began making transitions toward both democratic political systems and, simultaneously, market economies. But as the euphoria that followed the fall of the Berlin Wall and the lifting of the Iron Curtain began to fade into memory, most of these countries experienced growing pains in the early stages of democratization and the shift to a capitalist economic system. But not all of the former Warsaw Pact nations experienced these growing pains equally. In the process, the transition from communism to capitalism, and from autocracy to democracy, appeared quite fragile.

For decades, political scientists, especially those with interests in the cross-national study of politics, have investigated why citizens express support for democracy. Citizens in some fledgling democracies have been very supportive of the democratization process, whereas others, according to survey results, are not at all optimistic about the benefits of democracy. One of the primary explanations for why different societies exhibit more or less enthusiasm for democratic government has been the variation in economic experiences.[4] In particular, in so-called *transition societies* like those in Eastern Europe, for which both democracy and markets are relatively new experiences, Przeworski (1991) argued that politicians motivated by electoral success will promise much, but be able to deliver relatively little. Citizens' sentiments about democracy, then, are often a function of

---

[4] See, for example, Przeworski (1991). Before economic explanations for support for democracy came to prominence, cultural explanations were dominant. In those theories, countries with a history of a democratic culture were most likely to have citizens that supported democratic government, and hence to have thriving democracies. See Almond and Verba (1963).

the public's experiences with the market economy and how these actual experiences differ from their expectations. If the public's expectations are exceeded, they will be supportive of democratization; if not, support will wane. As the economic pie grows, so the thinking goes, then more and more ordinary citizens have a stake in the stability and success of the democratic political arrangement. In essence, the public is linking the benefits (or lack thereof) of democratization to economic success.

On the other hand, some researchers have theorized that citizens' evaluations of the pros and cons of democracy will be based primarily on visible evidence that the new democratic institutions are working to represent citizens' interests. That is, instead of relying on economic evaluations, citizens base their evaluations of democracy on how well they see the polity functioning. If people perceive that government works to benefit everyone, that everyone has a meaningful voice in elections, that government cares what they want and is responsive to their needs, then they will be supportive of democracy. But if, in contrast, people perceive government to be benefiting a narrow range of interests, responsive to the few instead of the many, and uncaring, then people will not view democracy positively at all. In essence, it is political factors, not economic ones, that determine how people feel about democracy.

Geoffrey Evans and Stephen Whitefield investigated these questions in a 1993 survey in nine countries, formerly a part of the Soviet bloc, all of which were new democracies (Evans and Whitefield 1995). In each of the nine countries – Bulgaria, Estonia, Hungary, Lithuania, Poland, Romania, Russia, and Ukraine – Evans and Whitefield asked a representative sample of citizens about their experiences with the economy, about their experiences with their new democratic government, and about their overall commitment to democracy in their country. In all, they surveyed approximately 15,000 respondents. Their dependent variable, commitment to democracy, is measured by the following survey question:

> How do you feel about the aim of introducing democracy in [respondent's country], in which parties compete for government? Are you a . . . strong supporter, supporter, opponent, strong opponent, neither supporter nor opponent?

Evans and Whitefield performed a multivariate regression analysis to examine whether political or economic factors are the best predictors of support for or opposition to democratic government. A portion of their results is shown in Table 12.2. The results in column A of the table are consistent with the theory that economic evaluations will affect support for democracy, showing that increases in a respondent's perceptions of the performance of the free market lead to increases in his or her support for

Table 12.2. Excerpts from the table of Evans and Whitefield on the relationship between the economy and support for democracy

Parameter	A	B
Market evaluation	0.14*	0.05*
Democratic evaluation	–	0.20*
R^2	.09	.15
n	14,808	14,808

Note: The coefficients in the table are standardized; * = $p < 0.05$. Other variables were estimated as a part of the regression model but were excluded from this table for ease of presentation.

democracy. The coefficients in the table are standardized, so the coefficient of 0.14 means that a 1-standard-deviation increase in a respondent's evaluation of the market is associated with a 0.14-standard-deviation increase in support for democracy, controlling for the other factors in the model (which are not shown to keep the table a manageable size).

Compare the results in column A, however, with those in column B, which includes a control for how the respondent evaluates the workings of democracy. Two things are notable. First, because the parameter estimates are standardized, we can compare their magnitudes to see which effect is stronger. In this case, the effect of a respondent's evaluation of democracy is four times as large (0.20) as their evaluation of the market (0.05) in shaping their overall support for democratic government. Both effects, it is worth keeping in mind, remain statistically significant predictors of a citizen's support for democracy; their political evaluations, though, are a stronger predictor than are their economic evaluations.

Second, notice how the parameter estimate for the evaluation of the market shrank from column A to column B. The reduction from 0.14 to 0.05 indicates that, once the effect of a person's beliefs about the functioning of democracy is controlled for, the effect of their views of the market fall by roughly two-thirds.

Reflecting back on the lessons learned in Chapter 10, we see that the results here clearly indicate that the relationship between citizens' attitudes about markets and their attitudes about the functioning of democracy are related, and that both of these contribute to support for or opposition to democracy as a system of government (at least in these nine developing democracies). It is equally clear that, given the discrepancy between the results in columns A and B of Table 12.2, the situation more closely resembles that of Figure 10.1, in which the variances of the two independent variables overlap, than that of Figure 10.2, in which they do not. As a result, omitting any one of the variables – as we omitted democratic evaluations in column A – is likely to produce misleading estimates about the variables in the model.

12.4 EXAMPLE 3: COMPETING THEORIES OF HOW POLITICS AFFECTS INTERNATIONAL TRADE

What are the forces that affect international trade? Economists have long noted that there are economic forces that shape the extent to which two nations trade with one another.[5] The size of each nation's economy, the physical distance between them, and the overall level of development have all been investigated as economic causes of trade.[6] But in addition to economic forces, does politics help to shape international trade?

Morrow, Siverson, and Tabares (1998) investigate three competing (and perhaps complementary) political explanations for the extent to which two nations engage in international trade. The first theory is that states with friendly relations are more likely to trade with one another than are states engaged in conflict. Conflict, in this sense, need not be militarized disputes (though it may be).[7] Conflict, they argue, can dampen trade in several ways. First, interstate conflict can sometimes produce embargoes (or prohibitions on trade). Second, conflict can reduce trade by raising the risks for firms that wish to engage in cross-border trading.

The second theory is that trade will be higher when both nations are democracies and lower when one (or both) is an autocracy.[8] Because democracies have more open political and judicial systems, trade should be higher between democracies because firms in one country will have greater assurance that any trade disputes will be resolved openly and fairly in courts to which they have access. In contrast, firms in a democratic state may be more reluctant to trade with nondemocratic countries, because it is less certain how any disagreements will be resolved. In addition, firms may be wary of trading with nondemocracies for fear of having their assets

---

[5] Theories of trade and, indeed, many theories about other aspects of international trade are usually developed with pairs of nations in mind. Thus all of the relevant variables, like trade, are measured in terms of pairs of nations, which are often referred to as "dyads" by international relations scholars. The resulting **dyadic data** sets are often quite large because they encompass each relevant pair of nations.

[6] Such models are charmingly referred to as "gravity models," because, according to these theories, the forces driving trade resemble the forces that determine gravitational attraction between two physical objects.

[7] See Pollins (1989) for an extended discussion of this theory.

[8] See Dixon and Moon (1993) for an elaboration of this theory.

Table 12.3. Excerpts from the table of Morrow, Siverson, and Tabares on the political causes of international trade

Parameter	A	B	C	D
Peaceful relations	1.12*	–	–	1.45*
	(0.22)	–	–	(0.37)
Democratic partners	–	1.18*	–	1.22*
	–	(0.12)	–	(0.13)
Alliance partners	–	–	0.29*	−0.50*
	–	–	(0.03)	(0.16)
GNP of exporter	0.67*	0.57*	0.68*	0.56*
	(0.07)	(0.07)	(0.07)	(0.08)
R^2	.77	.78	.77	.78
n	2631	2631	2631	2631

Note: Standard errors are in parentheses; * = $p < .05$.
Other variables were estimated as a part of the regression model but were excluded from this table for ease of presentation.

seized by the foreign government. In short, trading with an autocratic government should raise the perceived risks of international trade.

The third theory is that states that are in an alliance with one another are more likely to trade with one another than are states that are not in such an alliance.[9] For states that are not in an alliance, one nation may be reluctant to trade with another nation if the first thinks that the gains from trade may be used to arm itself for future conflict. In contrast, states in an alliance stand to gain from each other's increased wealth as a result from trade.

To test these theories, Morrow, Siverson, and Tabares look at trade among all of the major powers in the international system – the United States, Britain, France, Germany, Russia and Italy – during most of the twentieth century. They consider each pair of states – called *dyads* – separately and examine exports to each country on an annual basis.[10] Their dependent variable is the amount of exports in every dyadic relationship in each year.

Table 12.3 shows excerpts from the analysis of Morrow, Siverson, and Tabares.[11] In column A, they show that, as the first theory predicts,

---

[9] See Gowa (1989) and Gowa and Mansfield (1993) for an extended discussion, including distinctions between bipolar and multipolar organizations of the international system.

[10] This research design is often referred to as a time-series cross-section design, because it contains both variation between units and variation across time. In this sense, it is a hybrid of the two types of quasi-experiments discussed in Chapter 3.

[11] Interpreting the precise magnitudes of the parameter estimates is a bit tricky in this case, because the independent variables were all transformed by use of natural logarithms.

increases in interstate peace are associated with higher amounts of trade between countries, controlling for economic factors. In addition, the larger the economy in general, the more trade there is. (This finding is consistent across all estimation equations.) The results in column B indicate that pairs of democracies trade at higher rates than do pairs involving at least one nondemocracy. Finally, the results in column C show that trade is higher between alliance partners than between states that are not in an alliance with one another. All of these effects are statistically significant.

So far, each of the theories received at least some support. But, as you can tell from looking at the table, the results in columns A through C do not control for the other explanations. That is, we have yet to see results of a fully multivariate model, in which the theories can compete for explanatory power. That situation is rectified in column D, in which all three political variables are entered in the same regression model. There, we see that the effects of reduced hostility between states is actually enhanced in the multivariate context – compare the coefficient of 1.12 with the multivariate 1.45. Similarly, the effects of democratic trading partners remains almost unchanged in the fully multivariate framework. However, the effect of alliances changes. Before controlling for conflict and democracy, the effect of alliances was (as expected) positive and statistically significant. However, in column D, in which we control for conflict and democracy, the effect flips signs and is now *negative* (and statistically significant), which means that, when we control for these factors, states in an alliance are less (not more) likely to trade with one another.

The article by Morrow, Siverson, and Tabares represents a case in which synthesizing several competing explanations for the same phenomenon – international trade – produces surprising findings. By using a data set that allowed them to test all three theories simultaneously, Morrow, Siverson, and Tabares were able to sort out which theories received support and which did not.

12.5 CONCLUSIONS

One of the fascinating features of social science research is that new theoretical developments come along from time to time to replace old theories. That is, a scholar questions the received wisdom, proposes an alternate explanation, and then investigates how his or her new explanation fits in with the old ones. Sometimes, the explanations are complementary; that is, a new explanation does not replace the old one so much as it adds to the old one. Other times, however, the new explanations contradict the old ones, and the evidence ends up favoring the new theory. In this chapter, we have seen some examples of each type, as well as one example – the one involving international trade – in which a new analysis synthesized three theories that had not previously been tested against one another. These are some of the typical uses of multiple regression in political science.

CONCEPTS INTRODUCED IN THIS CHAPTER

consumer confidence   presidential popularity
dyadic data

EXERCISES

1. Find an example in the political literature in which the introduction of a new variable changes the results of a regression model. Explain how this result has an impacted on our understanding of the relevant causal relationships.

2. In footnote 4 we discussed how previous theories about public support for democracy were about culture. Is the research design of Evans and Whitefield (1995) appropriate for testing such a theory? Why or why not?

3. In Table 12.1, column A, calculate the cumulative effect of a 1% increase in the unemployment rate on a president's approval rating.

Critical Values of χ^2

df	Level of significance				
	.10	.05	.025	.01	.001
1	2.706	3.841	5.024	6.635	10.828
2	4.605	5.991	7.378	9.210	13.816
3	6.251	7.815	9.348	11.345	16.266
4	7.779	9.488	11.143	13.277	18.467
5	9.236	11.070	12.833	15.086	20.515
6	10.645	12.592	14.449	16.812	22.458
7	12.017	14.067	16.013	18.475	24.322
8	13.362	15.507	17.535	20.090	26.125
9	14.684	16.919	19.023	21.666	27.877
10	15.987	18.307	20.403	23.209	29.588
11	17.275	19.675	21.920	24.725	31.264
12	18.549	21.026	23.337	26.217	32.910
13	19.813	22.302	24.736	27.688	34.528
14	21.064	23.685	26.119	29.141	36.123
15	22.307	24.996	27.488	30.578	37.697
20	28.412	31.410	34.170	37.566	45.315
25	34.382	37.652	40.646	44.314	52.620
30	40.256	43.773	46.979	50.892	59.703
35	46.059	49.802	53.203	57.342	66.619
40	51.805	55.758	59.342	63.691	73.402
50	63.167	67.505	71.420	76.154	86.661
60	74.397	79.082	83.298	88.379	99.607
70	85.527	90.531	95.023	100.425	112.317
75	91.061	96.217	100.839	106.393	118.599
80	96.578	101.879	106.629	112.329	124.839
90	107.565	113.145	118.136	124.116	137.208
100	118.498	124.342	129.561	135.807	149.449

Critical Values of *t*

df	Level of significance					
	.10	.05	.025	.01	.005	.001
1	3.078	6.314	12.706	31.821	63.657	318.313
2	1.886	2.920	4.303	6.965	9.925	22.327
3	1.638	2.353	3.182	4.541	5.841	10.215
4	1.533	2.132	2.776	3.747	4.604	7.173
5	1.476	2.015	2.571	3.365	4.032	5.893
6	1.440	1.943	2.447	3.143	3.707	5.208
7	1.415	1.895	2.365	2.998	3.499	4.782
8	1.397	1.860	2.306	2.896	3.355	4.499
9	1.383	1.833	2.262	2.821	3.250	4.296
10	1.372	1.812	2.228	2.764	3.169	4.143
11	1.363	1.796	2.201	2.718	3.106	4.024
12	1.356	1.782	2.179	2.681	3.055	3.929
13	1.350	1.771	2.160	2.650	3.012	3.852
14	1.345	1.761	2.145	2.624	2.977	3.787
15	1.341	1.753	2.131	2.602	2.947	3.733
20	1.325	1.725	2.086	2.528	2.845	3.552
25	1.316	1.708	2.060	2.485	2.787	3.450
30	1.310	1.697	2.042	2.457	2.750	3.385
40	1.303	1.684	2.021	2.423	2.704	3.307
50	1.299	1.676	2.009	2.403	2.678	3.261
60	1.296	1.671	2.000	2.390	2.660	3.232
70	1.294	1.667	1.994	2.381	2.648	3.211
75	1.293	1.665	1.992	2.377	2.643	3.202
80	1.292	1.664	1.990	2.374	2.639	3.195
90	1.291	1.662	1.987	2.368	2.632	3.183
100	1.290	1.660	1.984	2.364	2.626	3.174
∞	1.282	1.645	1.960	2.326	2.576	3.090

The Λ Link Function for BNL Models

	Translating negative $X_i\hat{\beta}$ values into predicted probabilities $\hat{P}_i$									
$X_i\hat{\beta}$	−0.00	−0.01	−0.02	−0.03	−0.04	−0.05	−0.06	−0.07	−0.08	−0.09
−4.5	0.0110	0.0109	0.0108	0.0107	0.0106	0.0105	0.0104	0.0103	0.0102	0.0101
−4.0	0.0180	0.0178	0.0176	0.0175	0.0173	0.0171	0.0170	0.0168	0.0166	0.0165
−3.5	0.0293	0.0290	0.0287	0.0285	0.0282	0.0279	0.0277	0.0274	0.0271	0.0269
−3.0	0.0474	0.0470	0.0465	0.0461	0.0457	0.0452	0.0448	0.0444	0.0439	0.0435
−2.5	0.0759	0.0752	0.0745	0.0738	0.0731	0.0724	0.0718	0.0711	0.0704	0.0698
−2.0	0.1192	0.1182	0.1171	0.1161	0.1151	0.1141	0.1130	0.1120	0.1111	0.1101
−1.9	0.1301	0.1290	0.1279	0.1268	0.1256	0.1246	0.1235	0.1224	0.1213	0.1203
−1.8	0.1419	0.1406	0.1394	0.1382	0.1371	0.1359	0.1347	0.1335	0.1324	0.1312
−1.7	0.1545	0.1532	0.1519	0.1506	0.1493	0.1480	0.1468	0.1455	0.1443	0.1431
−1.6	0.1680	0.1666	0.1652	0.1638	0.1625	0.1611	0.1598	0.1584	0.1571	0.1558
−1.5	0.1824	0.1809	0.1795	0.1780	0.1765	0.1751	0.1736	0.1722	0.1708	0.1694
−1.4	0.1978	0.1962	0.1947	0.1931	0.1915	0.1900	0.1885	0.1869	0.1854	0.1839
−1.3	0.2142	0.2125	0.2108	0.2092	0.2075	0.2059	0.2042	0.2026	0.2010	0.1994
−1.2	0.2315	0.2297	0.2279	0.2262	0.2244	0.2227	0.2210	0.2193	0.2176	0.2159
−1.1	0.2497	0.2479	0.2460	0.2442	0.2423	0.2405	0.2387	0.2369	0.2351	0.2333
−1.0	0.2689	0.2670	0.2650	0.2631	0.2611	0.2592	0.2573	0.2554	0.2535	0.2516
−.9	0.2891	0.2870	0.2850	0.2829	0.2809	0.2789	0.2769	0.2749	0.2729	0.2709
−.8	0.3100	0.3079	0.3058	0.3036	0.3015	0.2994	0.2973	0.2953	0.2932	0.2911
−.7	0.3318	0.3296	0.3274	0.3252	0.3230	0.3208	0.3186	0.3165	0.3143	0.3112
.6	0.3543	0.3521	0.3498	0.3475	0.3452	0.3430	0.3407	0.3385	0.3363	0.3340
−.5	0.3775	0.3752	0.3729	0.3705	0.3682	0.3659	0.3635	0.3612	0.3589	0.3566
−.4	0.4013	0.3989	0.3965	0.3941	0.3917	0.3894	0.3870	0.3846	0.3823	0.3799
−.3	0.4256	0.4231	0.4207	0.4182	0.4158	0.4134	0.4110	0.4085	0.4061	0.4037
−.2	0.4502	0.4477	0.4452	0.4428	0.4403	0.4378	0.4354	0.4329	0.4305	0.4280
−.1	0.4750	0.4725	0.4700	0.4675	0.4651	0.4626	0.4601	0.4576	0.4551	0.4526
−.0	0.5000	0.4975	0.4950	0.4925	0.4900	0.4875	0.4850	0.4825	0.4800	0.4775

(continued)

Appendix C (*continued*)

$X_i\hat{\beta}$	Translating positive $X_i\hat{\beta}$ values into predicted probabilities $\hat{P}_i$									
	+0.00	+0.01	+0.02	+0.03	+0.04	+0.05	+0.06	+0.07	+0.08	+0.09
0.0	0.5000	0.5025	0.5050	0.5075	0.5100	0.5125	0.5150	0.5175	0.5200	0.5225
0.1	0.5250	0.5275	0.5300	0.5325	0.5349	0.5374	0.5399	0.5424	0.5449	0.5474
0.2	0.5498	0.5523	0.5548	0.5572	0.5597	0.5622	0.5646	0.5671	0.5695	0.5720
0.3	0.5744	0.5769	0.5793	0.5818	0.5842	0.5866	0.5890	0.5915	0.5939	0.5963
0.4	0.5987	0.6011	0.6035	0.6059	0.6083	0.6106	0.6130	0.6154	0.6177	0.6201
0.5	0.6225	0.6248	0.6271	0.6295	0.6318	0.6341	0.6365	0.6388	0.6411	0.6434
0.6	0.6457	0.6479	0.6502	0.6525	0.6548	0.6570	0.6593	0.6615	0.6637	0.6660
0.7	0.6682	0.6704	0.6726	0.6748	0.6770	0.6792	0.6814	0.6835	0.6857	0.6878
0.8	0.6900	0.6921	0.6942	0.6964	0.6985	0.7006	0.7027	0.7047	0.7068	0.7089
0.9	0.7109	0.7130	0.7150	0.7171	0.7191	0.7211	0.7231	0.7251	0.7271	0.7291
1.0	0.7311	0.7330	0.7350	0.7369	0.7389	0.7408	0.7427	0.7446	0.7465	0.7484
1.1	0.7503	0.7521	0.7540	0.7558	0.7577	0.7595	0.7613	0.7631	0.7649	0.7667
1.2	0.7685	0.7703	0.7721	0.7738	0.7756	0.7773	0.7790	0.7807	0.7824	0.7841
1.3	0.7858	0.7875	0.7892	0.7908	0.7925	0.7941	0.7958	0.7974	0.7990	0.8006
1.4	0.8022	0.8038	0.8053	0.8069	0.8085	0.8100	0.8115	0.8131	0.8146	0.8161
1.5	0.8176	0.8191	0.8205	0.8220	0.8235	0.8249	0.8264	0.8278	0.8292	0.8306
1.6	0.8320	0.8334	0.8348	0.8362	0.8375	0.8389	0.8402	0.8416	0.8429	0.8442
1.7	0.8455	0.8468	0.8481	0.8494	0.8507	0.8520	0.8532	0.8545	0.8557	0.8569
1.8	0.8581	0.8594	0.8606	0.8618	0.8629	0.8641	0.8653	0.8665	0.8676	0.8688
1.9	0.8699	0.8710	0.8721	0.8732	0.8744	0.8754	0.8765	0.8776	0.8787	0.8797
2.0	0.8808	0.8818	0.8829	0.8839	0.8849	0.8859	0.8870	0.8880	0.8889	0.8899
2.5	0.9241	0.9248	0.9255	0.9262	0.9269	0.9276	0.9282	0.9289	0.9296	0.9302
3.0	0.9526	0.9530	0.9535	0.9539	0.9543	0.9548	0.9552	0.9556	0.9561	0.9565
3.5	0.9707	0.9710	0.9713	0.9715	0.9718	0.9721	0.9723	0.9726	0.9729	0.9731
4.0	0.9820	0.9822	0.9824	0.9825	0.9827	0.9829	0.9830	0.9832	0.9834	0.9835
4.5	0.9890	0.9891	0.9892	0.9893	0.9894	0.9895	0.9896	0.9897	0.9898	0.9899

APPENDIX D

The Φ Link Function for BNP Models

	Translating negative $X_i\hat{\beta}$ values into predicted probabilities $\hat{P}_i$									
$X_i\hat{\beta}$	−.00	−.01	−.02	−.03	−.04	−.05	−.06	−.07	.08	−.09
−3.4	.0003	.0003	.0003	.0003	.0003	.0003	.0003	.0003	.0003	.0002
−3.0	.0013	.0013	.0013	.0012	.0012	.0011	.0011	.0011	.0010	.0010
−2.5	.0062	.0060	.0059	.0057	.0055	.0054	.0052	.0051	.0049	.0048
−2.0	.0228	.0222	.0217	.0212	.0207	.0202	.0197	.0192	.0188	.0183
−1.9	.0287	.0281	.0274	.0268	.0262	.0256	.0250	.0244	.0239	.0233
−1.8	.0359	.0351	.0344	.0336	.0329	.0322	.0314	.0307	.0301	.0294
−1.7	.0446	.0436	.0427	.0418	.0409	.0401	.0392	.0384	.0375	.0367
−1.6	.0548	.0537	.0526	.0516	.0505	.0495	.0485	.0475	.0465	.0455
−1.5	.0668	.0655	.0643	.0630	.0618	.0606	.0594	.0582	.0571	.0559
−1.4	.0808	.0793	.0778	.0764	.0749	.0735	.0721	.0708	.0694	.0681
−1.3	.0968	.0951	.0934	.0918	.0901	.0885	.0869	.0853	.0838	.0823
−1.2	.1151	.1131	.1112	.1093	.1075	.1056	.1038	.1020	.1003	.0985
−1.1	.1357	.1335	.1314	.1292	.1271	.1251	.1230	.1210	.1190	.1170
−1.0	.1587	.1562	.1539	.1515	.1492	.1469	.1446	.1423	.1401	.1379
−.9	.1841	.1814	.1788	.1762	.1736	.1711	.1685	.1660	.1635	.1611
−.8	.2119	.2090	.2061	.2033	.2005	.1977	.1949	.1922	.1894	.1867
−.7	.2420	.2389	.2358	.2327	.2296	.2266	.2236	.2206	.2177	.2148
−.6	.2743	.2709	.2676	.2643	.2611	.2578	.2546	.2514	.2483	.2451
−.5	.3085	.3050	.3015	.2981	.2946	.2912	.2877	.2843	.2810	.2776
−.4	.3446	.3409	.3372	.3336	.3300	.3264	.3228	.3192	.3156	.3121
.3	.3821	.3783	.3745	.3707	.3669	.3632	.3594	.3557	.3520	.3483
−.2	.4207	.4168	.4129	.4090	.4052	.4013	.3974	.3936	.3897	.3859
−.1	.4602	.4562	.4522	.4483	.4443	.4404	.4364	.4325	.4286	.4247
−.0	.5000	.4960	.4920	.4880	.4840	.4801	.4761	.4721	.4681	.4641

(continued)

Appendix D (*continued*)

$X_i\hat{\beta}$	Translating positive $X_i\hat{\beta}$ values into predicted probabilities $\hat{P}_i$									
	+.00	+.01	+.02	+.03	+.04	+.05	+.06	+.07	+.08	+.09
+.0	.5000	.5040	.5080	.5120	.5160	.5199	.5239	.5279	.5319	.5359
+.1	.5398	.5438	.5478	.5517	.5557	.5596	.5636	.5675	.5714	.5753
+.2	.5793	.5832	.5871	.5910	.5948	.5987	.6026	.6064	.6103	.6141
+.3	.6179	.6217	.6255	.6293	.6331	.6368	.6406	.6443	.6480	.6517
+.4	.6554	.6591	.6628	.6664	.6700	.6736	.6772	.6808	.6844	.6879
.5	.6915	.6950	.6985	.7019	.7054	.7088	.7123	.7157	.7190	.7224
+.6	.7257	.7291	.7324	.7357	.7389	.7422	.7454	.7486	.7517	.7549
+.7	.7580	.7611	.7642	.7673	.7704	.7734	.7764	.7794	.7823	.7852
+.8	.7881	.7910	.7939	.7967	.7995	.8023	.8051	.8078	.8106	.8133
+.9	.8159	.8186	.8212	.8238	.8264	.8289	.8315	.8340	.8365	.8389
+1.0	.8413	.8438	.8461	.8485	.8508	.8531	.8554	.8577	.8599	.8621
+1.1	.8643	.8665	.8686	.8708	.8729	.8749	.8770	.8790	.8810	.8830
+1.2	.8849	.8869	.8888	.8907	.8925	.8944	.8962	.8980	.8997	.9015
+1.3	.9032	.9049	.9066	.9082	.9099	.9115	.9131	.9147	.9162	.9177
+1.4	.9192	.9207	.9222	.9236	.9251	.9265	.9279	.9292	.9306	.9319
+1.5	.9332	.9345	.9357	.9370	.9382	.9394	.9406	.9418	.9429	.9441
+1.6	.9452	.9463	.9474	.9484	.9495	.9505	.9515	.9525	.9535	.9545
+1.7	.9554	.9564	.9573	.9582	.9591	.9599	.9608	.9616	.9625	.9633
+1.8	.9641	.9649	.9656	.9664	.9671	.9678	.9686	.9693	.9699	.9706
+1.9	.9713	.9719	.9726	.9732	.9738	.9744	.9750	.9756	.9761	.9767
+2.0	.9772	.9778	.9783	.9788	.9793	.9798	.9803	.9808	.9812	.9817
+2.5	.9938	.9940	.9941	.9943	.9945	.9946	.9948	.9949	.9951	.9952
+3.0	.9987	.9987	.9987	.9988	.9988	.9989	.9989	.9989	.9990	.9990
+3.4	.9997	.9997	.9997	.9997	.9997	.9997	.9997	.9997	.9997	.9998

Bibliography

Achen, Christopher H. 1982. *Interpreting and Using Regression*. Beverly Hills, CA: Sage.

Almond, Gabriel A. and Sidney Verba. 1963. *The Civic Culture: Political Attitudes and Democracy in Five Nations*. Princeton, NJ: Princeton University Press.

Arrow, Kenneth. 1951. *Social Choice and Individual Values*. New York: Wiley.

Belsley, David A., Edwin Kuh, and Roy E. Welsch. 1980. *Regression Diagnostics: Identifying Influential Data and Sources of Collinearity*. New York: Wiley.

Brady, Henry E. 2002. "Models of Causal Inference: Going Beyond the Neyman–Rubin–Holland Theory." Paper presented at the annual meeting of the Political Methodology Society, Seattle, WA.

Brady, Henry E. 2004. "Introduction." *Perspectives on Politics* 2:295–300.

Campbell, Donald T. and Julian C. Stanley. 1963. *Experimental and Quasi-experimental Designs for Research*. Chicago: Rand McNally.

Dahl, Robert A. 1971. *Polyarchy: Participation and Opposition*. New Haven, CT: Yale University Press.

Danziger, Sheldon and Peter Gottschalk. 1983. "The Measurement of Poverty: Implications for Antipoverty Policy." *American Behavioral Scientist* 26:739–756.

Dixon, William and Bruce Moon. 1993. "Political Similarity and American Foreign Trade Patterns." *Political Research Quarterly* 46:5–25.

Edmonds, David and John Eidinow. 2003. *Wittgenstein's Poker: The Story of a Ten-Minute Argument Between Two Great Philosophers*. New York: Harper Perennial.

Elkins, Zachary. 2000. "Gradations of Democracy? Empirical Tests of Alternative Conceptualizations." *American Journal of Political Science* 44:293–300.

Evans, Geoffrey and Stephen Whitefield. 1995. "The Politics and Economics of Democratic Commitment: Support for Democracy in Transition Societies." *British Journal of Political Science* 25:485–514.

Fenno, Richard F. 1973. *Congressmen in Committees*. Boston: Little, Brown.

Fiorina, Morris P. 1989. *Congress: Keystone to the Washington Establishment*, 2nd ed. New Haven, CT: Yale University Press.

Gallagher, Michael, Michael Laver and Peter Mair. 2006. *Representative Government in Modern Europe*, 4th ed. New York: McGraw-Hill.

Gibson, James L. 1992. "Alternative Measures of Political Tolerance: Must Tolerance Be 'Least-Liked'?" *American Journal of Political Science* 36:560–577.

Gowa, Joanne. 1989. "Bipolarity, Multipolarity, and Free Trade." *American Political Science Review* 83:1245–1256.

Gowa, Joanne and Edward D. Mansfield. 1993. "Power Politics and International Trade." *American Political Science Review* 87:408–420.

Granger, Clive W.J. and Paul Newbold. 1974. "Spurious Regressions in Econometrics." *Journal of Econometrics* 26:1045–1066.

Green, Donald P. and Ian Shapiro. 1994. *Pathologies of Rational Choice Theory: A Critique of Applications in Political Science*. New Haven, CT: Yale University Press.

King, Gary. 1986. "How Not to Lie with Statistics: Avoiding Common Mistakes in Quantitative Political Science." *American Journal of Political Science* 30: 666–687.

Kuhn, Thomas S. 1962. *The Structure of Scientific Revolutions*. Chicago: University of Chicago Press.

Inglehart, Ronald. 1988. "The Renaissance of Political Culture." *American Political Science Review* 82:1203–1230.

Iyengar, Shanto and Donald R. Kinder. 1987. *News that Matters: Television and American Opinion*. Chicago: University of Chicago Press.

Lazarsfeld, Paul F., Bernard Berelson, and Hazel Gaudet. 1948. *The People's Choice: How the Voter Makes Up His Mind in a Presidential Campaign*. New York: Columbia University Press.

Lewis-Beck, Michael S. 1997. "Who's the Chef? Economic Voting Under a Dual Executive." *European Journal of Political Research* 31:315–325.

Luskin, Robert C. 1987. "Measuring Political Sophistication." *American Journal of Political Science* 31:856–899.

MacKuen, Michael B., Robert S. Erikson, and James A. Stimson. 1992. "Peasants or Bankers: The American Electorate and the U.S. Economy." *American Political Science Review* 86:597–611.

Mayhew, David R. 1974. *Congress: The Electoral Connection*. New Haven, CT: Yale University Press.

Morrow, James D., Randolph M. Siverson, and Tressa E. Tabares. 1998. "The Political Determinants of International Trade: The Major Powers, 1907–90." *American Political Science Review* 92:649–661.

Mueller, John. 1973. *War, Presidents, and Public Opinion*. New York: Wiley.

Munck, Gerardo L. and Jay Verkuilen. 2002. "Conceptualizing and Measuring Democracy: Evaluating Alternative Indices." *Comparative Political Studies* 35:5–34.

Niemi, Richard G. and M. Kent Jennings. 1974. *The Political Character of Adolescence: The Influence of Families and Schools*. Princeton, NJ: Princeton University Press.

Pearl, Judea. 2000. *Causality: Models, Reasoning, and Inference*. New York: Cambridge University Press.

Piazza, Thomas, Paul M. Sniderman, and Philip E. Tetlock. 1990. "Analysis of the Dynamics of Political Reasoning: A General-Purpose Computer-Assisted Methodology." *Political Analysis* 1:99–120.

Pollins, Brian M. 1989. "Does Trade Still Follow the Flag?" *American Political Science Review* 83:465–480.

Poole, Keith T. and Howard Rosenthal. 1997. *Congress: A Political-Economic History of Roll Call Voting*. New York: Oxford University Press.

Przeworski, Adam. 1991. *Democracy and the Market*. New York: Cambridge University Press.

Putnam, Robert P. 2000. *Bowling Alone*. New York: Simon & Schuster.

Riker, William H. 1982. *Liberalism Against Populism: A Confrontation Between the Theory of Democracy and the Theory of Social Choice*. San Francisco: Freeman.

Riker, William H. and Peter C. Ordeshook. 1968. "A Theory of the Calculus of Voting." *American Political Science Review* 62:25–42.

Rogers, James R. 2006. "Judicial Review Standards in Unicameral Legislative Systems: A Positive Theoretic and Historical Analysis." *Creighton Law Review* 33(1): 65–120.

Salmon, Wesley C. 1993. "Probabilistic Causality." In *Causation*, edited by Ernest Sosa and Michael Tooley. Oxford: Oxford University Press, Chapter 8, pp. 137–153.

Sniderman, Paul M. and Thomas Piazza. 1993. *The Scar of Race*. Cambridge, MA: Harvard University Press.

Stouffer, Samuel C. 1955. *Communism, Conformity, and Civil Liberties*. New York: Doubleday.

Tijms, Henk. 2007. *Understanding Probability: Chance Rules in Everyday Life*, 2nd ed. Cambridge: Cambridge University Press.

Sullivan, John L., James Piereson, and George E. Marcus. 1979. "An Alternative Conceptualization of Political Tolerance: Illusory Increases 1950s–1970s." *American Political Science Review* 73:781–794.

Weatherford, M. Stephen. 1992. "Measuring Political Legitimacy." *American Political Science Review* 86:149–166.

Index